GW00729942

The Virtual Reality Construction Kit

Joe Gradecki

John Wiley & Sons, Inc.
New York ■ Chichester ■ Brisbane ■ Toronto ■ Singapore

Publisher: Katherine Schowalter
Editor: Tim Ryan
Associate Managing Editor: Jacqueline A. Martin
Editorial Production: Impressions, a Division of Edwards Brothers, Inc.
Interior Design: Jane Tenenbaum
Icon Illustrations: Andy Ewen

Designations used by companies to distinguish their products are often claimed as trademarks. In all instances where John Wiley & Sons, Inc. is aware of a claim, the product names appear in Initial Capital or ALL CAPITAL letters. Readers, however, should contact the appropriate companies for more complete information regarding trademarks and registration.

This text is printed on acid-free paper.

Copyright © 1994 by John Wiley & Sons, Inc.

All rights reserved. Published simultaneously in Canada.

This publication is designed to provide accurate and authoritative information in regard to the subject matter covered. It is sold with the understanding that the publisher is not engaged in rendering legal, accounting, or other professional service. If legal advice or other expert assistance is required, the services of a competent professional person should be sought. FROM A DECLARATION OF PRINCIPLES JOINTLY ADOPTED BY A COMMITTEE OF THE AMERICAN BAR ASSOCIATION AND A COMMITTEE OF PUBLISHERS.

Reproduction or translation of any part of this work beyond that permitted by section 107 or 108 of the 1976 United States Copyright Act without the permission of the copyright owner is unlawful. Requests for permission or further information should be addressed to the Permissions Department, John Wiley & Sons, Inc.

Library of Congress Cataloging-in-Publication Data:

Gradecki, Joseph D.
    The virtual reality construction kit / by Joseph D. Gradecki.
       p. cm.
    Includes index.
    ISBN 0-471-00953-9
      1. Human-computer interaction. 2. Virtual reality. I. Title.
QA76.9.H85G715 1994
006—dc20   93-48253
                                   CIP

Printed in the United States of America

10 9 8 7 6 5 4 3 2

This book is dedicated to my wife, Waverly, our son Matthew, and our precious Jesus Christ. Without you, this book would mean nothing. Thank you for allowing me to spend countless hours writing and developing the hardware and software presented in this book.

Acknowledgments

When I agreed to write this book, I thought my experience at publishing a magazine and writing a 250-page thesis would have prepared me. I was wrong. No matter how good or bad a book may be, the author deserves credit for just getting through it. It is an experience that I will never forget. I wish to thank Tim Ryan for asking me to write this book. His energy and excitement about this technology helped to get me through the slow parts.

My thanks to Gregory Everitt for editing the manuscript and making it look like I can write. My thanks also to Claire Huismann and Impressions for all the work that went into creating this book.

Contents

Introduction

Have you ever heard the expression, "Champagne taste on a beer budget"? It means a lot in the virtual reality industry. The media force-feeds us with the idea that virtual reality is defined by the computer-generated sequences in movies like *The Lawnmower Man*. I liked the movie itself, but the so-called virtual reality sequences took hundreds of hours to produce on computer systems costing hundreds of thousands of dollars. That's way beyond my budget—how about yours?

That doesn't knock us out of the game—we just have to be creative. Welcome to the cutting edge in "garage" VR. In this book, you'll find projects for building motion trackers, 3-D goggles, a 3-D mouse, 3-D sound systems, and more—all from scratch. There are also projects for converting existing hardware to work on your PC, including a PowerGlove, the new VictorMaxx StuntMaster goggles (designed for the Sega games system), Logitech's CyberMan, and more.

No programming or electronics experience is required!

Immerse yourself in the virtual "worlds" included on disk by using your mouse and monitor or, better yet, combine any of the 14 hardware projects described in this book for a total virtual reality experience.

What's on the Disk?

The disk included with this book gives you all the software to make the projects work on a PC as well as many virtual worlds, complete and ready to run (for programmers I've included the source code and a lot of programming tips). Here are a few of the things you'll be able to do in the virtual worlds on disk:

- ❏ *Play an exciting game of virtual racquetball*
- ❏ *Wrap yourself in power armor and engage in a deadly combat game that you can play over modems*
- ❏ *Roam a midnight world of towering monoliths and find your armed opponent before s/he finds you*
- ❏ *"Bicycle" through a relaxing virtual reality park*

This is a hands-on book. You are not going to read about some theoretical foundation of VR. I present down-and-dirty, garage-level virtual reality. I expect you to "get dirty." Build the projects, hook them up to your PC, load the software (it's on the disk, ready to run), and experience state-of-the-art homegrown VR. All the projects that I explain in this book are proven to work. I have personally built all of them, including writing or testing every line of code.

How This Book Is Organized

Each chapter focuses on a specific hardware project with an explanation of how the device works, what parts you'll need and where to buy them, clear steps and lots of pictures to guide you through building it, and instructions on how to use it with the software on disk.

Chapter 1 is a quick overview of what we need to have a full-blown virtual reality experience.

Chapter 2 starts off with a discussion of the input devices and the sense of touch. I explain how true VR is created through object manipulation. We then build an interface of the Mattel Power Glove so you can hook it up to your PC.

Chapter 3 illustrates how to build a 3-D input device using an ordinary mouse and parts from a Power Glove.

Chapter 4 describes using the Global 3-D Controller and Logitech CyberMan input devices in virtual reality. Programmers will also find a lot of tips for writing their own drivers.

Chapter 5 presents the world of feedback. We explore tactile, force, and thermal feedback systems and look at ways we can build our own systems.

Chapter 6 brings our eyes into focus. We begin by looking at the theory of stereo pairs and the techniques necessary to generate them. We conclude with instructions for building an interface that connects a pair of shutter glasses to the PC.

Chapter 7 helps us interface the VictorMaxx StuntMaster to our PC. A simple cable is all it takes.

Chapter 8 discusses building a functional 3-D head-mounted display. The theory behind the hardware and step-by-step instructions are given for constructing your own.

Chapter 9 opens our ears to the theory and practice of simulating three-dimensional sound.

Chapter 10 is an introduction to the advanced Gravis Ultrasound 3D card and tells you how to build your own 3-D sound system using just a few components. We also look at how sound is generated and talk about software necessary to produce sound from our sound system.

Chapter 11 is a brief look at how we can add voice recognition to our virtual environment. Just imagine being able to speak to other virtual creatures, and have them reply!

Chapter 12 shows how to really put yourself in a virtual world. Using parts found in any hardware store, you'll build an arm-based head tracker for under $30 that will allow you to track where your head is turning or the position of your hand.

Chapter 13 looks at a different angle for head tracking. Using part of the Power Glove, we are able to build a simple head tracker.

Chapter 14 gives a general but in-depth look at the software necessary to control the virtual environments that we wish to interact in.

Chapter 15 describes the virtual racquetball game included on disk. Programmers will benefit from the lengthy notes on designing this virtual world.

Chapter 16 shows you how to hook up a bicycle, exercise bike, or treadmill to your PC and take a virtual stroll through the park.

Chapter 17 discusses the dark, midnight world of danger where a virtual opponent seeks you out for termination.

Appendix A discusses installation of the software disk.

Appendix B is a list of current VR-related companies.

Appendix C is a list of sources for further VR information.

Appendix D is a list of electronic part sources.

Appendix E discussed *PCVR Magazine*—the magazine dedicated to PC-based virtual reality.

Appendix F gives you tips on building the projects in the book.

This is the real thing. Grab your tool box, find a project you want to build, and immerse yourself in VR!

Difficulty Level of Projects ❗❗❗

Next to each project title in this book you will see a number of screwdriver icons that represents how difficult the project is. One screwdriver indicates that it's easy; five screwdrivers indicates a difficult project.

Virtual Reality You Can Afford

1

Imagine a long stretch of beach. Roll your pant legs up to your knees and stand at the edge of the water. Every so often, take a step toward the ocean. Your feet get wet, and soon you are waist deep. At some point, the water comes crashing against your body, throwing you backward. Now look up at the sea gulls flying above your head. You think to yourself, Are they trying to use me as a target? The sun is setting on the distant horizon, coloring the ocean red as it sets. Oh, by the way, you are on a deserted island hundreds of miles from civilization, which means you have no electricity. Before you know it, the sun sets, and all is pitch black. The only light comes from the moon—a big, bright, full moon clearly visible high up in the sky and to your right.

This is reality! Your reality. The description of the scene above wasn't super-detailed, yet you probably painted a beautiful picture in your mind of that island. That's human nature. Now let me ask you a question about that picture you just painted: Was it three-dimensional? Could you see the sun out on the far horizon or the moon way out in space? If you could, then was this picture in your mind reality or not? Was imagining it kind of like being there? This type of mental activity greatly relaxes many people. They feel they are in a tropical paradise instead of a busy office. They are creating a new reality; it just happens to be in their minds. How much more real this new reality would be if you could see your hand pickup a seashell if the image were crystal clear. You could say you were actually there.

This is the intent of the technology called *virtual reality*. It is a reality because you are there. You can see parts of your body and other objects and better yet, you can manipulate them. The word *virtual* comes into play because it is a perceived reality in which you can do things you couldn't do in the real world. In order to arrive at a clear-cut definition of virtual reality, we need to look at what a virtual reality is made of.

 ## Virtual Worlds

Virtual worlds are where we experience new realities. They hold all of the objects we can see and manipulate; they also enable us to experience things that aren't possible in the real world. How many times have you walked through a tree? Speaking of trees, Figure 1.1 shows an example of a virtual world. This particular world comes from the virtual reality (VR) program that you will develop in Chapter 16.

FIGURE 1.1 *Actual rendered park scene*

In the virtual reality community, there is a debate surfacing as to what exactly certain commonly used terms mean. We are all familiar on some level with word processors. These examples of computer software are commonly called *applications* and are used to write text. We have pieces of software called *computer games* that give us entertainment. We also have computer software called *tools* that help us or our computers to do their jobs a little better. A program that formats a hard drive is a tool. So in the general computer community, of which I am a member, there is widespread acceptance of these terms.

But in the VR community, any computer software that deals with VR is called a *world*. These worlds typically do not do anything. You just navigate through them and explore things. This mess is further confused by software houses putting the words "virtual reality" on just about anything that has a three-dimensional feel to it. To end the confusion, I would like to propose the following definitions for different pieces of VR software. But wait a minute— how can we put definitions on computer software that proposes to be VR when we don't even know what constitutes a VR program and what exactly a virtual reality experience is?

 ## What Goes into Creating a Virtual Reality Experience?

A great deal of thought has to go into determining what constitutes a new technology, so there is going to be a great deal of arguing between the experts in the field. I present my verdict on the nature of a VR program from the viewpoint of having worked at the garage level. I've had to write applications, games, tools, and worlds just to determine what is what, so I feel I have them straight in my mind; now it's time to stir the pot again.

There are two basic components that a *true* virtual reality program *must* contain:

1. *A first-person user viewpoint that has complete movement at will in real time*
2. *The ability to manipulate and/or change the virtual environment in real time*

The virtual reality hardware projects and the software included on disk are all designed to give you a first-person perspective on the virtual world and to enable you to walk around the world and manipulate objects you find in real time.

The Importance of a First-Person Perspective

In order to explain the importance of this concept, allow me to set up a situation. You are looking at a computer monitor, and the image you see is the park scene shown in Figure 1.1. However, the trees have brown bark and green foliage, the grass is green, and the sky is blue. All of the other objects are colored as you would normally expect. Your view is represented as though you were looking out of your own eyes into the park (you are not looking at the top of a little figure that represents you). Directly in front of you is an object that is a representation of your hand. You have now established a *first-person user viewpoint*. This is a fairly common part of most three-dimensional games on the market such as Ultima VI or Castle Wolfenstein.

Now for the second part of the component: We must have the ability to move the viewpoint to *any* position in the three-dimensional coordinate system that surrounds the park scene, just as you can move around, stand on your toes, or crouch down in the real world to get different views. Remember that a VR park scene is not just a bunch of flat, two-dimensional bitmaps—it's a bunch of three-dimensional objects that you can walk around.

I'll let you in on a little secret. The "three-dimensional" objects in games such as Castle Wolfenstein are simply bitmaps that have been drawn from four to eight different angles. Imagine for a minute that we take one of the trees from Figure 1.1 and place it in the middle of a stop sign, as shown in Figure 1.2. The Wolfenstein-type games only allow you to see the tree from the eight sides of the stop sign. You cannot move just a little bit in any direction, only to another of the eight different positions. In a true VR program, you can move anywhere that you wish. For example, you can become an ant on the base of the tree and look into the foliage as in Figure 1.3. You can even start walking up the trunk of the tree while you look around for a nasty spi-

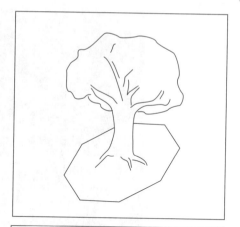

FIGURE 1.2 ***Eight possible views with bitmaps***

der. Or you could become an eagle. You could swoop down on an unsuspecting tourist, fly to the top of the tree, and sit comfortably on a branch as in Figures 1.4–6.

There is other software available (called *visualization programs*) that gives you the ability to change your views, but it doesn't allow you to do it in real time. Real-time viewpoint movement is crucial to simulating how we walk

FIGURE 1.3 ***An ant's view of a virtual tree***

FIGURE 1.4 *First scene of an eagle's flight*

FIGURE 1.5 *Second scene of an eagle's flight*

FIGURE 1.6 ***Third scene of an eagle's flight***

around in real life. With VR software, you do not passively follow some prepro-grammed path. If you want to walk forward and suddenly turn to the left and fly 30 feet in the air, you can do it.

Now to be fair, I must point out that by using the technique of selective bitmaps like Wolfenstein employs, you can have very high-quality graphics. The detail in Wolfenstein's objects is much better than even some high-level VR equipment. But when a program calls for "at will" movement in real time, noth-ing can substitute for VR. With that understood, I begin my explanation of the second VR component.

The Importance of Manipulating the Virtual Environment in Real Time

The second basic requirement for a program to be called VR is more profound than the first. Many programs let you move around in real time, but few enable you to directly manipulate objects in the virtual world.

In your reality, you have the ability to affect the things around you every second of the day. If you want to drive to the store, you get in your car and go. If you want to walk, you walk. But in the process of making the decision to change your environment, you generally manipulate the objects around you. If you want to drive to the store, you must first find your keys, and once you have them, you need to lock the front door. This continues until you return from the store, when it starts all over again because you have to decide what to do with the objects you purchased.

Throughout this entire process, you are manipulating objects. If you move to a virtual reality, you must have this same capability. The beautiful part about VR is that you can determine just what is manipulable and what is not. If you want to build an environment that lets you find your car keys but doesn't allow you to get close enough to pick them up, you can do it. If you want to be able to move mountains, you can do that as well.

This component of a VR program is by far the most important. The developer of the environment is in control of how objects interact with each other and are manipulated. This control can be very beneficial. NASA is in the process of creating the space station *Freedom*, which will be a complete laboratory and living center for U.S. astronauts. During the development of this station, all of the components must be tested in a zero-gravity situation in order to determine how they will respond. Although scientists have come up with ways to simulate zero gravity, none of them is perfect for all situations. Take, for instance, power generation. It's a good bet that *Freedom* will be run by solar power as well as some sort of atomic reactor. They work good in submarines, so why not in space? But there's a bit of a problem when it comes to testing an atomic reactor. Some of the options are (1) build a reactor and test it in the water tank, (2) build a reactor and put it in space for some period of time to determine the effects of zero gravity, or (3) use VR. The first option is reasonable if we just consider the effects of zero gravity on the production of power from the reactor. Whether or not it could operate in a zero-gravity environment could be determined. But what about the survivability of the reactor itself in space? What if the space station was suddenly showered by meteors? Would the reactor take the punishment? Not only would this be quite difficult to simulate in a water tank, but also what happens if the reactor is seriously damaged and explodes? We can look at option 2 as a possible solution.

With option 2, we would build a working reactor, transport it to space, and turn it on. We would have a way to monitor power generation as well as physical condition, be it by camera or other means. Now we would be doing a real test, except for the tiny detail of when the meteor shower is expected to occur. What if the reactor is in space for three years and one hasn't occurred yet? Do we consider the test successful? Let's say that we do get a meteor shower. What happens if the reactor cannot take all of the punishment and explodes? There are many scientists who have made predictions as to the effects an atomic explosion in space would have on the earth—for example, the gravitational pull between the planets might be disrupted, and satellites could be destroyed or sent out of orbit. So this really isn't a good option. Now comes option 3: VR.

In a virtual environment, we create a reactor object and all of its associated parts; in other words, we create a running simulation of the reactor. Seeing as how the reactor is in VR, we can move and observe it from any angle. This is something present in option 1 but missing from option 2. Because we are in VR, we can simulate any type of disaster that could strike the reactor. We could have a meteor shower occur naturally, or we could throw the meteors ourselves. We could pick the reactor up and rotate it, or we could shut it off. We could remove parts of the reactor as if they had fallen off during a storm. Along comes another meteor shower—what effect will the missing piece have on the survivability of the reactor? We can create so many different test conditions that actually using them all would be impossible. But by being able to manipulate our virtual environment, we have created a system that can defy physical laws. We have given power to an engineer such as no other tool can provide.

Just as in the first requirement, it is very important that this manipulation capability be in real time. It doesn't make much sense to leave our virtual environment, do something, and then come back. We have to have a system that feels somewhat like our real world.

Now that we have an idea of what I feel a program must contain to be called a true VR program, let's look at our program definitions again.

So What Is the Purpose of VR?

VR technology can be applied to many situations, from enabling executives to take part in across-the-globe-teleconferences, to helping medical students practice surgery, but we should never forget the energy and creativity that can be brought to life in a virtual world. With that in mind, I would like to give my definition of VR: an interactive three-dimensional playground. This definition incorporates the two basic components of a VR program (first-person perspective and the ability to manipulate objects) as well as giving us the freedom of a playground where there are no rules. We are there to have fun. This is what VR is all about. We can take a completely different look at things. Even if VR is used in the workplace, it will be fun. Where else can you go and play on the moon one minute and the next be taking a stroll on a beach in Maui?

A Look Behind the Stage

We are going to work with the assumption that all of our virtual realities will be created with a computer. And because we are visually oriented, computer graphics are of extreme importance. But creating detailed real-time graphics is one of the most challenging things a computer can do.

Ivan Sutherland, one of the first pioneers of modern-day virtual reality, used a computer, some other hardware he designed, and very crude *wireframe* graphics to enter a new reality. Figure 1.7 is an example of a cube that has been drawn using wireframe graphics. Now, this wireframe cube can be interpreted several different ways. Where exactly is the front of the cube? I know where it is because I drew it, but you may not be able to determine where I put the front. As computer graphics became more advanced, it was discovered that we have to employ a technique called *hidden-line removal,* which eliminates the lines that would be hidden by the surfaces of the cube. If I take my paint program to the cube in Figure 1.7, you will be able to see exactly which side is the front. Figure 1.8 shows the new cube.

Now we have a complete cube, and we know its orientation as well. These wireframe graphics give us the ability to create, interact with, or manipulate just about any sort of object; for example, sea gulls and the setting sun. By simply drawing three-dimensional objects, we can create a new reality. But wait a minute—that cube doesn't look very good. It's a white box with a black outline. Or is it a clear box with a black outline? I guess we will never know, but the point is that we have to be able to better represent these objects if we are going to create a virtual reality that closely matches our *real* reality.

This is where advanced graphics techniques come into play. A technique called *rendering* allows us to create better graphics than what can be accomplished using wireframes. Through rendering, you can color an object, shine a light on it, and shade it appropriately. Rendering takes a bunch of numbers that represent an object and converts them into a three-dimensional graphical representation on the computer screen. Figure 1.9 is an example of a rendered object, a rook from a virtual chess game.

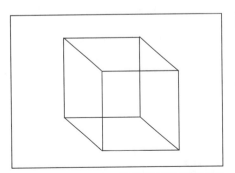

FIGURE 1.7 *A simple wireframe cube without hidden lines removed*

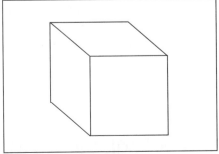

FIGURE 1.8 *A simple cube with hidden lines removed*

FIGURE 1.9 *Example of a three-dimensional object: a rook*

Notice that the rook displays different shades of gray. This is not something that the printers did when they printed the book; it's a result of the rendering software and the virtual light source that was shining down on the rook. Figure 1.10 shows the actual series of numbers that make up the rook.

When software renders an object, it builds the object from a series of polygons, which are geometric figures created from three or more points arranged such that if you connected all of the points, no two lines would intersect each other. A triangle is a polygon and so is a square. If you look back at Figure 1.9, you will see that there are basically five vertical sections to the rook. The very top and bottom are composed of four rectangular polygons made into a cube. A lid is put on the top and a base is put on the bottom of the cube. If we move toward the middle, there are two more identical sections that slope inward. This entire object is made up of 22 rectangular polygons; the numbers in Figure 1.10 actually describe their shapes.

The numbers at the beginning of the list are the actual points, or *vertices*, for the polygons in space. Because we are working in three dimensions, each vertex has to be described in terms of x, y, z coordinates. If you think about this, each of the polygons has four vertices. There are a total of 22 polygons, so there should be 88 total vertices in the list, but there are only 24. This is because all of the polygons share vertices with four other polygons, and we can eliminate duplicate numbers. After describing all of the vertices, we begin a second list for the polygons. Each line describes the color of the polygon, how many vertices it contains, and which vertices in the first list should be used to construct it.

By using the renderer and describing our objects as numbers, we can create quite complex scenes for our virtual reality. But once we have all of these objects, we need to put them somewhere. If we move back to our usual reality, where are all of the real objects located? On our world, of course. If we extend this notion to VR, we can create virtual worlds.

Defining Virtual Reality Software

Three-dimensional programs are pieces of computer software that employ three-dimensional graphics, whether bitmaps or rendered objects; have limited viewpoint movement; and do not allow manipulation of the environment in real time. These last two characteristics mean that three-dimensional programs aren't really in the realm of virtual reality software.

Walkthroughs are a common demonstration tool that many VR companies use to demonstrate their graphics software. These programs simply allow you to walk through a house or other object. Thus, a walkthrough is a three-dimensional program that includes all of the above characteristics but allows full viewpoint movement in real time. But because you can't change or manipulate the environment in real time, walkthroughs also fail the virtual reality test.

A *world* is a three-dimensional program that allows full viewpoint movement and object manipulation in real time. This is an example of a true virtual

```
castle 24 22

28 60 -28
28 60 28
-28 60 28
-28 60 -28
28 40 -28
28 40 28
-28 40 28
-28 40 -28
14 20 -14
14 20 14
-14 20 14
-14 20 -14
14 -20 -14
14 -20 14
-14 -20 14
-14 -20 -14
28 -40 -28
28 -40 28
-28 -40 28
-28 -40 -28
28 -60 -28
28 -60 28
-28 -60 28
-28 -60 -28

0x1FDF 4 5 1 0 4
0x1FDF 4 6 2 1 5
0x1FDF 4 7 3 2 6
0x1FDF 4 4 0 3 7
0x1FDF 4 9 5 4 8
0x1FDF 4 10 6 5 9
0x1FDF 4 11 7 6 10
0x1FDF 4 8 4 7 11
0x1FDF 4 13 9 8 12
0x1FDF 4 14 10 9 13
0x1FDF 4 15 11 10 14
0x1FDF 4 12 8 11 15
0x1FDF 4 17 13 12 16
0x1FDF 4 18 14 13 17
0x1FDF 4 19 15 14 18
0x1FDF 4 16 12 15 19
0x1FDF 4 21 17 16 20
0x1FDF 4 22 18 17 21
0x1FDF 4 23 19 18 22
0x1FDF 4 20 16 19 23
0x1FDF 4 0 1 2 3
0x1FDF 4 23 22 21 20
```

FIGURE 1.10 **Vertices and polygons for the rook**

reality program. There is, however, one additional characteristic. A world is simply used for exploration. There is typically nothing really to do except explore the objects in the world and move them around, which makes worlds great for demonstration purposes. Because there is not a lot to do in the world, the user cannot get into much trouble.

Finally, we have *virtual reality programs*, which, by definition, must incorporate both of the basic VR components but must also present or allow a specific task to be accomplished. In a world, there is not much that has to be done. In contrast, a good example of a VR program would be one that allows architects to design buildings virtually; constructing, moving, and stretching walls just by using a virtual hand or some other tool.

While these are not profound definitions in the world of virtual reality, they will allow me to get my points across more easily in later chapters of this book.

Now that we know what worlds and VR programs are, we need to look at how they are created. Just how do you make a virtual world? If only it was as easy as using Legos. But really, in a way it is. All software development is just a matter of fitting the right pieces together to create the system in mind. In developing your virtual world, there are several questions that you must ask yourself:

What's to be in my scene?
What are my input devices?
What are my output devices?
What software am I using?
What level of detail should I use?

This book gives you all the information you need to build VR hardware, and with it you also get a disk full of utilities and VR worlds. You even get a lot of programming tips and mathematics. I don't spend a great deal of time telling you how to program a virtual world, because that depends a lot on what software you're using. However, I would like to touch on this topic briefly.

The questions above are just the first of many that must be considered when designing a virtual world. Unlike members of the general PC community, who commonly have a mouse and modem attached their computer, those using or experimenting with VR do not have common devices. It is more common for users not to have any device attached to their computers that has been specifically designed for VR use. This is typically due to the price of VR peripherals. We will do our best to change that situation with this book.

On the subject of software to use in building your virtual world, there is simply not enough competition in this field. There are about five complete software development packages that allow you to build worlds and programs, and their costs range from free to well over six thousand dollars. Some of these packages cannot even use the VGA card; instead, you must purchase a separate graphics card for $2,500. The main reason for their not using the VGA card is speed.

If you build a virtual world out of very simple objects with no fancy features, the speed (or lack thereof), of the VGA card is not a big problem, but if you decide that you want to incorporate a great deal of detail into your world, then the card simply cannot keep up. A separate graphics card, while expensive, has the capability to do the computing necessary for detailed graphics on its own processor. The detail of an object is usually described by whether or not *textures* are used. A texture is a pattern applied to the surface of an object in order to make it more realistic. An easy example would be a kitchen cabinet. A cabinet with no detail might look like a brown block hanging on the side of a wall. If we add a texture to the cabinet, it will appear to have a wood grain. It is this wood grain that is the texture. It makes the cabinet look like a cabinet.

By using textures, the complexity of the calculations necessary to render the objects is increased hundreds of times. Normally, the renderer would just fill in a polygon with the same color pixels. The front of the cabinet would be all the same color brown. With textures, the system has to go to a buffer and determine how to copy the texture onto the cabinet, taking the user's viewpoint into consideration. This requires a great deal of calculation.

What all this means is that when you are designing a virtual world, you have to scale your ideas back to the level of the users. You have to take into consideration what equipment they will have at their disposal and what level of detail is appropriate.

Once we have an idea of what we want to put in our virtual world and what computer equipment it will use, we have to design our graphics. There are three basic ways to do so:

Use a World Editor
Use CAD
Do it by hand

World Editor

A World Editor is a piece of software that allows you to build worlds interactively. You are typically given a blank screen with menu bars at the top and/or bottom of the screen. You are able to create objects by simply selecting them from a menu; specific characteristics can be added to the objects using the menus as well. Just a click of the mouse and an object is a different color or has the ability to be moved. Objects can be combined to make more complex objects or deleted altogether. This is probably the easiest way to develop VR worlds. However, World Editors are specific to the rendering package with which they are included. While conversion to a different renderer would not be impossible, programs to accomplish this are not available at this time.

CAD

By far the most popular CAD program is Autocad from Autodesk. This program allows you to make complex three-dimensional models that can be exported and used in most rendering packages. Although not as easy as a World Editor, using a CAD program is much better than the third method. 3D Studio, also by Autodesk, can be an excellent tool for creating virtual worlds.

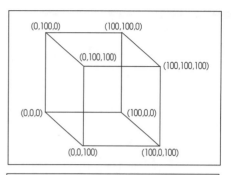

FIGURE 1.11 **Fully vertexed cube**

By Hand

The alternative is to do the drawing yourself. Simply draw a square, draw a second square that is off-set from the first, connect the corners, and you have a representation of a three-dimensional cube on paper. Because the renderer needs vertices and their locations, we give each vertex a triplet number corresponding to the x, y, and z positions in the three-dimensional coordinate system. Figure 1.11 is an example of a fully vertexed cube object.

Conclusion

It's time to dive in and start building your own virtual world. Pick a project that interests you (the Mattel Power Glove, and Logitech's CyberMan and 3D Mouse are all good places to start). After you have built some of the hardware projects, load the software from the disk and explore new worlds. If you want to jump right to the software, that's cool, too—each world on the disk supports a regular monitor, mouse, and joystick. If you don't have any experience wielding a soldering iron, don't worry. Read Appendix F for some pointers and then jump right in—that's what VR is all about!

Hooking Up a Mattel Power Glove to Your PC

Remember what the first home video game was? If you said Atari Pong, you were right. It wasn't much, but it was a beginning. A small knob on the game's console was used to maneuver a small rectangular "paddle" on the screen to hit a smaller rectangular "ball." Later, that same company brought us the Atari home entertainment system. Now we had our choice of either using a paddle or a joystick. Between that time and now, we've seen a lot of other input devices, including the thumb joystick from Mattel Intellivision and the cursor joystick from Nintendo. What was missing was an input device that took advantage of the way our bodies really move. This was particularly important for karate and streetfighter-type games—if you want to hit somebody on the screen, it's more natural to make a fist and throw a punch, not press a little plastic button marked "X."

Some years ago, several companies were thinking along these lines, and thus the Power Glove was invented. The Power Glove is a peripheral for the Nintendo home entertainment system. It allows the computer to determine where the user's hand is in 3-D space, if he or she is making a fist or not, and if the hand is being rotated. What a perfect input device for a violent society like ours. Kids loved it. My research shows that over 1 million Power Gloves had been sold by the end of 1990, and the projections were for 2 million to be sold by the end of 1991. The Power Glove had a retail price of $100. Even at discounted prices, the Power Glove brought in a total of over $100 million dollars, which is not bad for a video game input device. Figure 2.1 shows what a Power Glove system looks like.

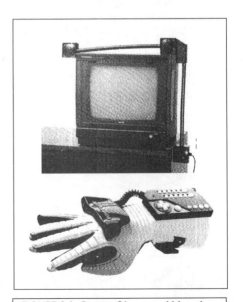

The Making of the Power Glove

Sometime around 1991, a guy named Thomas Zimmerman became curious about computer music and if there was some way he could really make music by playing air guitar. What was needed was a device that would mimic the gestures of the human hand. He got an idea, ran down to a local store, and purchased a regular glove and some plastic tubing. Using a tech-

FIGURE 2.1 *Power Glove and triangle sensor*

nique found in fiber optics, Zimmerman created an input device that would correctly replicate the movements of fingers. By placing the tubing in a special way down each of the fingers, he could tell when they were bent and to what degree. Figure 2.2 shows a simplistic view of the glove tubing. At one end of the tubing is a light source. If the hand were kept flat, the majority of the light would be registered at the other end of the tubing. Measuring the amount of source light relative to the amount that made it to the other end would tell Zimmerman how much a finger was being bent. Obviously, if a finger was bent in a fist, the resulting light would be minimal. In 1982, Zimmerman was granted a patent on his invention: number 4,542,291.

Sometime thereafter, Zimmerman came in contact with Jaron Lanier, who was very much interested in music

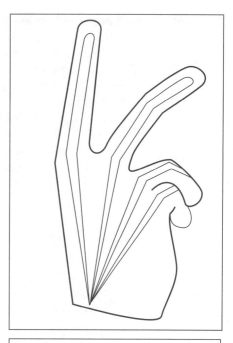

FIGURE 2.2 *View of tubes on glove used to detect finger bending*

and had some thoughts on using the glove invention. In the years to follow, the company VPL was founded. In October 1987, *Scientific American* featured a VPL Dataglove on its cover. The Dataglove used advanced fiber optics to measure the bend of the fingers. In addition, it incorporated a tracking mechanism that allowed a computer to tell where in space the glove was located and identify three different angular positions; pitch, roll, and yaw. The tracker was developed by Polhemus and used magnetic fields to determine these properties. The price of the Dataglove was $8,800, just a bit out of the average hobbyist's budget.

Enter the Mattel Power Glove

In late 1987, AGE (Abrams-Gentile Entertainment) had connections to the toy manufacturers. Using skills from both VPL and Mattel, the Power Glove was developed. Even though the Power Glove was designed for the Nintendo, it is typically referred to as the Mattel Power Glove. When it was distributed, a lawsuit developed between the different developers. Once settled, VPL ended up sharing profits with AGE from Mattel.

The designers of the Power Glove wanted it to be a partial replacement to the plastic control pad used with the Nintendo. To accomplish this, the Power Glove can mimic a joystick. To track this movement, an ultrasonic positioning system is used. Although not very accurate, it worked for the game industry. The Power Glove turned out to be quite heavy and cumbersome for use as a joystick. The designers had also planned on releasing a number of games that would take advantage of a special "high-res" (short for high-resolution) mode of the glove. This mode allowed the glove to respond to x, y, and z movement; finger movement; and hand roll. That's all great, but a hardware product without software is dead. One of the first games was called Mike Tyson Boxing, in which the Power Glove was used to knock out an opponent. A second game called Super Ball was just a glorified break-out back from Pong days. As you might have guessed, the Power Glove failed as the excitement fell off when new games weren't released.

Availability

The Power Glove was discontinued by Mattel in late 1991. Fortunately, there are a number of stores that still carry the glove in varying quantities. The most common places to find Power Gloves are

- *Toys' R' Us*
- *K-Mart*
- *Walmart*
- *KayBee and other mall toy stores*
- *The discount houses such as Walgreens, Woolworth, and so on*
- *Mail order from various VR companies (see Appendix B)*
- *PCVR Magazine ($25 plus $5 shipping for the U.S. and Canada—$16 overseas; see Appendix E)*

You should be able to find the glove priced anywhere form $12.95 to $59.95, depending on how aware the department manager is about technology. In addition to stores, the Power Glove has been seen in many younger kid's toy boxes (remember that most kids did like using it with the games that were available), pawn shops, and thrift stores. In a small town of 24,000 in the middle of Wyoming, there were gloves in both a pawn shop and the thrift store.

Converting the Power Glove to Work on a PC

As you know, the Power Glove was designed for the Nintendo, not the PC. In 1990, an article in *Byte* magazine discussed how to interface the Mattel Power Glove to any IBM or IBM-compatible PC. A complete source code was included that interpreted the joystick mode of the glove, now called the *low-res* mode. Once this news spread, everyone hooked up a glove and worked at a feverish pace to crack the secret high-res mode. In late 1991, a series of messages appeared on a network mailing list called the "glove-list" and in the USENET newsgroup sci.virtual-worlds. A number of people had cracked the high-res mode and were releasing code into the public domain for everyone to use. Since then, others have taken the code and refined it into more useful forms. Some of those people are Greg Alt, Dave Stampe, Bernie Roehl, and Mark Pflaging. All are thanked for their contributions. We continue the chapter with an in-depth look at the Power Glove, how it works, and the availability of hardware and software interfaces for the IBM or IBM-compatible PC. This begins our quest into garage VR.

Converting the Power Glove consists of two parts: doing some minor rewiring on the glove itself and using the software included on the disk in this book. There are two ways to rewire the glove based on whether you want to connect it through the serial or parallel port of your computer. We'll discuss both these methods, but you should seriously consider using the parallel port method because most software designed to run the Power Glove only works if the glove is connected there.

Parallel Port Method

This is the preferred method—it is easier and less expensive, and more software supports the Power Glove in this configuration.

Parts List for the Power Glove Parallel-Port Interface

For the parallel port of your PC to hook up to the Power Glove, you will need the following items:

- ❑ PC, of course
- ❑ Power Glove
- ❑ Extension Cable, not necessary but a good idea
- ❑ A bidirectional parallel port in your PC
- ❑ DB-25 male parallel connector, crimp or solder version (RS-232)
- ❑ DB-25 connector hood (RS-15)
- ❑ A few feet of 18-gauge type wire
- ❑ Wire cutters or X-acto knife
- ❑ Regular screwdriver
- ❑ Power supply (your options will be examined later in this chapter)
- ❑ Soldering iron and solder (optional)
- ❑ A multimeter (optional)

Note: The Power Glove–to–PC interface is available from *PCVR Magazine* for $19.95 plus $2.50 shipping for the U.S. and Canada ($4.50 shipping overseas).

Figure 2.3 depicts the completed Power Glove interface.

It is crucial that you have a *bidirectional* parallel port in your PC. When the PC was originally designed, the parallel port was meant only to allow for data to be output from the computer to a printer. It just so happens that the parallel port has several features that make it useful for input as well. As the clone manufacturers started expanding into peripherals, they designed their generic parallel and multiport card to be bidirectional, meaning that information can be transferred in both input and output modes. In our case, we will be sending data to the Power Glove and receiving data back. Therefore, if your glove and interface do not work and you have followed the troubleshooting guide at the end of this chapter, then your parallel port is probably not bidirectional. In most cases nowadays, computers are being supplied with bidirectional parallel ports.

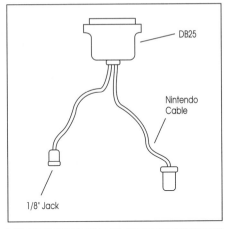

FIGURE 2.3 *The Power Glove interface*

For the adventurous, if your parallel port turns out to not be bidirectional, there have been articles in electronics magazines that explain how to convert your standard model. However, a new parallel-port card would only cost around ten to twenty dollars. You might think that the time and effort you would need to put into the conversion process would make that sound like a bargain. The problem with the documentation for the conversion is that most parallel ports have different circuitry, and you will probably make an adjustment that is not wise. So go buy a parallel port that is bidirectional.

It is important to consider the use of Nintendo extension cable. First, the cable only costs about ten dollars. Second, it gives an obvious extension to the short cables supplied with the Power Glove itself. Third, if you make a mistake, you only have to throw out a cheap, widely available extension cable and not an entire Power Glove.

Examining the Power Glove's Wiring

The first thing that you need to do is determine which of the wires in the Power Glove cable are connected to what pins in the end connector. If you are using the original connector and no extension cable, locate the box at the end of the triangle receivers. There should be a short cable coming out of the box. Cut the end of this cable about 0.5 inch from the end connector (as shown in Figure 2.4). If you are using an extension cable, connect the end of the extension cable to the end connector coming out of the box, and then cut the remaining end off the extension cable.

Strip back the black insulation until about 1.5 inches of all wires are exposed. Strip off the insulation from the individual wires until about 0.75 inch of actual wire is exposed.

Using the Original Cable

Follow this section if you are using the original cable (not the extension cord); otherwise, skip to the section entitled "Detective Work." Begin the connection process by looking at the colored wires coming from the end of the wire you just cut. You should see

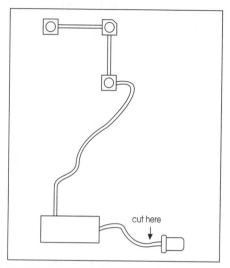

cut here

FIGURE 2.4 *Cutting the Power Glove cable*

wires of these colors: black, orange, yellow, green, and red. There are two other wires, but we are not concerned with them right now. Each of these colors refer to a particular pin on the connector (see Table 2.1). Verify that you have the five colors mentioned: and that they connect to the correct pin. If so, skip to the section entitled "Connection." If you are missing a color or the colors are different than those above, move on to the next section.

Detective Work

If you don't have the colors mentioned in the previous section, find the Nintendo connector that you cut off from the end of the small box or from the end of the

Table 2.1. **The Power Glove's Wiring**		
Pin #	**Color**	**Function**
1	Black	Ground
2	Orange	Clock
3	Yellow	Latch
4	Green	Out
5		nothing
6		nothing
7	Red	+5 Volts

extension cable. Cut the black insulation back until you have an inch or two of colored wires. Strip a half inch or so of the colored insulation back from each of the wires, but be sure to leave some of the colored insulation as you are going to need it to identify the wires. For the next operation you are going to need a multimeter set on resistance, or something like the circuit in Figure 2.5.

Using the multimeter or lamp circuit and the loose Nintendo connector, attach one of the probes to one of the colored wires. Now, on a piece of paper write down the color of wire you have attached to the probe. With the

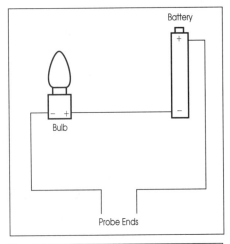

FIGURE 2.5 *Circuit to test Power Glove leads*

other probe, touch each of the pins inside the Nintendo connector until either your multimeter shows that resistance is present or the lamp lights up. When the multimeter or lamp registers, the colored wire you are touching and the pin the other probe is touching are related. Now create a chart (like that in Table 2.1) by writing the wire color and the pin number that you are currently touching with the probe. Repeat this operation for each of the wires. Once you are done, you will have a map of the relationship between the wires and the pins.

The PC Connection

Next, we have to wire the glove to the parallel port. For this part of the interface, you will want to use a DB-25 male connector. The easiest to use are the ones with the crimp pins, though one drawback is that they are not as sturdy as the solder type. You will also need to cut two pieces of wire, approximately 6 inches long to use for powering the glove. Connect the Power Glove wires and the two 6-inch wires to the parallel port as shown in Figure 2.6.

When you are finished, you should have the following wiring scheme:

Power Glove Pin #	Connects to
Pin 1	Pin 18 of the parallel connector and ground (to power supply)
Pin 2	Pin 2 of the parallel connector
Pin 3	Pin 3 of the parallel connector
Pin 4	Pin 13 of the parallel connector
Pin 7	+5 volts (power supply)

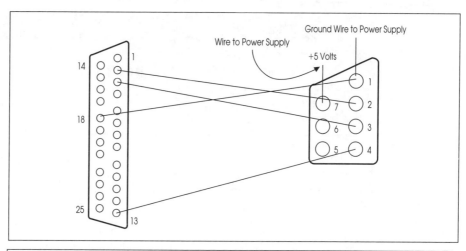

FIGURE 2.6 *Power Glove to DB-25 interface pinouts*

Connecting the Power

There are four different ways that power can be connected to the glove. (1) from the keyboard, (2) from an external source, (3) from an internal peripheral connector, or (4) from a battery. There are reasons for choosing each of the options. If you want to be able to move the glove from one computer to another, then the keyboard and external source are best.

Whatever your choice, make sure that you use only +5 volts, that the ground is wired to pin 1 (or the associated color), and that the +5 volts is wired to pin 7 (or the associated color). This is *very* important. If the polarity of the wires is turned around, there is a good possibility that you will damage your computer's motherboard once the Power Glove is connected to the parallel port. A friend of mine in Australia blew a 486 motherboard because his electronics pal wired the interface with the wrong polarity. It is a simple but costly mistake to make. Let's look at each of the options separately.

Keyboard Power !

There are several reasons to choose the keyboard connector for your power options. The first is that if you have your computer, you have power for the Power Glove, which isn't the case with an external source. Second, the keyboard connection into the computer is usually in an easy-to-reach location. If you chose the keyboard options, you are faced with building a feed-through–type adapter. We need to access the power lines located in the keyboard connector but also allow the computer access to the keyboard itself.

Keyboard Power Supply

You will need to purchase
- ❏   1 male 5-pin DIP connector, like the one on your keyboard
- ❏   1 female 5-pin DIP connector
- ❏   A few feet of wire
- ❏   A soldering iron and solder

One note of caution: Not all computers are designed the same. If the keyboard–and–Power-Glove combination draws too much power from the keyboard connector, unknown damage could occur. Our goal is to create an adapter such as that shown in Figure 2.7.

To wire the connectors correctly, we need to determine which pins on the DIPs are +5V and GND (ground). Pin 5 is +5V and pin 4 is GND. Figure 2.8 gives an example of the DIP connector and the numbering of the pins from the viewpoint of looking at the female DIP connector head-on. Now that we know the numbering of the power pins, the connection becomes very easy. Just remember to follow the pins' numbers.

Note that you need to put the black cases through the wires before you start soldering; otherwise, you will have to cut and resolder the wires. Begin by soldering a wire to both pins 4 and 5 of one of the DIP connectors. Once finished, attach two wires to the end of each of the wires coming from the first connector (see Figure 2.7). One set of wires will go to the other connector, and the other set will be attached to the glove. Take one wire from each set, follow to the opposite DIP connector, and attach to the *same* pin number. Repeat this step for the other wire. This is very important because you can damage your computer and glove if you supply it with the wrong voltage.

You should now have an adapter for the keyboard; one end plugs into the computer's socket for the keyboard, and the keyboard plugs into the other end of the adapter. In addition, there are two wires coming off the adapter; one con-

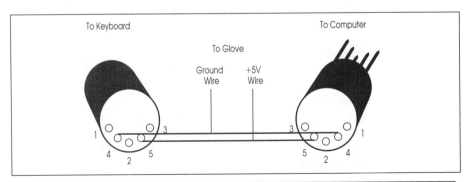

FIGURE 2.7 *Complete keyboard adapter power source for Power Glove*

nected to pin 4 and the other connected to pin 5. Take the wire that is
connected to pin 5 of the DIP connectors and attach it to the +5V wire from
the Power Glove. Take the wire that is
connected to pin 4 of the DIP connectors and attach it to the GND wire
from the Power Glove. Now do the
same for the other wire. Keyboard
power is now available for your Power
Glove.

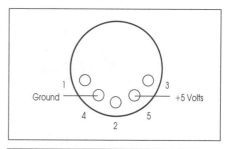

FIGURE 2.8 **Pinouts for inside section of DIP connector**

External Power

One of the easiest ways to supply power to the Power Glove is through an external source. However, one problem is locating an inexpensive system that supplies 5 volts. For my Power Gloves, I used an external power supply that I purchased from a surplus electronics store. Specifically, the power source was used
for the old Coleco Adam computer. See Appendix D for a list of the places that
report still having the supplies, as well as other places with 5-volt transformers.
Although some have suggested that 4.5 or 6 volts can be used on the glove, I
would not recommend it because the electronics expect 5 volts and there is the
possibility that the glove will be affected.

External Power Supply

You need the following:
- ☐ Transformer that outputs 5 volts
- ☐ ⅛" mono plug
- ☐ ⅛" mono jack

Note: You can purchase a +5V power supply from *PCVR Magazine* for $20 plus $5
shipping for the U.S. and Canada ($20 overseas). See Appendix E for ordering
information.

There are two ways to connect the power supply to the glove itself. In the
case of the Coleco model, the connector on the end was useless; therefore, it
had to be cut off. This allows the supply to be directly connected to the glove.
The other choice, especially when using a new supply, is to use a matching
plug-and-jack system. This also allows for quick removal of the power supply
for disassembly purposes. Figure 2.9 shows the connection.

The first step is to determine if you need to attach a plug to the power supply. If you purchase a surplus power supply, chances are that the connector on
the end will not be usable. We need to attach a standard ⅛-inch mono plug to
the +5V line and the GND line. The power supply will usually have a diagram

FIGURE 2.9 **Plug and jack for external power supply**

on it that will tell you which wires are what voltages. Find the GND line and attach it to the long part of the plug (see Figure 2.10).

Find the +5V line and attach it to the small part of the plug. To verify that the connection is correct, use a multimeter to take a voltage reading from the plug. The positive probe, usually red, should touch the tip of the plug and the negative, usually black, should touch the base of the plug. The multimeter should give you a read of +5V when the power supply is turned on.

Next you have to connect a jack to the Power Glove wires. Do exactly the same things as above, except that you should use the +5V and GND wires of the Power Glove. See Figure 2.11 for an example of the connection.

Peripheral Power

The next power supply is again the computer, but it is channeled through one of the peripheral connectors in the back of the computer, as shown in Figure 2.12. These connectors are commonly used to attach power to hard and floppy drives. The easiest way to connect this power to your glove is to extend the power from the back of the computer through a slot opening (or some other opening) and attach a plug to the wires. A socket would then be placed on the end of the Power Glove. You can purchase power cable extenders from a variety of mail-order computer companies such as JDR or Jameco.

Peripheral Power Supply

You need the following:
❑ Male PC power connector

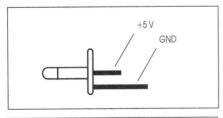

FIGURE 2.10 **GND and +5V connection to plug**

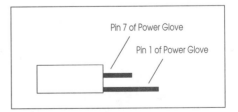

FIGURE 2.11 **Jack connection to Power Glove**

When you purchase the power extender cables, you will receive the male power connector as well as a foot of wire already attached to it. All you need to do for the Power Glove connection is attach the +5V wire of the Power Glove to one of the red wires coming from the male power connector. Then attach the GND wire of the Power Glove to the black wire coming from the male power connector. Snake the connector through the back of the PC, attach it to an empty connector coming from the PC's power supply, and you now have Power Glove power.

FIGURE 2.12 **Computer peripheral power source for Power Glove**

Battery Power !

The last option is to use battery power. I would recommend that you use rechargeable batteries. Using four D-size rechargeable batteries, it is possible to get a total voltage of 4.8 to 5.0 volts for an extended period of time. Again, Radio Shack sells the batteries as well as a battery pack that holds four D cells like in Figure 2.13. The pack is attached to the glove just as in all the other options. Just check to make sure that the polarity is correct between the glove interface and the battery pack.

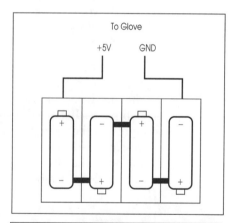

FIGURE 2.13 **Battery-pack power source for Power Glove**

If you purchase the battery pack from Radio Shack, it will come to you with two wires attached to it. The red wire is +5V and the black wire is GND. Attach the red wire to the +5V wire from the Power Glove and the black wire to the GND wire of the Power Glove. Charge the batteries and put them into the battery pack. This makes for a great power supply when using the Power Glove with a portable computer.

Battery Power Supply

You need the following:
- ❏ 4 D-cell battery pack
- ❏ 4 D-cell rechargeable batteries
- ❏ Battery Recharger

Firing it Up

Once power has been supplied to the glove, it is time to test it out. Before running a full-scale test, you want to verify the power connection so that you don't risk harming your computer. If you already plugged the parallel connector into your computer, unplug it. There should be no physical connection between your computer and the glove at this time. If you used an extension cable for the glove, unplug the glove from the extension cord. Attach the power source to the glove. Once you put power to the glove, you should hear a single beep, and the lights on the sensor triangle may or may not not light up. If they do light up, they will not necessarily all be on. If you do *not* hear the beep, then something is wrong.

If smoke begins to fill the air, then something is obviously wrong. Double-check your work with a multimeter; check for a correct voltage on the Nintendo connector by touching pin 7 of the Nintendo cable with the positive probe and touching pin 1 with the negative probe. You should get a reading of 5 volts. If you do not, check your power source. If your multimeter reads a negative value, then it would appear that you have incorrectly wired your power supply. Use the multimeter to test the power supply and make sure that a +5V is going to pin 7 and GND to pin 1.

Once you have verified that the correct voltage is present on the Nintendo cable, recheck all your connections. Attach the entire Power Glove assembly to the interface and plug the DB-25 connector to your parallel port. Turn on your computer. If everything is working correctly, the glove should beep and the lights on the receiver triangle should blink once or twice. If this happens, then you are ready to run some of the software included on disk (see Chapters 14, 15, or 16). If the glove does not start up properly, refer to the section of this chapter entitled "Troubleshooting the Power Glove and Connection."

Serial Interface Method

The interface we built above is based on the parallel-port method. It is the preferred method because most of the software available (and provided with this book) only works with it. A number of people have developed interfaces for the serial port. These are more complicated because the serial lines are based on +12 and −12 volts instead of +5 volts. All of the serial interfaces are based on a separate microprocessor that does the actual interfacing with the Power Glove and simply sends the final data to the computer through the serial lines. There are currently three serial interfaces available: 3DTV, PGSI, and Menelli.

3DTV

3DTV offers several interface packages for the Power Glove and shutter glasses as well. The product called the PC-VR (no relation to *PCVR Magazine*) includes an interface that works on the serial or parallel port and includes shutter glasses and a Power Glove at an additional cost as well as a VR rendering package for $350 without the glove and $500 with the glove. They are also selling an already-assembled Power Glove and interface cable for $175.

PGSI

The PGSI is a serial–port–based interface that gives you a Power Glove interface, a shutter-glasses interface, and several I/O lines for $90. This system was created by the University of Illinois ACM chapter, and it comes assembled and tested. Their address can be found in Appendix B.

Menelli

The final serial interface is a build-it-yourself project. All of the information about this interface is included on the enclosed disk in the file menelli.zip. I have personally built the interface, and it does work quite well. It does a much better job at controlling the Power Glove, but, it does cost much more than the simple parallel-port interface.

Troubleshooting the Power Glove and Connection

Because we are dealing with a commercial product and a home-built interface, there may be complications. In this section, I have tried to identify some of the problems that can occur with the glove interface and the software on the enclosed disk.

If you are having problems with the glove not responding to any of the programs, we need to create a troubleshooting path. The first thing to do is connect the glove to the parallel port and turn your machine on.

Do you hear a beep? If the answer is yes, then this is a good sign that the interface is getting power to the glove. If no, then there is a good chance that the glove is not getting power. Make sure that all of your power connections are okay. Use a multimeter to verify that the glove is getting power. The best way to do this is to check at the point where you cut off the Nintendo connector. If you are using the extender cable, just touch pins 1 and 7 inside the connector itself. If you have power going to the glove and there's still no beep, then the glove is probably not operational. You can check this by plugging it into a Nintendo machine and testing it. If the glove works with the Nintendo system, check all of your connections. There is probably a break somewhere.

Once you have a beep, execute the program called TEST.EXE on the enclosed disk. This program will tell use whether or not the computer is communicating with the glove. If nothing appears on the glove, then your connections are probably backward or have broken off. Check them with the original diagram and retry the program. If there's still nothing, verify that your Power Glove is attached to LPT1, the primary parallel port of the PC. The majority of the software requires that the glove be on the first parallel port and not LPT2 or LPT3, which are the secondary parallel ports.

If everything is okay, the program will begin to display numbers on the bottom of the monitor. When you move the glove in different directions, the numbers should change values, both positive and negative.

Perhaps your glove works with one program and not another. The most common reason for this is that one program allowed the glove to be on another parallel port besides LPT1. Make sure you are on LPT1 for all of the programs. The next reason for this problem is timings. Remember in our discussions about the software interface, the timings for the glove are tricky and one software developer may have done something a little different than another. Also remember that most of the glove code was written before there were 486dx2 machines, let alone the 486dx50. I would recommend that you look at the documentation for the specific piece of software that does not work and adjust the software controls the documentation talks about.

Power Glove Fun

Now that you have wired and tested your Power Glove, it's time to put it to use. On the enclosed disk is a program called JET.EXE that will allow you to control the operation of a very simple jet plane using the Power Glove. The program is executed by typing JET JET.WLD and pressing the RETURN key. Make sure that you have the Power Glove connected to parallel port LPT1 and that power has been connected to it.

Controlling the jet is very simple. Once the program starts, you will see a control stick in the lower middle part of the screen. This is what controls the jet. To move, place your virtual hand on the top of the control stick and grip. Once you have done this, you can move your hand in the direction that you want to go. To stop moving, simply release your grip.

To change the speed of the jet, use the index finger of the virtual hand to touch the top red button to the right of the control stick. A floating menu will appear that allows you to change the speed of the jet. Touch the top button to increase the speed, touch the middle button to decrease the speed, and touch the bottom button when you are finished.

In addition to moving around, you can fire a missile. Press B on the keyboard, and an explosion will appear in the distance. If you press the middle button on the main control panel, another floating menu will appear that will allow you to change the missile's range. The last button allows you to leave the menu. It is possible to hit and remove the different mound formations that appear in the landscape, but it's not easy.

The bottom button on the control panel allows you to leave the simulation, which you can also do by pressing Q on the keyboard.

Technical Notes on the Power Glove

When you look at the glove, there are three things to note on its top. The first is the control panel. There are a number of keys as well as a plastic cursor joystick common to the Nintendo control pads. Inside the hard plastic casing are the electronics that control the Power Glove. The second thing to note is the two ultrasonic transmitters enclosed in plastic just above where your knuckle would be. We will talk about the ultrasonic positioning later.

The third thing to note is the plastic pieces running down each of the fingers and the thumb. Inside each of these pieces of plastic are thin strips of metal that are coated with an electrically conductive ink. When the metal is flexed, the resistance of the electricity is changed. The idea behind the metal is just as simple as the fiber-optic Dataglove. If we apply 5 volts to one side of the metal sensor, we should get a reading of 5V on the other side, if the metal is not flexed. Now if we flex the metal, the properties of the metal change, and a lesser voltage is measured on the sensor. This corresponds to the Dataglove, where a bent finger caused less light to be received through the fiber-optic line looping on the glove. In order for the Power Glove's electronics to use the voltage to determine if a finger is bent or not, it needs to convert the analog nature of the voltage to a digital form. The original design of the Power Glove did not require a great deal of resolution in the fingers. The result was a single byte of data to convey all of the information concerning the fingers and the thumb. The format of this byte is

```
ThumbM ThumbL IndexM IndexL MiddleM MiddleL RingM RingL
```

where ThumbM is the most significant bit of the byte and RingL is the least significant. If you study this byte, you will notice two things. The first is that there is no sensor for the pinkie. The second is that each finger has 2 bits of resolution, or four different positions. If you consider that fully open and fully closed are two of the positions, there is not much range in the Power Glove's fingers and thumb. We can work out the voltage swing of the fingers quite simply.

The voltage supply of the Power Glove is 5 volts. If we assume that the glove uses some type of analog-to-digital converter that has 8 bits of resolution, then we know that there are 256 possible steps over which the 5 volts can be converted. When we divide 5 volts by 256 steps, we get 0.02 volts per step. This means that the voltage swing of the finger sensors as used in the Power Glove is 0.6–0.8 volts. Reports have shown that when measured, the voltage swing is about 0.8 volts.

Once each finger sensor is converted to a digital form, they are all rolled into a single byte and transmitted to the Nintendo game system for processing. It would appear very easy to use the metal strips in the Power Glove and separate analog-to-digital converts to gain the full 8 bits of resolution per finger. We will explore this idea in a later chapter.

The Ultrasonic Positioning System

The ultrasonic positioning system consists of two ultrasonic transmitters located on top of the Power Glove and three receivers arranged in a triangular fashion. The twenty-dollar question is this: How does the system convert the information received from the ultrasonics to x, y, z and roll positions? First we'll look at the math and then at an example. If it wasn't for a programming contest several years ago and help from Bernie Roehl, I would have made this harder than it looks.

The ultrasonic receivers for the Power Glove are arranged in a triangle, as shown in Figure 2.14. We will label each of the receivers with the letters R1, R2, and R3. R1 is the receiver in the upper left, R2 is the receiver in the upper right, and R3 is the receiver in the lower right corner. If we assume that receiver R1 is at position 0,0,0, then we can determine the position of the other two receivers. The distance from receiver R1 to R2 is 16 units, which means R2 is at position 16,0,0. Receiver R3 is 16 units from R1 and 16 units from R2; thus, it is at position 16,16,0. Notice that all of the positions have a zero for the z coordinate. This is because the three receivers are in the x-y coordinate plane.

Imagine for a moment that each of these receivers are the center points for three separate spheres. What we are trying to find out is the x, y, z position of the ultrasonic transmitter. This position is located on each of the spheres. The electronics from the Power Glove gives us the distance from a transmitter to each of the three receivers. Let's call these values R1d, R2d, and R3d, representing the distance from each of the receivers to one of the transmitters. If this is the case, then R1d is the radius of the sphere with center point R1 and the transmit-

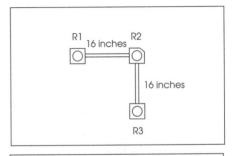

FIGURE 2.14 *Location of ultrasonic receivers*

ter location x, y, z. This is the case for each of the other two receivers. The problem we have is to find the x, y, z values that satisfy the equation of a sphere for each of the receivers. The equation of a sphere is:

$$\text{Radius}^2 = (x-x_{center})^2 + (y-y_{center})^2 + (z-z_{center})^2$$

If we substitute the coordinates for all three receivers, we have three sphere equations as such

$$R1^2 = (x-x1_{center})^2 + (y-y1_{center})^2 + (z-z1_{center})^2$$
$$R2^2 = (x-x2_{center})^2 + (y-y2_{center})^2 + (z-z2_{center})^2$$
$$R3^2 = (x-x3_{center})^2 + (y-y3_{center})^2 + (z-z3_{center})^2$$

Now if we substitute the above information about the origins of all three receivers, we obtain the equations

$$R1^2 = (x)^2 + (y)^2 + (z)^2$$
$$R2^2 = (x-16)^2 + (y)^2 + (z)^2$$
$$R3^2 = (x-16)^2 + (y-16)^2 + (z)^2$$

We can solve for the y and z unknowns in the first and second equations to obtain the equation

$$R1^2 = R2^2 + 32x - 256$$

Solving for x gives us

$$x = \frac{(R1^2 - R2^2 + 256)}{32}$$

We repeat the above procedure for each of the remaining equations to obtain the following:

$$y = \frac{(R2^2 - R3^2 + 256)}{32}$$

and

$$z = \text{SQRT}(R1^2 + x^2 + y^2)$$

If we look at our unknowns, we see that once the receiver has the R1, R2, and R3 distances, the electronics can determine where the transmitter is located and therefore where the hand is located.

Now let's run this through with some numbers. Assume that the receivers have the following distances: R1d = 25, R2d = 30, and R3d = 10. By substituting into the last equations, we determine that the glove is at position (0,33,41). This is a deceptive value because it is based on the position in space where the glove was centered.

Roll

The roll of the glove is much simpler. Remember that we have *two* transmitters on the glove. The only reason for this is to determine the roll of the glove. We must first locate the positions of both transmitters using the technique above. Using just a bit more math, we can see that if we take the difference of the x values and divide by the difference of the y values, we have the tangent of the roll angle.

$$\tan (\text{roll angle}) = \frac{(y_{t1} - y_{t2})}{(x_{t1} - x_{t2})}$$

Now all we need to do is a simple tangent function and we have the desired angle. But tangent functions are expensive computationally, so we will create a reference table with the precomputed tangent values. The electronics search this table for a close match to the value obtained in the above equation. Each of the precomputed values has a number associated with it from 0 to 11. The numbers and the roll positions of the glove are

0—Glove is positioned with palm down
3—Glove is positioned with palm facing left
6—Glove is positioned with palm up
9—Glove is positioned with palm to the right
11—Glove is just about in position of 0 above

These values are all approximate. If you have the glove in a position with the palm facing to the left, the numbers will vary from 2 to 4. That's all the math necessary for a decent ultrasonic tracker. Next we have to look at the Nintendo connector.

 # Programming the Power Glove

Now that you have the hardware finished for our Power Glove interface, you have to look at how to control the Power Glove through software. One of the first things to notice about the hardware interface is that everything is controlled through a clock, latch, and data line. I implied before that you were going to be able to get positioning and roll information from the glove. The glove sends this information in a serial fashion, one bit at a time. On top of that, there are specific timings involved that must be coordinated between the glove and the computer. But let's not get too carried away. We begin by looking at the low-res joystick mode of the Power Glove.

Low-Res Mode

Software for the low-res mode was included in the original *Byte* article on the parallel interface. The code was written in assembly language. What we will do here is look at a C version of the code and try to understand just what is involved in communicating with the glove.

The parallel port on the PC is located at hex 378. This is the *data output location*. When communicating with a printer, this is where we would output a character. Location 379 hex is a status register. It reads a status byte from the printer. This bit is really made up of five status lines that the printer can either set to 0 volts or 5 volts to indicate a problem.

In the low-res mode of the Power Glove, the glove is designed to emulate a joystick. Using a simple algorithm, we can ask the glove what it is doing, and it will respond with a single byte value that gives us the necessary information. The algorithm for accessing the low-res information is

```
Loop
        signal glove
        loop for 8 bits
        use 8 bits
end loop
```

Signal Glove

The glove is signaled by sending a value to the latch and clock signals of the interface. We begin by setting the latch line to 0 and keeping the clock line set at `outportb (0x378,1);`. The `outportb` command sends the send parameter, a byte, to the first parameter, an address. After the latch has been cleared, we load the latch line and pulse it: `outportb (0x378,3);`. The signaling is concluded by clearing the latch line: `outportb (0x378,1);`. The glove is now aware that we would like to receive information about its current position.

Loop for 8 Bits

As soon as we signal the glove for information, it will begin sending the information to us one bit at a time. We need to be able to receive the bits and form a complete byte out of them. The code to do this could look like the following:

```
b=0;
for(i=0;i<8;i++)
{
        b <= 1;
        b+=(inportb(0x379)&0x16)>>4;
        outportb (0x378,0);
        outportb (0x378,1);
}
b^=0xFF;
```

We begin by setting the variable in which we want the information to be stored to zero - `b=0;`. Next, we enter the loop for a total iteration count of 8 - `for(i=0;i<8;i++)`. Any information that is contained in our variable is shifted to the left to make room for another bit value - `b<=1;`. We read the parallel port and add the bit value to our variable - `b+=(inportb(0x379)&0x16)>>4;`. The loop iteration is ended by pulsing the clock line of the glove - `outportb(0x378,0); outportb(0x378,1);`.

Use 8 Bits

The last thing we do is use the 8 bits of data that have been returned to us. The meanings of each bit in our storage variable are as follows:

> *Bit 7—A value of 1 indicates that information is valid*
> *Bit 6—Set to 1 if glove is gripped or a button is pressed*
> *Bit 5—Set to 1 if SELECT button is pressed*
> *Bit 4—Set to 1 if START button is pressed*
> *Bit 3—Set to 1 if glove is moved up*
> *Bit 2—Set to 1 if glove is moved down*
> *Bit 1—Set to 1 if glove is moved to the left*
> *Bit 0—Set to 1 if glove is moved to the right*

Software

A compiled program is available on the enclosed disk called LOWRES.EXE. This program, when executed, will display the eight data bits coming from the glove. To start the glove in the correct mode, press the PROG key, then 0, 5, and ENTER. The glove will beep, and the numbers will begin to change. Now hold the glove in one position and press the CLEAR button. This will center the glove to the location you have it. If you move the glove to the left, out of this clear location, the movement will register on the screen.

The low-res mode of the Power Glove is useful for the purpose intended, a joystick emulator. However, it has very limited capability when applied to the task at hand, which is virtual reality. For this reason, we need to investigate the high-res mode of the Power Glove.

High-Res Mode

The high-res mode of the Power Glove is more complicated than the low-res mode. The main reason is that the glove expects information to be transferred to it according to a specific timing pattern. The glove operates in a give-and-take fashion. You give it a clock pulse and it will give you a bit (literally) of data.

The first step in getting any high-res data out of the glove is to put it into high-res mode. All of the public domain software agrees that the initialization algorithm for high-res mode is

```
Send a reset pulse to the glove
Read 4 bits from the glove and discard
Establish communication with the glove
using the clock and latch lines
Output a 7-byte code—0x06, 0xC1, 0x08,0x00, 0x02, 0xFF, 0x01
Delay
Drop reset line
Delay for awhile
```

For something closer to C code:

```
      // Send a reset pulse to the glove
      outportb (0x378, 0x01);
      outportb (0x378,0x03);
      delay (3-4 microseconds); // NOTE not milliseconds
      outportb (0x78, 0x02);
//    read four bits and discard
      delay (304 microseconds);
      outportb (0x378, 0);
      outportb (0x378, 0x01);
      delay (304 microseconds);
      outportb (0x378, 0);
      outportb (0x378, 0x01);
      delay (304 microseconds);
      outportb (0x378, 0);
      outportb (0x378, 0x01);
      delay (304 microseconds);
      outportb (0x378, 0);
      outportb (0x378, 0x01);
//    Establish communications
      outportb (0x378, 0x01);
      delay (7212 microseconds);
      outportb (0x378, 0x03);
      delay (2260 microseconds);
//    Send 7 bytes
      hi_res_codes[7] = {0x06, 0xC1, 0x08, 0x00,0x02, 0xFF, 0x01};
      for (i=0;i<7;i++)
      { x = hi_res_code[i];
       for (j=0;j<8;j++)       // output 8 bits at a time
       {
         if (x&0x80)
         {
          outportb(0x378,0x03);
          outportb ( 0x378, 0x02);
          outportb (0x378, 0x03);
         }
         else
         {
          outportb (0x378,0x01);
```

```
     outportb (0x378, 0x00);
     outportb (0x378, 0x01);
    }
    x=x<<1;
    delay(3-4 microseconds);
   }
   delay (85-150 microseconds);
}
delay(892 microseconds);
outportb (0x378, 0x01);
delay (50000 microseconds);
```

Let's look at a couple components of this code. The first is the output to the parallel port.

A read of a bit from the glove is accomplished by setting both the clock and the latch to a zero state; outportb (0x378, 0); . After this, the clock line is set high; outportb (0x378, 0x01). Then the bit is read from the data line of the glove, inportb(0x379)&0x01. Recall that the clock line of the Power Glove is attached to bit 0 of the parallel port.

The glove is reset using a pulse of the latch line. The latch line is set to zero state, but the clock is kept high; outportb (0x378, 0x01); . Then the latch line is set high along with the clock; outportb(0x378, 0x03); . A delay is made to allow the glove to read the latch line, and then the latch line is set back to the zero state, outportb (0x378, 0x01); .

A bit is sent to the glove using two different clock/latch combinations depending on whether the bit is a 1 or a 0. If the bit is a 1, the clock and latch lines are set high: outportb (0x378, 0x03); . Next, the clock is pulsed by setting it to zero and then back to the high state: outportb (0x378, 0x02); outportb (0x378, 0x03). If the bit is a 0, the same sequence is performed, but the latch is kept in the zero state: outportb (0x378, 0x01); outportb (0x378, 0x00); outportb (0x378, 0x01); . Between each bit there is a 3–4 microsecond delay, and between each byte there is an 85–150 microsecond delay.

Delay

At this point it would be a good idea to talk about the microsecond delays that must occur in the data transfer sequences. The glove was originally designed to work with a single microprocessor in the Nintendo machine. This processor is a 6502, the same processor as in the APPLE II series of microcomputers. This means that the designers could set up the bit transfers at the speed of the 6502 and that they did not have to worry about other machines. Since the interface to the PC, software designers have wrestled with the delays. The typical solution was to use a timing loop along with two variables that could increase or decrease the timing loop based on the machine being used. This works but is a hassle because there is no guarantee that the software will always work with the new PC on the block. A considerable portion of the timing problem was solved with a package called the OOGLOVE system by Mark Pflaging. He used a simple method that does calculations on the machine that the software is executing in order to find the values needed for the timing loops. This greatly enhanced the reliability of the Power Glove and the PC interface.

Glove Read

The last thing we have to do with the software interface is actually start reading data. The glove is set up to follow an algorithm:

```
Loop
        When read to send data output a 0xA0 value
        send X position
        send Y position
        send Z position
        send Rotation value
        send Fingers value
        send Buttons value
Endloop
```

The code for this algorithm is

```
while (!kbhit())
{
  while ((a = get_glove_byte()) != 0xA0)
    delay(2000-4000 microseconds);
  x = get_glove_byte();
  y = get_glove_byte();
  z = get_glove_byte();
  rot = get_glove_byte();
  fingers = get_glove_byte();
  buttons = get_glove_byte();
  discard = get_glove_byte();
  discard = get_glove_byte();
}
```

In order to use this code, we need the function get_glove_byte();. This function is

```
unsigned char get_glove_byte();
{
//Reset glove
  outportb(0x378,0x01);
  outportb (0x378,0x03);
  delay (3-4 microseconds);
  outportb (0x378,0x01);
//the above reset also triggers to glove to sending data because we
already saw the 0xA0
//read 8 bits
  for (i=0;i<8;i++)
  {
    val = val<<1;
```

```
    val += inportb(0x379) & 0x01;
    outportb (0x378,0x00);
    outportb (0x378,0x01);
  }
  delay(85-150 microseconds);
  return x;
}
```

Once the 0xA0 value has been detected and all bytes read from the glove, we can use them for whatever purpose necessary. Because of the interface to the PC, reading data from the glove is not simple yet not too complex. There are a number of public domain libraries available that are based on the examples above. Included on the enclosed disk is the file: glove.c—the very first software for the PC interface. This file has been enhanced by a number of different people. All of the source code is included for your experimentation.

Now that we know everything about how the Power Glove communicates and have code that will allow us to do the communication, it is time to write software that actually does something.

Power Glove Programming Example

For the simple examples that we are going to build, we will use the routines in the file glove.c. There are basically three files we will need. The first is a C header file. We will be using C for all of the examples in this book, it is by far the most widely used programming language in the VR field. In fact, most all of the code has been written with the Borland line of C compilers in mind. Unfortunately, I am not aware of any Pascal-based systems. The C header file we need from the disk is called glove.h. The second file we need is the actual C code compiled into an object file. This file is called glove.obj and is compiled in the large memory model.

Test.C

The third file we are going to use is actually the first of our example programs, which is the simplest possible test of the functionality of your glove. The main function is

```
void main()
        {
        glove_data glov;
        glove_init(IHIRES, NULL);
        printf("\n\n");
        while(!kbhit())
                if (glove_ready()) {
                        glove_read(&glov);
                        printf("%+4d %+4d %+4d %+4d %02.2X %02.2X \r",
                                glov.x, glov.y, glov.z, glov.rot,
```

```
                                        glov.fingers & 0xFF, glov.keys & 0xFF);
                      }
            else
                      glove_delay();
      getch();
      glove_quit();
      }
```

The code begins by setting up a variable called `glov` which is of type `glove_data`. `glove_data` is a simple data structure that holds some basic information about the glove and the data received. The glove is initialized with the statement `glove_init(IHIRES,NULL);`. The parameter `IHIRES` tells the initialization code to use an interrupt system to handle the timings. This is an enhancement of the original code. After the glove is initialized—this routine is basically the same as the code above for putting the glove into hires mode; it just has the interrupts added—we are ready to begin accepting data. The next part of the program should look familiar. We start by determining if the glove is ready to send data to us. If not, we just do a delay and try again. If the glove is ready to send data, we receive it using the statement `glove_read(&glov);`. After we have the data, we print out the details and loop to do it all again.

To execute this program, compile it using the Borland command-line compiler with the command `bcc(tcc) -o test.c glove.obj` or just type the command `test` at the command-line prompt to execute the precompiled version. The LEDs on the receiver should blink a couple of times and then begin blinking in a steady fashion. The screen should go blank, and a row of changing numbers will appear at the bottom of the screen. Point the glove toward the receiver triangle and press the CENTER button. By pressing CENTER, you are telling the glove that its current position is 0,0,0 and to begin all new readings from there.

If the only numbers that appear at the bottom are zeroes, then the computer is not communicating with the glove properly. Check the section "Troubleshooting the Power Glove and Connection" for help. If this is not the case, there should be six numbers rapidly changing as you move the glove. The first three numbers represent the x,y,z position to the glove, which allows a single byte for each of the x,y,z coordinates. In order to show movement in both directions along an axis, the glove responds with a positive value for one and a negative value for the other direction. This limits the total value to 127 and -127 for the three coordinates. Move the glove and observe the number changes.

The next number is the roll value for the glove. If you stand in front of the receiver triangle with your hand positioned palm down, the rotation number should be in the range of 3 to 5. If you twist your hand toward the left, the numbers will drop to 0 and if you twist to the right, the numbers will increase to 12.

The number following the rotation value is the position value for the fingers. When you start any program that uses the Power Glove, it is a good idea to make a grip several times to calibrate the system. After you do this, the computer should respond with the value 0 when your fingers are fully extended. If you slowly make a fist, the values will increase until they reach 255.

REND386 Examples

Now that we know what the Power Glove circuitry is sending to us and how the final values look to an application program, let's investigate a slightly more complex example. Sometime ago, a freeware rendering package was introduced for the PC. This package is called REND386 and was developed by Bernie Roehl and Dave Stampe. It consists of several hundred Borland C library routines that allow for the creation, viewing, and manipulation of three-dimensional objects; the scenes shown in the first chapters were created using it. One of the highlights of REND386 is its ability to interface with many different types of input devices, including the Power Glove. In this section, we will look at a simple program that mimics the action of the Power Glove using a virtual hand on the screen, and we will discuss the interface code necessary for the REND386 program. The majority of the REND386 program will be discussed in a later chapter.

The Hand

In order to realistically mimic your physical hand using the Power Glove, you need to have some type of virtual representation on the computer screen. There are many different choices, such as a tool or a block cursor, but the most rational choice is a hand. Figure 2.15 shows what our virtual hand will look like.

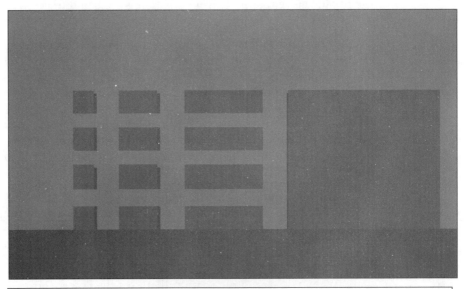

FIGURE 2.15 *Virtual hand created with REND386 objects*

The hand was created from an object format called *plg*. A plg object format is a simple way to represent a three-dimensional object using numbers. An example of a cube represented as a plg object is shown below (see Figure 2.16 for the actual cube):

```
cube  8  6
  0    0  100
  0  100  100
100  100  100
100    0  100
  0    0    0
  0  100    0
100  100    0
100    0    0
0x13EF  4  0  1  2  3
0x13EF  4  1  5  6  2
0x13EF  4  5  4  7  6
0x13EF  4  0  3  7  4
0x13EF  4  4  5  1  0
0x13EF  4  7  3  2  6
```

The actual meaning of the plg object format will be discussed in Chapter 14, so we will hold off talking about it here. Just remember that the plg files are a numerical representation of a three-dimensional object. In addition to plg files, REND386 supports an additional file format called the fig file, which allows the user to join some number of plg files to make a more complex object.

FIGURE 2.16 *Rendered view of cube represented in code above*

The fig files are unique in that they allow joints to be associated with any two objects. For instance, if we are going to model the human hand, then each of the fingers must be described in a manner that allows them to perform naturally. If we tap one of our fingers on the desk, we are not just moving a single piece of the finger; there are actually three different segments, each separated by a joint. By developing our virtual hand in a fig file, we can represent each of the segments and joints accurately without much overhead. We will represent our hand as shown in Figure 2.17.

The complete code for the virtual hand is shown below (see Figure 2.15 for a look at the actual hand). Now that we have a virtual representation for our hand, we have to learn how to communicate with the Power Glove using the REND386 renderer.

```
{
    name=hand;
    plgfile=metlcube.plg scale 4,3,0.5 shift 0,0,0;
    pos=0,0,0;
    {
        name=first1;
        plgfile=redcube.plg scale 2,0.5,0.5 shift 0,0,0;
        pos=-250,0,0;
        {
            name=first2;
            plgfile=bluecube.plg scale 1,0.5,0.5 shift 0,0,0;
            pos=-150,0,0;
            {
                name=first3;
                plgfile=grencube.plg scale 0.5,0.5,0.5 shift 0,0,0;
                pos=-100,0,0;
            }
        }
    }
    {
        name=second1;
        plgfile=redcube.plg scale 2,0.5,0.5 shift 0,0,0;
        pos=-250,85,0;
```

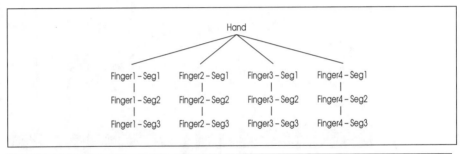

FIGURE 2.17 *Flowchart for segment representation of virtual hand*

```
    {
       name=second2;
       plgfile=bluecube.plg scale 1,0.5,0.5 shift 0,0,0;
       pos=-150,0,0;
       {
          name=second3;
          plgfile=grencube.plg scale 0.5,0.5,0.5 shift 0,0,0;
          pos=-100,0,0;
       }
    }
 }
 {
    name=third1;
    plgfile=redcube.plg scale 2,0.5,0.5 shift 0,0,0;
    pos=-250,170,0;
    {
       name=third2;
       plgfile=bluecube.plg scale 1,0.5,0.5 shift 0,0,0;
       pos=-150,0,0;
       {
          name=third3;
          plgfile=grencube.plg scale 0.5,0.5,0.5 shift 0,0,0;
          pos=-100,0,0;
       }
    }
 }{
    name=fourth1;
    plgfile=redcube.plg scale 2,0.5,0.5 shift 0,0,0;
    pos=-250,250,0;
    {
       name=fourth2;
       plgfile=bluecube.plg scale 1,0.5,0.5 shift 0,0,0;
       pos=-150,0,0;
       {
          name=fourth3;
          plgfile=grencube.plg scale 0.5,0.5,0.5 shift 0,0,0;
          pos=-100,0,0;
       }}}}
```

Power Glove/REND386 Connection

Both of the authors of REND386 are responsible for several updates to the original glove code used in the "Power Glove Programming Example" section of this chapter. Therefore, it should come as no surprise that some of the glove code ended up in the initial releases of REND386; in fact, the first few releases used the exact same code before it was rewritten for a subsequent release.

This simple program works using the following algorithm:

```
Initialize the REND386 system
Initialize the Power Glove
Read the current position of the glove and store
Loop
```

```
        put stored position of glove in temp storage
        read the current position of the glove and store
        move the virtual hand the difference between the temp position
        and current position
        if (glove_grip) and (not in a fist)
                grip glove
        else if (in a fist)
                ungrip glove
End loop
Release everything
```

The most important part of the algorithm is calculating the difference between the current position of the glove and the old position. This subtraction will give us the number of units that the glove has moved relative to its old position, which is the number of units that we must move the glove.

Execution

The program that performs the above algorithm is called GLOVREND.EXE and can be found on the enclosed disk. To execute the program, type GLOVREND at the command prompt and press RETURN. Note that you must have your Power Glove attached to the parallel printer port LPT1 on your computer in order for the program to work correctly.

3

Using a Regular Mouse and Building a 3-D Mouse

Now wait a minute. Why would we consider using a mouse as a virtual reality input device? The reason is simple—most people have one, which means that a lot of people will be able to experiment with virtual reality by using this simple but effective little device.

 The Mouse

As you know, the mouse is normally used as a pointing device that allows us to make selections in an application without having to use the keyboard. We want to do the same thing in VR, but we aren't going to represent the mouse on screen with a little arrow; furthermore, our mouse will be 3-D. Whether the user has a serial or a bus mouse, a mouse driver is loaded when the computer is first booted. The mouse driver converts the mouse's raw information into something useful for an application. DOS uses software interrupt number 33 to act as an interpreter between our application and the mouse driver. The complete list of interrupt 33 services is listed in Figure 3.1.

The services we will be using are 0, 3, and 11. Before we can use the mouse, we have to determine if a mouse driver using service 0 has been installed. In order to access service 0 of interrupt 33, we must load the CPU's AX register with a value of 00, execute the interrupt, and look for the results of the service in registers AX and BX. The Borland C code to perform this is

```
union REGS r;
r.x.ax = 0;
int86 (0x33, &r, &r);
if (r.x.ax == 0) THEN NO DRIVER INSTALLED
else  AX = FFFF (indicating that a driver is present)  and
      BX = number of buttons on mouse
```

That's all there is to it. Once we have determined that the mouse driver is installed, we are ready to receive data about the mouse's position, which can be completely supplied by interrupt 33 services 3 and 11. Service 3 has two purposes, the first of which is to report the condition of the buttons on the mouse and the second, to return the current position of the mouse based on a 640 x 200 resolution grid. Upon return from the interrupt, the CX register will contain the current x position of the mouse in units from 0 to 639, whereas the DX register will tell us the y position of the mouse in units from 0 to 199. The BX register will tell us the condition of the buttons. The bits of BX are given the values shown in Figure 3.2.

```
INT 33,0    Mouse Reset/Get Mouse Installed Flag
INT 33,1    Show Mouse Cursor
INT 33,2    Hide Mouse Cursor
INT 33,3    Get Mouse Position and Button Status
INT 33,4    Set Mouse Cursor Position
INT 33,5    Get Mouse Button Press Information
INT 33,6    Get Mouse Button Release Information
INT 33,7    Set Mouse Horizontal Min/Max Position
INT 33,8    Set Mouse Vertical Min/Max Position
INT 33,9    Set Mouse Graphics Cursor
INT 33,A    Set Mouse Text Cursor
INT 33,B    Read Mouse Motion Counters
INT 33,C    Set Mouse User Defined Subroutine and Input Mask
INT 33,D    Mouse Light Pen Emulation On
INT 33,E    Mouse Light Pen Emulation Off
INT 33,F    Set Mouse Mickey Pixel Ratio
INT 33,10   Mouse Conditional OFF
INT 33,13   Set Mouse Double Speed Threshold
INT 33,14   Swap interrupt subroutines
INT 33,15   Get mouse driver state and memory requirements
INT 33,16   Save mouse driver state
INT 33,17   Restore mouse driver state
INT 33,18   Set alternate subroutine call mask and address
INT 33,19   Get user alternate interrupt address
INT 33,1A   Set mouse sensitivity
INT 33,1B   Get mouse sensitivity
INT 33,1C   Set mouse interrupt rate (InPort only)
INT 33,1D   Set mouse CRT page
INT 33,1E   Get mouse CRT page
INT 33,1F   Disable mouse driver
INT 33,20   Enable mouse driver
INT 33,21   Reset mouse software
INT 33,22   Set language for messages
INT 33,23   Get language number
INT 33,24   Get driver version, mouse type & IRQ number
```

FIGURE 3.1 **Mouse driver services available**

If a button is pressed, the appropriate bit will have a value of 1 instead of 0. For our virtual reality work, only the button information from this service will be used. The position information is not of much use because of the small unit grid it returns.

Software

The program MOUSE1.EXE on the enclosed disk gives a short demonstration of how to use the mouse and the two interrupt services. It will simply output the current location of the mouse and the status of the buttons.

Motion Counters

Because we cannot use the positioning information from the mouse using service 3, we need to look at service 11, which returns the counts from motion

```
            CX = horizontal (X) position
            DX = vertical (Y) position
            BX = button status:

                    |F-8|7|6|5|4|3|2|1|0|  Button Status
                    | | | | | | | |       +-- left button
                    | | | | | | | |    +--- right button
                    | | | | | | | | +----- middle Button
                    +--------------- unused
```

FIGURE 3.2 *Service 3 return values for Interrupt 33*

counters inside the mouse. Each count (or *mickey*, as they are sometimes called) is equivalent to 0.005 inch. Each time service 11 is called, the mickey counts for the horizontal and vertical movements are returned, and the counters are reset to zero. The call to the service is basically the same as the previous call, so we will not demonstrate it here.

What we need to do is talk about a little problem. The mouse is a two-dimensional input device. It returns to us the position or movement in the horizontal, or x, coordinate and the vertical, or y, coordinate but has no way of giving information about the z axis. It would be pretty tough to push the mouse into the mouse pad and tabletop. Several companies have solved this problem by developing three-dimensional mice, but these input devices are still quite expensive. So we have two options: simulate the third dimension or build a 3-D mouse. We will do both.

 # Simulating 3-D with a Regular Mouse

Actually simulating the z coordinate using the mouse is quite easy. All PC mice have a minimum of two buttons. We will reserve the left button for a purpose detailed later on in the chapter, which leaves the right mouse button open for any other use. When we use the mouse normally, the left and right motions correspond to the x coordinate and the forward and backward motions to the y coordinate. In our scheme, pressing the right mouse button will indicate to the software that any forward and backward movement should be interpreted as movement in the z coordinate axis. Let's assume that the variables `mouse_x`, `mouse_y`, and `mouse_z` hold the current movement of the mouse. The following code would then give us movement in all three planes:

```
union REGS r;
r.x.ax = 3;
int86(0x33,&r,&r);
mouse_buttons = r.x.bx;
r.x.ax = 11;
int86 ( 0x33, &r, &r);
mouse_x = (int) r.x.cx;
if (mouse_buttons & 0x02)
        mouse_z = (int)r.x.dx;
else
        mouse_y = (int)r.x.dx;
```

The program MOUSEZ.EXE on the enclosed disk gives an example of using the mouse as a 3 degree of freedom (DOF) input device. Degree of freedom refers to a device's range of movement. Those that are able to move up and down have 1 DOF; those that can also move right and left have 2 DOF; and those with the capability to move forward and backward, too, have 3 DOF. The program will output the current state of the mouse buttons as well as the counters for the motion counters.

Building a 3-D Mouse ❗❗

Figure 3.3 shows what our Power Glove 3-D mouse is going to look like. Basically, it is the Power Glove without the finger mechanisms and with your mouse. By converting the Power Glove as we have, it will provide us with a system that can be used for various tracking duties. You will see a reference to this conversion in Chapter 13.

Before we start the actual conversion, I want to let you know that the following procedure will be very destructive to the Power Glove. You will not be able to use it as we did in Chapter 2. We are only interested in the Power Glove's ultrasonic tracking mechanism, so we will be throwing out the finger sensors. If you do not have an extra glove lying around, you may not want to do this conversion.

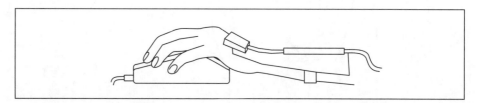

FIGURE 3.3 **The 3-D mouse**

3-D Mouse Parts

You will need the following:
- ❑ 1 Power Glove
- ❑ 1 Mouse
- ❑ 1 Phillips screwdriver
- ❑ 1 Knife or scissors

The first step is to disassemble the Power Glove. We will begin by removing the ultrasonic transmitter enclosure. On the underside of the enclosure are four screws that need to be removed. The fourth screw is hidden behind a plastic flap on the thumb side (see Figure 3.4). Just pull the plastic, and you will have access to the screws. Carefully remove the top of the enclosure.

Next, unscrew all five screws inside the enclosure (see Figure 3.5). Notice that two of the screws help to hold the circuit board to the cover. After you have all of the screws out, the circuit board and the bottom part of the enclosure should be loose. They will not come off because of the wires for the finger metal.

We do not need the finger sensors for our 3-D mouse, so clip the wires that run to the circuit board as close as possible to the board itself. Better yet, use a soldering iron to remove the wires completely. After you have done this, the ultrasonic enclosure will move away from the glove but not completely because

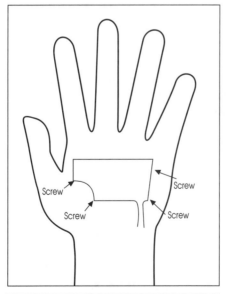

FIGURE 3.4 *Screws outside ultrasonic enclosure*

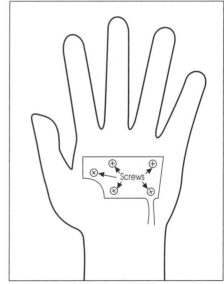

FIGURE 3.5 *Screws inside ultrasonic enclosure*

it is attached to the computer module on the glove's "forearm." Before continuing, place the circuit board back into the bottom part of its enclosure and replace the top, but be careful of the plastic tube with the wires running to the computer module. Be sure to place the plastic into the slot in the enclosure. Once the top is replaced, screw the enclosure together using the screws we removed in the first step.

If you turn the glove over, you should see a small piece of plastic with a black bottom. This is the piece to which the enclosure was attached. Remove it and set it aside; we will need it later. We will now remove the computer module. This step is not entirely necessary, but it makes working with the glove much easier; anyway, it's not hard to remove. Turn the glove over and look for the four screws in the corners of the forearm part of the glove (see Figure 3.6). Unscrew these screws, and the computer module will come off. The back cover to the module will come off as well. This will give you a chance to look at the computer chips that handle the math we did in Chapter 2. You can set the entire unit to the side as we will be working with the plastic glove.

We now need to remove the finger metals. This can be a bit tricky. What we have are four pieces of thin metal that run down the first three fingers and the thumb. Each of the pieces has two wires attached to it. These wires are glued to the top plastic of the glove and snake out of the opening on top. To remove the metal, pull up on the top opening and cut to the right of the glove with a pair of scissors (see Figure 3.7). You should be able to pull the plastic up enough to see what you are cutting. Once you have done this, you should be able to pull the plastic up enough to detach the ring finger wires from the glove. Once you have the wires detached, wiggle the finger metal from the ring finger. To remove the other metal, just keep cutting toward the fingers, removing the wires and metal.

Once we have the metal fingers removed, we want to remove the cloth glove on the underside of the Power Glove. It will detach from the plastic with a little force. I found it easiest to remove by starting at the base of the fingers and pulling at one of the edges (see Figure 3.8). After that, the glove

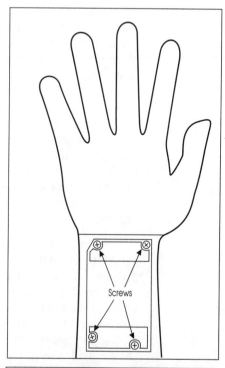

FIGURE 3.6 **Screws on underside of glove**

will pull right off. You should now have a Power Glove plastic shell. We are now going to remove the fingers. With the top of the glove facing you, notice the five holes in the center of the glove; this is where the ultrasonic enclosure attaches to it. We want to preserve this part of the glove. Using scissors again, cut a line toward the fingers from the back of the glove (see Figure 3.9). In other words, once cut, the thumb is no longer on the glove, and a section of the pinkie has been removed. The glove should be of equal width. Next, cut off the fingers about a quarter to half an inch from the top holes in the glove (see Figure 3.10). Now we just reassemble the glove. Begin by putting the ultrasonic enclosure back on. You will need to open the enclosure up to do this. Once open, place the small piece we removed from the underside of the glove back into place. The longer posts on the piece should be to the right of the glove. Once through, place the bottom of the enclosure over the posts and replace the circuit board. Screw the five screws into place and the enclosure is attached. Replace the cover and screw the four screws into it. The last step is to replace the computer module with its four screws, and the 3-D mouse is finished.

In order to test the system, the program 3DMOUSE.EXE has been put on the enclosed disk. This program will display the current position of the mouse and the status of the mouse buttons. There is no additional wiring necessary because your 3-D mouse will use the interface from Chapter 2. The system is a Power Glove without the fingers, which are

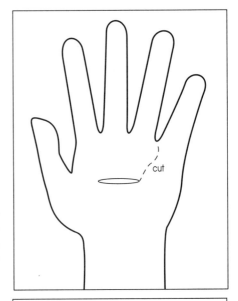

FIGURE 3.7 **Top opening and right cut**

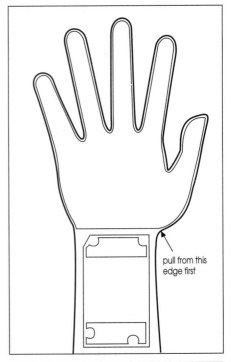

FIGURE 3.8 **Removing the cloth glove**

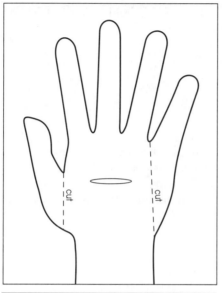

FIGURE 3.9 **Cut thumb and pinkie off**

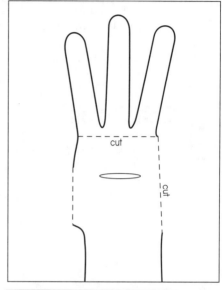

FIGURE 3.10 **No more fingers**

replaced by the mouse buttons. The majority of the weight of the Power Glove has been removed and you will find that it is not hard to use the 3-D mouse or type with the tracker section attached to your forearm.

Complete Hand

We have looked at several different mouse systems, discussed their software interfaces, and executed programs that display what the mouse is doing. The last thing we need to do is look at a system that allows the mouse to mimic a virtual hand. The programs RENDMS1.BAT and RENDMS2.BAT are REND386 programs that, like the Power Glove program discussed in Chapter 2, allow the mouse to control a virtual hand. RENDMS1.BAT uses the ordinary mouse without the Power Glove position tracker and RENDMS2.BAT is for the 3-D mouse. Not much changes between the programs except that we no longer have fingers to bend that cause the virtual hand fingers to bend as well. We need a way to do this with our mice. Remember that we were going to reserve the left mouse button for a specific purpose, and this is it. When using your mouse and this program, press the left mouse button, and the virtual hand will

grip and remain gripped as long as you hold it down. As soon as you let up on the button, the hand will ungrip.

Conclusion

The mouse provides a very simple and easy-to-use interface for virtual reality. In addition, most computer systems come with mice, so the potential market for VR applications is huge. By using the functionality of the Power Glove, we can create a usable version of equipment that costs over a thousand dollars.

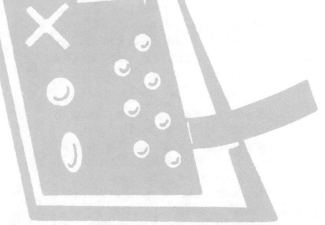

4

The Global 3D Controller and Logitech's CyberMan

*T*he lack of input devices for virtual reality has led many companies to create products to fill the void. One such product that we need to discuss is called the Global 3D Controller (GDC) from Global Devices (see Appendix B for a list of manufacturers of VR-related equipment). This input device, shown in Figure 4.1, is unique because it allows for a total 6 DOF input to the computer.

The program G3DMATE.EXE on the enclosed disk is a virtual chess game that allows the Global 3D Controller to manipulate a virtual hand. Appendix A explains how to execute this program.

Operation

The GDC is a digital device that tells the computer the position of many different ent switches. On the base of the unit is a joystick mechanism that reports the status of five switches that monitor the forward, backward, left, right, and vertical positions.

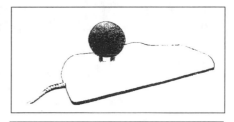

FIGURE 4.1 *The Global 3D Controller*

The mechanism in Figure 4.2 is just a basic design for a joystick. When the joystick is moved in any of the four directions, a connection is made between a specific pair of contacts. The mechanism recognizes the contact and reports it to the host computer. To keep the joystick in the center, each of the four sides apply a slight pressure using springs.

To register the up-and-down movement of the joystick, a slightly different approach could be used. This is shown in Figure 4.3. The joystick would normally ride in a neutral position between two different sets of contacts using a set of springs. When the joystick is pulled up, a connection is made between the top contacts. The

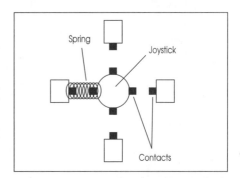

FIGURE 4.2 *Possible joystick mechanism for GDC*

spring will cause the joystick to be pulled back to a center position. The same is true when the joystick is pushed down. Keep in mind, however, that this is just my speculation about how the controller was designed.

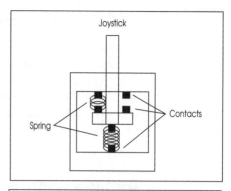

FIGURE 4.3 *Possible up/down switches for GDC*

Top Ball

In addition to the movements just mentioned, the GDC is able to report three additional movements: yaw, pitch, and roll. The controller is able to provide this information by means of a ball on top of the joystick that is allowed to rotate in those three movements. Each of the rotations requires a specific movement of the ball by the hand.

Yaw

The rotation of yaw is about the *y* axis. If you turn your head from left to right, you are yawing. In the case of the GDC, this action requires you to grab a racquetball positioned on top of the joystick in your hand and turn it left and right. Figure 4.4 is an illustration of what the contacts that detect this movement may look like.

According to Figure 4.4, a small platform with two contacts on each side could be attached to the ball. Just opposite of each contact would be another bar with contacts on it attached to the joystick. When the ball is rotated left, the contacts between one of the bars and the ball contacts would connect. If the ball was rotated to the right, the other contacts would connect. Again, a couple of springs could be used to help bring the ball back to its original position.

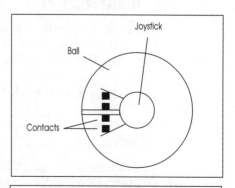

FIGURE 4.4 *Possible contacts needed for yaw*

Pitch

The pitch of the ball is measured when the hand tilts the ball either forward or backward. Figure 4.5 illustrates possible contact positions. When the hand tilts the ball, it moves just enough in each direction to create a connection between the appropriate contacts.

Roll

The roll of the ball is measured when the hand rotates the ball from side to side. The possible contact positions are the same as for yaw except that they are on the left and right sides of the ball.

Tactile Feedback

The Global 3D Controller has a unique feature for tactile feedback that will be explained in more detail in Chapter 5.

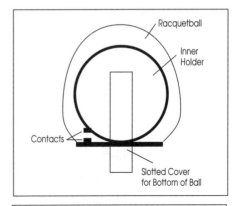

FIGURE 4.5 ***Possible contacts for pitch rotation***

Programming the Global 3D Controller

The Global 3D Controller is attached to the computer through an RS-232 port. Inside the GDC is a microprocessor that monitors all of the switches and relays the data to the computer through the serial line. In order for the host computer to read the data, it must establish communication with the GDC. Information is transmitted at a rate of 9600 baud with `no parity` and `1 stop bit`. The only signals used in the serial line are `transmit`, `receive`, and `ground`.

Initialization

The first thing that has to be done is initializing the controller. To determine if the controller is available for use, the host sends the value `0x8F` to the controller. If the controller is available, it will respond with one of six possible return codes: `0x35`, `0x3A`, `0x3E`, `0x34`, `0x3B`, or `0x3F`. Each of the return codes defines a specific mode the controller could be in.

0x35

This return code indicates that the controller is in a 3-byte polled mode and that there are no buttons on the controller. This is the default mode when the controller is powered up. When the host computer requests the status of the controller in this mode, the controller returns 3 bytes—*linear, rotational,* and *button*.

0x3A

This return code indicates that the controller is in a 3-byte exception mode and that there are no buttons on the controller. If the controller is in this mode, it will return three bytes—again; linear, rotational, and button—whenever there is an action by the user.

0x3E

This return code indicates that the controller is in a single-byte exception mode and that there are no buttons on the controller. If the controller is in this mode, it will return a single byte depending on the action of the user. If the user makes a linear change, the linear byte is returned. If the user makes a rotational change, the rotational byte is returned.

0x34, 0x3B, and 0x3F

These are the same as return codes 0x35, 0x3A, and 0x3E, repectively, except that the controller has buttons.

Once we have determined that the controller is available and what mode it is in, we can either change the mode, request a piece of data, or activate the feedback mechanism.

Change Modes

We can change the mode of the 3-D controller by sending it one of the following bytes:

> 0x84—*puts the controller in 3-byte polled mode*
> 0x84—*puts the controller in 3-byte exception mode*
> 0x84—*puts the controller in single-byte exception mode*

After the controller receives the byte and changes modes, it returns a status byte as previously described.

Request Data

When requesting data from the controller, we have to be aware of what mode the controller is in. Each of the different modes requires a slightly different format for requesting and receiving the data.

The controller only has one mode that needs to be polled: the 3-byte polled mode. The other two modes send data based on the user's actions. To request data in the polled mode, the host computer sends the value 0x81 to the controller. The controller responds with a linear, rotational, and button byte. Each of the bytes returned from the controller has a specific purpose and is identified by the values in bits 6 and 7. The linear byte has a 0 in bit position 7 and a 1 in bit position 6. The rotational byte has a 1 in bit position 7 and a 1 in bit position 6. The button byte has a 1 in bit position 7 and a 0 in bit position 6.

Linear Status Byte

The remaining 6 bits of the linear status byte are defined as follows:

Bit 5—down
Bit 4—up
Bit 3—left
Bit 2—right
Bit 1—backward
Bit 0—forward

If any of the bits are set to 1, then the user has moved the controller. The bit will remain a 1 until the user no longer performs the movement.

Rotation Status Byte

The remaining 6 bits of the rotational status byte are as follows:

Bit 5—Roll counterclockwise
Bit 4—Roll clockwise
Bit 3—Pitch down
Bit 2—Pitch up
Bit 1—Yaw left
Bit 0—Yaw right

A value of 1 indicates movement as in the linear byte.

Button

Because the current models of the Global 3D Controller do not have buttons, all 6 remaining bits are undefined.

Activate Feedback

The last activity that we can do with the Global 3D Controller is the tactile feedback mechanism. In order to activate the feedback, the host computer sends a specific code to the controller that indicates which of two modes to use. The code bytes are differentiated by their upper nibbles. The two different modes are *variable intensity* and *timed pulse*.

Variable Intensity

The code byte to activate the variable intensity feedback has a binary value of 1010 in its upper nibble. The lower nibble corresponds to the intensity based on these values:

```
binary 0000. Feedback is OFF
binary 0001. Minimal intensity
       ....
binary 1111. Maximum intensity
```

Once the feedback mechanism has been turned on at the desired intensity, you must send another byte, 0xA0, to turn it off manually.

Timed Pulse

In the timed pulse mode, the upper nibble of the code byte is 1011. The lower nibble can have the values:

```
binary 0001. timed pulse of .05 seconds
 ....
binary 1111. timed pulse of .8 seconds
```

Because this mode works on a timer, there is no need to send a second byte to turn off the mechanism. If you send a second timed pulse code to the controller while it has the feedback mechanism activated, the timer will be reset to the new value.

Initialization Code

The C code necessary for the initialization of the controller is as follows:

```c
unsigned char initialize_3d_controller( int port )
{
 com_install ( port );
 com_set_speed ( 9600 );
 com_set_parity ( COM_NONE, 1 );
 com_tx ( 0x8f );
 return com_rx();
}
```

First, a piece of driver software has to be installed that will handle the communication between the computer and the serial port. It is set to the communication parameters specified in the controller's protocol, which are 9600 baud, no parity, 8 data bits, 1 stop bit.

Once the driver is installed, we send the CONFIG QUERY byte 0x8F to the controller. We will return the CONFIG STATUS byte sent by the controller to the calling routine.

Change Config Code

The next piece of code changes the current mode of the controller into a different mode based on a parameter from the user. The code for the operation is

```
unsigned char change_3d_controller_mode ( unsigned char mode )
{
 unsigned in;

 com_tx(mode);

 if ((in=com_rx()) == ( mode - 0x50 ))
   return 1;
 else
   return 0;

}
```

The routine works by sending the desired mode value to the controller. According to the protocol, the controller will respond with a CONFIG STATUS byte that tells us what mode the controller is now in. Because there are different models of the controller, we need to compare the status byte returned and the mode we asked the controller to go into. The comparison determines whether we return a 1 or a 0 to the calling routine.

Read Controller Code

Once the controller is initialized and the current mode set, we can begin reading data from it. The following code is able to read data using any of the modes.

```
void read_3d_controller ( G3D_STRUCT * info )
{
 unsigned linear, rotation, button, bytea, byteb, bytec;

 switch ( G3D_CONTROLLER_MODE )
 {
 case 0x35:
 {
  com_tx(0x81);

  while ( (bytea=com_rx()) == '\0' );
  while ( (byteb=com_rx()) == '\0' );
  while ( (bytec=com_rx()) == '\0' );
```

```
    if ( (bytea & 0xC0) == 0x40) linear = bytea;
    if ( (byteb & 0xC0) == 0x40) linear = byteb;
    if ( (bytec & 0xC0) == 0x40) linear = bytec;

    if ( (bytea & 0xC0) == 0xC0) rotation = bytea;
    if ( (byteb & 0xC0) == 0xC0) rotation = byteb;
    if ( (bytec & 0xC0) == 0xC0) rotation = bytec;
    }
  break;

  case 0x3A:
  {
   bytea=com_rx();
   if ( bytea != '\0' )
   {
    while ( (byteb=com_rx()) == '\0' );
    while ( (bytec=com_rx()) == '\0' );


    if ( (bytea & 0xC0) == 0x40) linear = bytea;
    if ( (byteb & 0xC0) == 0x40) linear = byteb;
    if ( (bytec & 0xC0) == 0x40) linear = bytec;

    if ( (bytea & 0xC0) == 0xC0) rotation = bytea;
    if ( (byteb & 0xC0) == 0xC0) rotation = byteb;
    if ( (bytec & 0xC0) == 0xC0) rotation = bytec;
    }
   }
  break;

  case 0x3E:
  {
   int i;

   bytea = com_rx();
   }
  break;
  }
 }
```

The code will perform three different actions based on the current mode of the controller. If the controller is in polled mode, the computer will send the byte code 0x81 to the controller and wait for 3 bytes to be returned to it. Upon reception, it tests bits 6 and 7 to determine which are the linear, rotational, and button bytes. Each of the bytes received is assigned to an appropriate variable.

If the controller is in the 3-byte exception mode, the host computer will make a quick check of the receive buffer of the serial port. If it is empty, there is no work to do. If the buffer contains characters, then we go through the same procedure as above.

If the controller is in the single-byte exception mode, we test the receive buffer; if there is a character available, we know that it is either the linear or rotational code byte. We determine which it is and make the appropriate assignment.

Tactile Feedback Code

The last code that we have to look at is for the tactile feedback mechanisms. Recall that there are two different ways to activate the feedback.

Intensity Mode

The code for the intensity mode of the feedback mechanism is

```
void set_3d_controller_tactile ( unsigned char intensity, int length )
{

 if ( intensity <= 0 )
   com_tx(0xA0);
 else if ( intensity >= 15 )
   com_tx(0xAF);
 else
   com_tx(0xA0|intensity);

 delay ( length );

 com_tx(0xA0);
}
```

For the intensity mode, we have to have both an intensity value and the length of time that we wish the feedback to occur. We begin by setting the current intensity. If the value given to us is less than 0, then we set the intensity to 0; if the intensity is greater than 15, then we set the intensity to 15. Otherwise, we set the intensity to the desired value.

After the intensity is set, we do a delay for the specified number of milliseconds. Once the delay is finished, we turn the feedback off.

Timed Mode

For the timed mode, we have this code:

```
void set_3d_controller_tactile_pulse ( unsigned char time )
{
 if ( time <= 0 )
   com_tx(0xB0);
 else if ( time >= 15 )
   com_tx(0xBF);
 else
   com_tx(0xB0|time);
}
```

For the timed tactile feedback mode, we simply determine if the time requested is less than 0. If it is, then we output the smallest time possible; if the time is greater than 15, then we output the largest time possible; and in all other cases we simply output the requested time amount.

Using the CyberMan for VR

Logitech has introduced a new low-cost (less than $90) input device. The CyberMan is a 3-D mouse with built-in tactile feedback (essentially a buzzer that can vibrate at different speeds as determined by the software running it). The driver that runs the CyberMan can also be used to run any standard mouse.

Refer to Appendix A to see how to activate the CyberMan with the software on the enclosed disk.

Programming the CyberMan

All of the following functions are available in source and object form on the enclosed disk (see Appendix A for installation instructions). The addition to the Logitech mouse driver is called SWIFT, or SenseWare InterFace Technology. The CyberMan is accessed through the SWIFT functions of software interrupt 33h. There are six basic functions necessary for controlling the CyberMan:

> *Get SWIFT static device data and driver support status*
> *Is CyberMan available?*
> *Get SWIFT dynamic device data*
> *Get absolute position, orientation, and button status*
> *SET/GET event handler*
> *Program tactile feedback*

We will look at each of the functions separately.

Get SWIFT Static Device Data and Driver Support Status

The static device data contains 10 bytes of data concerning any SWIFT device attached to the mouse driver. It is invoked using function 53C1h of software interrupt 33h. A 10-byte data area is provided to the interrupt in order to pass information about the controller to the calling routine. Upon return from the interrupt, the function will indicate the following:

> *1. If AX = 1, then the loaded driver supports SWIFT devices*
> *2. Device type—byte position 0*

3. *Major version number—byte position 1*
4. *Minor version number—byte position 2*
5. *X Coordinate descriptor—byte position 3*
6. *Y Coordinate descriptor—byte position 4*
7. *Z Coordinate descriptor—byte position 5*
8. *Pitch coordinate descriptor—byte position 6*
9. *Roll coordinate descriptor—byte position 7*
10. *Yaw coordinate descriptor—byte position 8*
11. *Reserved —Byte position 9*

The coordinate descriptors are

Bits 0-3—Bits of resolution
Bit 4—reserved
Bit 5—"Return to Center if 1" means device returns to center position when
    user releases device
Bit 6—1 = absolute, 0 = relative
Bit 7—Reserved

The code for this function would be something like this:

```
typedef struct _cyberman_static {
                        unsigned char  device_type,
                                       major_version,
                                       minor_version,
                                       x_coord,
                                       y_coord,
                                       z_coord,
                                       pitch_coord,
                                       roll_coord,
                                       yaw_coord,
                                       reserved;
                } cyberman_static_data;

int get_SWIFT_static(struct cyberman_static_data *data)
{
    struct REGPACK r;

    r.r_ax = 0x53C1;
    r.r_es = FP_SEG (data);
    r.r_dx = FP_OFF(DATA);
    intr(0x33, &r );

    if (r.x.ax == 1) return 1;
    else return 0;
}
```

Is CyberMan Available?

Using the function for getting the static data, we can determine whether or not a CyberMan is attached to the system by looking at the device type field of the static data. If device type is a 1, then a CyberMan is attached to the system. If device type is 0, no SWIFT device is attached. All other values are reserved for additional SWIFT devices. Our function would appear as

```
int cyberman_available()
{
    struct cyberman_static_data data;

    get_SWIFT_static (&data);
    if ( data.device_type == 1) return 1;
    else return 0;
}
```

Once we know a SWIFT device is attached, we can begin getting data about the device.

Get SWIFT Dynamic Device Data

The current dynamic device data defined for the CyberMan is whether or not external power is attached to the device and whether or not the power supply is too high. The external power supply is used for the tactile feedback motor. The CyberMan's tactile feedback will not operate when the external power is higher than recommended. The function is called by putting the value 53C2h in register AX and calling interrupt 33h.

Upon return, Bit 0 of the AX register is set to 1 if external power is attached to the CyberMan. Bit 1 of the AX register is set to 1 if the external power supply is too high. Bits 2–15 are reserved. Our code looks like this:

```
void get_SWIFT_dynamic(unsigned *data)
{
 struct REGPACK r;

 r.r_ax = 0x53C2;
 intr(0x33, &r);
 *data = r.r_ax;
}
```

Get Absolute Position, Orientation, and Button Status

In order to tell whether or not the user is doing something to the CyberMan, we have to ask it. Function 5301h does the asking for us. This function expects a seven-word buffer for the information. Once executed, our buffer will contain the following information:

> *Word 0—x Position: 254 distinct x values from −8128 to +8064 in increments of 64*
> *Word 1—y Position: 254 distinct y values from −8128 to +8064 in increments of 64*
> *Word 2—z Position: 3 values, −8192, 0, +8191*
> *Word 3—Pitch Position: 3 values, −8192, 0, +8191*

Word 4—Roll Position: 3 values, −8192, 0, +8191
Word 5—Yaw Position: 3 values, −8192, 0, +8191
Word 6—Button Status: Bit 0—Right Button, 1 = Pressed
Bit 1—Middle Button, 1 = Pressed
Bit 2—Right Button, 1 = Pressed
Bits 3–15—Reserved

Our code is

```
typedef struct _cyberman_information {
                                    int  x,
                                         y,
                                         z,
                                         pitch,
                                         roll,
                                         yaw,
                                         button;
                      }cyberman_information;
void get_cyberman_data(struct cyberman_information *data)
{
  struct REGPACK r;

  r.r_ax = 5301h
  r.r_es = FP_SEG(data);
  r.r_dx = FP_OFF(data);
  intr(0x33, &r );
}
```

An example of using the above routine would be in a main processing loop:

```
while ( execution )
{
  struct cyberman_information cyber_data;

  if ( keyboard ) check_keyboard;
  if ( joystick ) check_joystick;

  if (cyberman ) get_cyberman_data ( &cyber_data );

  if ( cyber_data.x ) then move_in_x_direction;
  .
  .
  .
}
```

This will work just fine. However, it will be a waste of time to ask the CyberMan for information and then determine if anything has changed between read times. The Logitech mouse driver gives us a better way to handle the CyberMan: using an event handler or interrupt.

SET/GET Event Handler

Function 53C0h of interrupt 33h allows us to set up a function in our program as an event handler for the CyberMan. The mouse driver will automatically call our designated function when any set of events occurs on the CyberMan. This function expects to find a six-word data structure that includes two call mask words, the segment and offset of the handler subroutine, and the segment/offset of a 12-word return information data structure. The two call mask words tell the mouse driver which events must occur on the CyberMan in order for the handler subroutine to be executed. These events include things like the left button pressed, left button released, *x* position changed, and so on.

When any of the desired events occurs, the mouse driver returns a 12-byte data structure with the *x*, *y*, *z*, pitch, roll, yaw, and button positions just like our get_cyberman_data function above, the dynamic device data, the two event bytes in the same format as the call mask bytes, and the *x,y* position of the cursor.

To determine what event has triggered the event handler, just look at the two event bytes returned in the data structure. If any of the bits are a 1, then that is the event that caused the handler to be executed.

The following code illustrates the routine necessary for setting up a CyberMan event. The parameter routine is the address of the function that will act as the servicing routine for this interrupt.

```
void set_cyberman_event(void *routine)
{

 cyberman_static_data data;
 struct REGPACK r;

 get_SWIFT_static (&data);

 r.r_ax = 0xC0;
 r.r_cx = 0xFFFF;
 r.r_es = FP_SEG(routine);
 r.r_dx = FP_OFF(routine);
 intr(0x33, &r);

/* Upon a call from the interrupt, the registers in the routine passed
above will have the following values:
     AX= Event bits    0—Mouse cursor changed
                       1—Left button pressed
                       2—Left button released
                       3—Right button pressed
                       4—Right button released
                       5—Middle button pressed
```

```
                    6—Middle button released
                    7—Other button pressed
                    8—Other button released
                    9—x coordinate changed
                   10—y coordinate changed
                   11—z coordinate changed
                   12—Pitch changed
                   13—Roll changed
                   14—Yaw changed
                   15—"Other" condition
       BX = button status
       CX = Horizontal cursor position
       DX = Vertical cursor position
       SI = Address of extended information block that contains the
       following data:
                    Word 0 = x coordinate value
                    Word 1 = y coordinate value
                    Word 2 = z coordinate value
                    Word 3 = Pitch value
                    Word 4 = Roll value
                    Word 5 = Yaw value
                    Word 6 = Button status
                    Word 7 = Dynamic device data word

  SS:SP = stack pointer
  DS = data segment of mouse driver - Save and load appropriately
*/
}
```

An example of an interrupt routine would be:

```
void interrupt cyberman_interrupt ( unsigned bp, unsigned di, unsigned
si,
                         unsigned ds, unsigned es, unsigned dx,
                         unsigned cx, unsigned bx, unsigned ax )
{

 if (ax & 0x0001) then left button pressed - handle it;
 etc.

}
```

Once we are finished using the interrupt event for the CyberMan, it should be removed by using the following routine:

```
void remove_cyberman_event()
{
 struct REGPACK r;
 r.r_ax = 0xC0;
 r.r_cx = 0;
 intr(0x33, &r);
}
```

Program Tactile Feedback

Triggering the tactile feedback on the CyberMan is performed using the interrupt 33 service 0x5330. The service is activated by the following code:

```
void tactile feedback (unsigned char duration,
                       unsigned char on,
                       unsigned char off)
{
 struct REGPACK r;

 r.r_ax = 0x5330;
 r.r_bh = on;
 r,r_bl = off;
 r,r_cl = duration
intr(0x33, sr)
}
```

The parameters of the function determine the amount and length of feedback. The feedback will be activated for the length of time specified by DURATION * 40 milliseconds. During this time, the tactile feedback mechanism is issuing repeated on/off cycles. The length of the on period is designated by the value of ON * 5 milliseconds. The length of the off period is designated by the value of OFF * 5 milliseconds.

Conclusion

The Global 3D controller and the Logitech CyberMan provide very useful input devices for virtual reality. By combining them with the right software, they can be used to control the movement of the viewer in the world. Both provide a single device for controlling all of the six degrees of freedom necessary for unlimited viewing.

5

Feedback and the Sense of Touch

There you are, sitting in the movie theater. You started the day by picking up the telephone, dialing your soon-to-be date, and immediately hanging up the phone. You quickly turn around and try to get ahold of yourself. What's wrong—it's just a phone call! Your palms are sweating, but you finally make the call, and the date is set. Back at the theater, the thought—no, the desire—comes over you to hold your date's hand. Your hand begins to shake and becomes very moist. In the dark theater, without looking, you reach over and begin to feel the skin on your date's hand. You continue until you find the curved space between the index finger and the thumb. Your hand stops and slowly squeezes, waiting for a response. The response is made; you feel your date squeezing back. Isn't life grand?

We have all experienced something similar, something purely based on the sense of touch and feedback. In this scenario you wanted to hold your date's hand, so your brain told your arm to begin moving your hand toward the other person's hand. Because it was dark, your brain relied on feedback from your hand to determine whether or not it had come into contact with your other hand. Once your hand felt the other person's skin, the brain responded to the feedback by moving your hand into a hand-holding position. When it felt the familiar form of the other person's hand, your brain sent signals that caused your hand to squeeze. You knew enough not to apply a full grip on the other person's hand but to squeeze slowly, waiting for feedback indicating that the other person was receptive. When your hand felt the other person's hand squeezing back, it was able to give the brain the desired feedback, and you were able to relax some.

Now let's relate this to a virtual environment. Let's say I have created a world with a cube in it. Using either the Power Glove, the mouse, or the 3-D mouse, your task is to pick up the cube. Simple enough—but did I mention that there is no light in the virtual world? Well, there isn't, so *only* by luck will you be able to pick it up. There is absolutely no feedback from the virtual hand to your brain to let you know that you are close to or even touching the cube. Virtual reality today would not even come close to simulating a real world without reproducing some sort of tactile sensation and feedback.

If you have played with the software for the Power Glove and mouse, you know that even with the various cues given to you by the virtual environment, they are inadequate. You used your eyes to see a virtual hand that you were controlling move toward a virtual cube. The hand got smaller the further away it was and even disappeared behind the cube when you went too far, but you felt nothing as the virtual hand went over the cube. Your brain was expecting a feedback cue from the hand, and nothing was received; therefore, your brain knew that something was not real about the situation (leaving out for the moment the fact that you were looking into a monitor).

How We Use Feedback

The entire system that our bodies use for receiving and making judgments about feedback is called the *haptic system,* which uses two different types of receivers for gathering feedback information: *mechanoreceptors* and *proprioceptors.*

Mechanoreceptors

The mechanoreceptors are used by the haptic system to sense pressure, which allows us to feel textures. This may need a bit of explanation. If you were to run your finger along the surface of a mirror, it would feel very smooth. If you were to magnify the surface of the mirror, you would see that it is very uniform. When you started to run your finger along the surface, you initially put a certain degree of pressure on the mirror and then moved your finger some distance. During this movement, the pressure you applied was fairly constant. Your mechanoreceptors felt an opposite pressure that was "reflected" back from the mirror's surface. Because the surface was uniform, the pressure or feedback never changed, and the mirror felt smooth.

Now imagine if you were to take a canister of salt, dump it on the mirror, and run your finger along the surface again. It would now feel rough. What happened is that your fingers felt the mirror's original surface between the salt granules, then ran over a certain number of salt granules, and then felt the mirror's surface once again. If you were to magnify the surface with the salt on it, you might see an image such as that in Figure 5.1.

Each time your finger ran across a piece of salt, the mechanoreceptors fed back to the brain a different pressure than that produced by the plain surface of the mirror. The surface felt the way it did because of the gaps between the different salt granules. In addition, the salt granules are made up of a substance that is hard and responds to your finger pressure differently than other substances. For

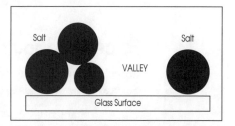

FIGURE 5.1 *Magnified view of salt on a glass surface*

instance, if you were to spread chocolate sauce on the mirror, feeling it would send yet another pressure reading to the brain.

It should be noted that if you were to close your eyes and run your finger through a bowl of chocolate sauce and then maple syrup, you would probably not know the difference. We know the difference between the two substances based on our senses of smell and sight.

Proprioceptors

The proprioceptors provide our brains with feedback based on forces from within our bodies, whereas the mechnoreceptors give us information about forces applied to our bodies from the outside. If you pick up an object, your fingers will give you some indication as to its weight, but the majority of the weight information will come from the proprioceptors in the muscles of the arm and hand.

Both the mechanoreceptors and the proprioceptors provide a degree of overlap in their feedback of information to the brain, and it is sometimes hard to judge which receptor is providing what information. What we want to do now is look at several different ways to simulate the sense of touch based on these two receptors. We will not try to separate them, just use them.

VR Feedback

Research in the area of the sense of touch has led to the development of several systems that provide some degree of simulated feedback that can be used in a virtual environment. Three of these systems are *force feedback*, *tactile feedback*, and *thermal feedback*.

Force Feedback

Force feedback is the term given to systems that convey a sense of weight. Several different uses are

1. *Molecular docking, in which the forces of the different atoms are felt*
2. *Picking up an object and determining if it is heavy or light*
3. *Picking up an object and determining if it is hard or soft*
4. *Providing resistance in things such as water*
5. *Resistance to solid objects such as walls*

A force-feedback system might be constructed in the following way. A mechanical system made up of motors and an exoskeleton, a structure that fits on the outside of your body, would be fitted to your arm and hand. During normal movements, the system would allow you to move as if nothing were attached to you. Let's say that you had the task of determining if a cube was light or heavy. Using a glove on your hand, as well as the exoskeleton, you would manipulate a virtual hand to pick up a virtual cube. You would grip the cube and try to pick it up. When you tried to move the cube upward to determine its weight, the exoskeleton would begin to restrict your arm movements. To simulate a very heavy cube, the exoskeleton would not allow your arm to move at all; if the virtual cube was light, the exoskeleton would provide just enough resistance to give you that impression.

In the case of the third use listed above, the exoskeleton would not allow your hand to grip very much if the virtual cube were solid. If the cube was composed of a spongy material, the exoskeleton would allow you to close your fingers around it even more, but not totally, because there would have to be room for the virtually scrunched-up cube.

In all of the situations above, the exoskeleton would provide a certain degree of resistance to any move you made in relation to the object you were manipulating. Research into force feedback has created two different systems; these are the mechanical arm, or GROPE, and pistons.

GROPE

By far the most widely known force-feedback system is the GROPE at the University of North Carolina (UNC) at Chapel Hill. The GROPE is a mechanical arm created by the Argonne National Lab for workers manipulating radioactive material. Figure 5.2 illustrates what a mechanical arm looks like. In its original use, a worker would manipulate a grip on one side of a glass enclosure, and a robot arm on the other side of the enclosure would mimic the worker's movements. Thus, it served as a natural extension of his or her arm and hand. Frederick Brooks at UNC modified it by removing the robot arm and replacing it with a *virtual* robot arm.

The new arm is a molecular docking system for chemists whose task it is to determine docking sites for molecules in the development of drugs. This is normally a grueling task, and it probably still is, but now it's somewhat easier with the GROPE. The chemists are now able to grab a section

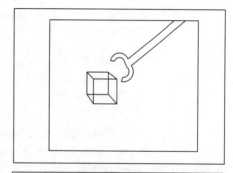

FIGURE 5.2 **Mechanical arm**

of molecule and try docking it into certain positions with a second molecule. The GROPE system allows the chemists to sense forces from both of the molecules during the docking sequences; the sensation is like holding two bar magnets in your hands and trying to bring the two positive or negative ends together. The repulsion can be strong; the same is true for the attraction when their opposite ends are brought together. The attractions and repulsions are used in conjunction with the software, which relays specific characteristics of the molecules.

Pistons

A second type of force-feedback device provides feedback for the hand only. Figure 5.3 shows an illustration of a system that uses a set of pistons to control the amount of resistance to the fingers. Although this type of system limits the range of possible feedback situations, it is less awkward. There are other force-feedback systems, but they all rely on some mechanical means to limit the movement of the hand and arm. For our purposes, these systems are much too expensive and cumbersome. Let's look at how we can add force feedback to our virtual environments.

Building VR Force Feedback with Software

Now that we know something about force feedback and some of its uses, let's build a couple of virtual environments that give us some level of feedback at minimal cost. We will begin with two software approaches.

Color

One of the simplest forms of feedback that can be accomplished with almost any computer program is color manipulation. To see how color can be used as a feedback tool, execute the GDCMATE.EXE program on the enclosed disk; see Appendix A for complete details on executing and using the program.

Once the game appears on your screen, you will see a chessboard and a complete set of chess pieces. You willl also see a virtual representation of your hand floating in front of you. Use

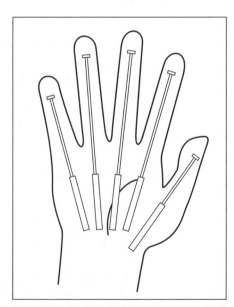

FIGURE 5.3 *Piston system*

the mouse to move the hand forward/backward and left/right. Now move the hand close to one of the chess pieces. Watch as the back of the hand turns blue. This is feedback; the system is letting you know that your hand is within grabbing distance of the chess piece. When you move your hand away from the piece, the back of the hand will return to its normal color.

Sound

Another approach we are going to take toward providing force feedback in software is the use of sound. We are all familiar with the feedback of sound. If you have ever gotten mad and slammed a door, you will remember that you received a huge sound cue when the door hit the frame. If you ever tried to drill into a material that was too tough for the motor of the drill, you probably noticed that it began to emit a grinding sound, your cue that you had ruined the drill and should stick to software development, not woodworking. We can do the same sorts of things in our virtual environments using sound.

The program FORCEFD3.BAT on the enclosed disk is an example of a virtual environment that uses sound. When you execute the program, you will see red and blue cubes. Your task is to pick up the red cube using the mouse and virtual hand. Because of the lack of cues in a normal virtual environment, it can be hard to put the hand in a position to grab a virtual object. In this program, when you go to pick up the red cube, a tone will be heard when you are in a position to pick it up. Once you have the cube in your grip, the tone will stop. Let go of the red cube and pick up the blue cube. Once you have it, move it up into the air using the right button as well as the left. A tone will begin, rising in pitch the higher you move the cube. A very high pitch indicates that the cube is very high; if there is no sound, the cube is on the floor.

Motion

When developing a virtual environment, we have complete control over any interactions that occur between the participant and the objects within the environment. This control allows us to simulate various systems such as force feedback. The program FORCEFD1.BAT on the enclosed disk is an example of a world that exhibits force feedback through software motion. The program uses a normal mouse to control a virtual hand. When you execute the program, you will be presented with two cubes, one red and one blue.

All you need to do is move the virtual hand into position over the red cube, press the left and right buttons at the same time, and move the mouse forward. Notice that the red cube moves into the air quite easily. It would appear that the red cube is very light. Now move the virtual hand into position over the blue cube, press both the left and right buttons, and move the mouse forward. Yikes! The cube hardly moved at all. It appears to be quite heavy. In fact, to move the cube as high in the air as the light cube, you have to move the mouse considerably more.

While this technique is not as strong as a true force-feedback mechanical system, it does allow for a certain level of response from the participant. I would like to thank John Williamson for this idea. Let's look at the very simple implementation. In the program, we have code that determines whether or not a collision has taken place with an object. When a collision has occurred and the participant presses the left button to grip the hand, we ask the system if the cube being gripped is the blue one; if that's the case, a variable is set indicating this situation. When the participant moves the virtual hand, the corresponding code checks to see if he or she is moving the blue cube; if so, each response from the mouse is divided by a factor of 10. For every real-world movement of the mouse, the blue cube and virtual hand react with $\frac{1}{10}$ of a normal move. We can change the weight of the object using a different divisor number.

Building VR Force Feedback with Hardware

We saw how the software approaches to force feedback relied on cues other than actual force. The opposite situation would be to create a system based on mechanical means that would provide actual force feedback. After much thought and some experimentation, I was not able to create a system that would be reproducible or useful.

Tactile Feedback

Now that we can determine the weight and density of an object, let's look at determining its texture. Tactile feedback presents the brain with the information necessary to determine if we are touching, for instance, a cat or a turtle. The majority of research into feedback and the sense of touch has gone into tactile feedback. I would assume this is true because force feedback is based on a physical property; the force or resistance applied to an object can be mathematically calculated. The force I apply to picking up a pencil is only proportionately smaller than the force I apply to picking up a bowling ball. However, the texture of the bowling ball is very much different than the texture of the pencil. There are as many different textures in the real world as there are objects. How can we possibly simulate all of them and be able to convey the necessary information to the participant's brain in real time? Here are some of the statistics for tactile feedback:

- ❏ *Our skin conforms to the surface of any objects with which it comes in contact*
- ❏ *The mechanoreceptors respond to the contact with electricity*
- ❏ *Impulses range from 50 to 100 millivolts*
- ❏ *The feedback should last 1 millisecond*
- ❏ *Tactile feedback can occur up to 500 times a second*

Now we cannot even produce video at 30 frames per second, so how are we going to produce impulses at up to 500 times a second? In addition, researchers have found that some textures can be classified in such a way that pattern recognition technique could be used to deliver simulated textures to participants. In other words, if you ran your virtual hand over a mirror with salt on it, the computer would output the impulse pattern it has stored, and you would have the feeling of running your hand over a mirror with salt on it. This is just another example of our body having been designed in a fashion so complex we cannot comprehend it. However, some research has produced promising results.

Virtual Sandpaper

Margaret Minsky has developed a system that allows a user to feel simulated textures (as well as the forces created by them) by using a joystick. Remember that it's hard to separate tactile and force feedback. The system works by not applying textures as if the user were touching them with his or her hand but as if he or she were holding a pencil or some kind of stick. In one experiment, users are given the feeling of running the pencil across a sheet of sandpaper. The technique used in the simulation of the sandpaper is the same as I described before about the salt and the mirror. It is as if you are running a pencil through many tiny hills and valleys. By using very minute levels of resistance, this sensation can be simulated.

In the end, what researchers and virtual reality engineers would like is a database of feedback responses. When a user picks up a glass, a specific action should occur in the force and tactile feedback areas. If the user puts the glass down, a different feedback structure should be used. Let's now look at ways that we can simulate tactile feedback.

Garage Level

Tactile feedback can be accomplished on a budget in several ways. We obviously cannot create the virtual sandpaper system, but we can provide some feedback for simple movements.

Global 3D Controller

The first system that we are going to look at is the Global 3D Controller described in Chapter 4. This is a 6 DOF input device that has the added feature of providing a simple feedback mechanism. At the developer's request, the 3-D controller will buzz the control ball. The buzz can be varied in time, thus changing the level of intensity. The program G3DMATE.EXE is a chess game that allows you to pick up chess pieces using a virtual hand. The Global 3D

Controller controls the movement of the hand and buzzes when you are in position to pick up the chess pieces. Because the Global 3D Controller has no buttons, you will have to press the **;** (semicolon) key with your other hand to grip and ungrip the virtual hand.

Air

A second form of tactile feedback involves the use of tiny air bladders embedded in a glove that a participant wears. When the participant picks up an object, the air bladders inflate to a specific pattern simulating the feel of the object picked up. Figure 5.4 shows an example of what such a glove might look like.

Although I cannot present you with a garage system , I can present the different ideas that have emerged about this approach. It should be noted that several companies, including the manufacturer of Virtuality, W Industries, have developed tactile gloves based on this principle. The main problem for us is finding an inexpensive alternative. What we want to do is have a compressor that is constantly running and providing a certain degree of air pressure to the main system hoses. Here's the plan: When a participant in a virtual environment grabs an object, the computer activates a certain number of electronic values that allow the pressurized air to enter specific air bladders. Each bladder has an intake valve and an exit valve. In the air bladders to be filled, these would be shut off, thereby keeping any air from escaping. If the participant grips the object harder, more air is forced into the air bladders. Once the participant lets go of the virtual object, the system shuts the intake valves and opens the exit valves.

The glove material is elastic enough both to allow the air bladders to inflate and to help with deflation. This is the main problem with the system—how do you get the air bladders to deflate completely? Suction could be used, but this adds another degree of complexity to the system. In addition, some have suggested that a liquid would be a better inflation substance. It is clear that this type of system could work, but developing one inexpensively is not so easy.

Piezo

Another alternative that we have for creating a garage-level feedback system can be accomplished using a sensor made from Kynar Piezo film, available from AMP Incorporated.

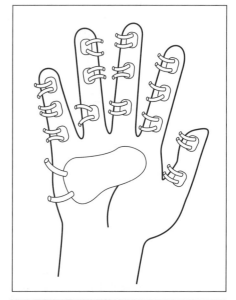

FIGURE 5.4 **The tactile glove**

This film comes in many different sizes and reacts to specific properties—for example, the application of force—by generating electricity. You can obtain a Basic Design Kit for $75 that includes a few samples of the film as well as a technical manual that discusses interfaces. One of the most basic uses of the film is as a switch. If you attach a multimeter to the film's contacts and apply a stress to it, a signal will register on the meter.

You can also make a simple microphone by attaching the film to the bottom of a paper cup and then attaching the contact leads to a recorder's microphone inputs. If you talk into the cup, the film will produce the appropriate signals, which are fed to the recorder. However, for our use, we want to be able to create a reaction from the film based on an input.

To show what the sensor can do, we hooked up a battery to the film. The film reacted by doing absolutely nothing. Once we hooked a preamp to the film, we had a reaction; in fact, the technical manual that comes with the basic kit includes the circuit and Radio Shack numbers necessary to build the preamp. Once you have it built, you can also use the film as a tiny speaker. It doesn't work too badly, but the bass response isn't too hot.

In order to use the film for feedback purposes, you will need to have a number of the film strips, an amplifier for each, and a way to drive the amplifiers. Unfortunately, I was unable to get a complete system operational in time to meet the book's deadline. The basic idea is to apply the film strips to the underside of a very thin glove. When the user comes in contact with a virtual object, the computer would fire up some of the amplifiers, which would in turn activate the film and provide a tiny buzzing sensation to the underside of the hand.

Thermal Feedback

As you begin to think about the many different types of feedback that just the hand and fingers provide, you will stumble upon some so basic that they are just second nature. One such feedback signal is temperature. Say you were in a virtual environment that consisted of a campground. There are trailers and tents all around, as well as people walking and doing things. In addition, there are campfires. As you walk up to one of the campfires, you feel nothing. You put out your hands to warm them, and they stay cold. Is this great virtual experience? Not entirely. It sure would be nice if your fingers started to get warm as you approached the fire. Well, you'll be happy to know that we can add this level of realism to any VR experience—but at a cost.

CM Research of League City, Texas, has developed a thermal feedback system that allows you to heat a part of the body using a small *thermode*, which is a small unit that consists of a heat pump, a temperature sensor, and a heat sink. The system operates through a control unit attached to a computer through the RS-232 port (I always knew I'd need 20–30 serial ports). The system can be programmed to supply a temperature in the range 10–35° Celsius. The unit activates the heat pump, which moves heat in or out of the heat sink to produce the desired temperature. The sensor is used to monitor the desired temperature at the thermode. You could now have a section of your virtual environment trigger the control unit, and the participant's fingers or other body parts would become warm or cool. The price of an eight-channel system is $10,000 and includes numerous safety features.

Garage Level

Now is there anything we can do to create a system of our own? One idea is to create a glove with very tiny hoses running through it. Yes, I know, we now have to wear a glove for input purposes, tactile feedback, and thermal feedback. Just think—we have no need for force feedback because with all of this stuff on our hands, we can't grip anything anyway!

If we had a glove with tiny hoses in it, we could circulate water through them. The water would either be heated or cooled, thus giving us the desired temperature. This works on basically the same principle as some heating systems that circulate warm water through hoses under the floor. While not practical, it does provide an opportunity for experimentation and would make a great demo.

 # Conclusion

Adding feedback mechanisms is by far the most complicated step for the garage-level virtual reality enthusiast. There are no simple ways to achieve a level of feedback from which the user will be able to draw a conclusion. By combining visual and auditory cues, however, the virtual environment in which a user is interacting can seem more true to life.

Connecting Shutter Glasses to the PC

As you know, we see in stereo. Look at the pages of this book—you are seeing two separate images even though you are probably not aware of it. We have all done the experiment of closing one eye and then the other. Well, let's do it again and think about it this time. Close your right eye and look at Figure 6.1. Now quickly open your right eye and close your left. Did you see the dot move? If you did, then you have stereo vision. The two different images that you see are called *stereo pairs*.

Our eyes are angularly displaced in our heads, which means we actually see two of everything from slightly different angles. When the images arrive at our brain, it fuses the two images into a single usable image. This fusing is called *convergence*, meaning that the two images join and become one image that contains an important depth cue called *binocular stereopsis* (or just stereopsis).

The purpose of presenting stereoscopic images in virtual reality is to create depth, thus making them more realistic. Graphics software engineers have many different tools for creating the illusion of depth on a computer screen. These include *occlusion*, *shading*, and *perceptive projection*, each of which will be discussed later. All of these techniques are very good at creating depth on the computer monitor, but what these techniques cannot do is "pull" the image out of the computer monitor so that we no longer seem to be looking at a window into a new world but instead are suddenly part of it. This is what stereo vision does for us.

In the real world there are many depth cues, and stereo vision is simply one more that the brain has to process. And indeed, there are people for whom stereo vision does not provide any extra sense of depth. The purpose of this chapter is to find ways to use stereo pairs so that we feel like we're actually inside—not just looking at—our virtual worlds. And all this will be possible by means of an overworked personal computer.

 ## The Challenge of Presenting Stereo Images in VR

What we are up against is somehow putting two different images on the computer screen—a screen that was originally designed to present only a single image. And this challenge is not just limited to the hardware; the software is responsible for creating the stereo pairs that have to be displayed.

This book will show you many ways to create 3-D images. Chapter 7 shows you how to modify the Victor Maxx StuntMaster 3-D goggles made for Nintendo, and Chapter 8 shows you how to build your own 3-D goggles from scratch. This chapter shows you how to modify the Sega shutter glasses (which use a method called *stereoscopic CRT display*) in conjunction with an ordinary computer monitor to view stereoscopic images. To do this, we will generate two angularly displaced views of

FIGURE 6.1 *A great big dot*

our graphics, flash them alternately on the computer monitor, and then use glasses with special opaquing lenses that are timed so that your left eye only sees the left view on the monitor and the right eye only sees the right view. By doing this, the participant is able to see a truly three-dimensional image. There are many different varieties of stereoscopic display; Figure 6.2 lists the majority of them.

Time-Multiplexed Displays

In our quest for stereo, we are going to use a time-multiplexed stereoscopic system. This means we are *not* going to show both left and right views of the images simultaneously; instead, we are going to generate our two different images and display them to the computer monitor in rapid sucession. At the same time, we will have the user wear a pair of shutter glasses that are plugged into the computer. The user puts on the shutter glasses and then looks at the computer monitor. When the left eye's image appears on the monitor, the computer will *opaque* (or shutter) the right lens of the glasses so that only the left

```
Stereoscopic Display Systems
        Time Multiplexed
                Electro-optical
                        Liquid Cystal
                                Active
                                Passive
                Mechanical
                        Tube
                        Shutter Glasses
        Time Parallel
                Anaglyph
                        red/green
                Separate
                        Split Screen
                        Dual Screen
                        Head Mounted
                        Hoods
```

FIGURE 6.2 *Breakdown of stereoscopic displays*

eye can see the monitor. When the right eye's image is displayed on the monitor, the left eye's lens closes.

Research has shown that for the time-multiplexed systems to operate without any annoying flickers, the computer monitor and shutter glasses must be able to display each image 60 times per second. This means that your monitor must have a refresh rate of 120 Hz allowing for 60 Hz per eye. In most cases, the monitors on IBM or IBM-compatible computers do not have this high of a refresh rate. Typically, they run at either 60 or 72 Hz. This means that at best, the monitor and shutter system will be able to deliver 30 images per second. In practice, the image that we are going to be able to produce with our PC and relatively inexpensive shutter glasses is quite good and very convincing.

When the shutter glasses interface presented in this chapter first appeared on the market, Sega was selling a pair of glasses for $39.95. These glasses were used as a peripheral for their home entertainment system several years ago. In fact, I have seen the system in some Toys' R Us stores, but never just the glasses. As time has progressed, Sega has quit selling the shutter glasses, and the supply now has to come from other sources. One company that has a supply of several different types of shutter glasses is 3DTV. They have the following equipment available:

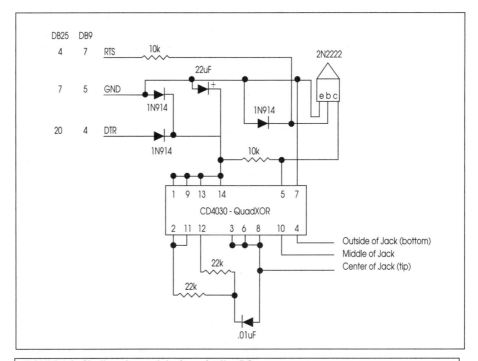

FIGURE 6.3 *Shutter glasses interface for the PC*

❑ *Sega Shutter Glasses*
❑ *Toshiba Shutter Glasses*
❑ *3DTV Shutter Glasses*

The 3DTV shutter glasses are produced in-house, and you can be confident that they will have glasses available for purchase when this book is published.

Interface for the Shutter Glasses ‼ !

The interface that you are going to build for the shutter glasses that will connect them to the serial port of your computer is illustrated in Figure 6.3. The serial port connection will give the computer control over the shutters in the glasses so that the opaquing lenses can be timed with the images on your monitor.

Parts List for the Sega Shutter Glasses Interface

You will need the following:
❑ Sega shutter glasses
❑ 1 CD4030 XOR Gate (do *not* use 74LS86 as a replacement)
❑ 1 2N2222 transistor
❑ 2 22k ¼ watt 5% resistors
❑ 2 10k ¼ watt 5% resistors
❑ 1 0.01 uf ceramic disc capacitor
❑ 1 22 uf electrolytic capacitor
❑ 3 1N914 diodes
❑ 1 Stereo ¼″ jack
❑ 1 DB25 or DB9 connector (depending on the serial port available on your computer)
❑ Perfboard
❑ Soldering iron and solder

Note: This interface is available, assembled and ready to use, from *PCVR Magazine* for $29.95 plus $3.50 shipping for the U.S. and Canada ($5.50 overseas). See Appendix E for ordering information.

There are several ways that the shutter interface can be constructed. By far the easiest is to build a Printed Circuit Board (PCB) and solder the parts to the board, although this is also the most expensive (see Appendix F for general guidelines on using PCB and solder). Figures 6.4 and 6.5 are the 2–1 masters for a PCB. Figure 6.6 shows the placement of parts on the board. The masters are the art-work used by a company to produce PCBs. Our masters are provided twice the size of the actual board. PCB manufacturers usually prefer 2-to-1 (or 2–1) sizes.

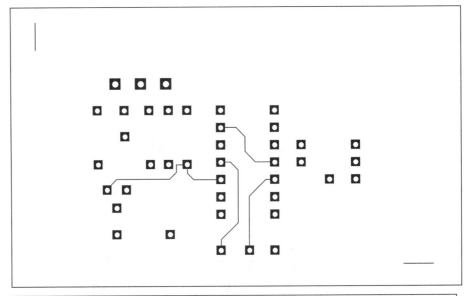

FIGURE 6.4 *Shutter glasses interface PCB top*

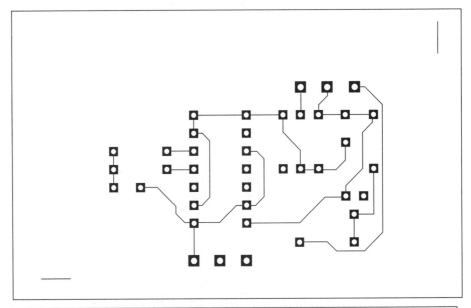

FIGURE 6.5 *Shutter glasses interface PCB bottom*

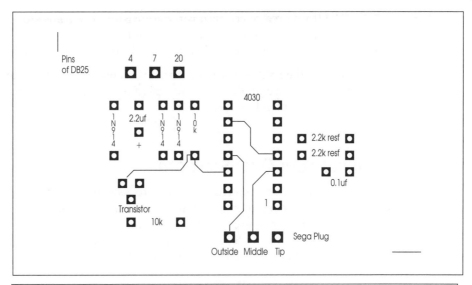

FIGURE 6.6 **Shutter glasses interface PCB parts placement**

If you do not have the capability to build a PCB, the next best way to build the interface is to wire-wrap the parts on a piece of breadboard. Radio Shack sells all of the components necessary for wirewrapping: the wire and the wrapping tool. Total cost is around $12. Another way to assemble the interface is point-to-point soldering.

No matter which way you assemble the unit, there are a few things you need to keep in mind. It would be a good idea to use a socket for the CD4030 integrated circuit (IC). This particular IC is sensitive to static and therefore can be damaged quite easily. If you use a socket, you will reduce the risk of damaging the IC as well as being able to replace it quickly if it goes bad.

There are three additional areas of concern, the first of which is the three diodes in the circuit. When you purchase the diodes, you will see that there is a small orange or yellow band around them with a black circle at one end. This black circle corresponds to the black lines in the diode representations in the shutter glasses interface circuit.

The second area of concern is the 22 uf electrolytic capacitor. Electrolytic capacitors have two leads on them; one is marked negative and the other, positive. On the glasses interface circuit, the positive lead is marked with a small plus sign (+). Be sure that the capacitor is wired with the leads in the proper order; otherwise, you risk having the capacitor explode.

The third area of concern is the transistor. The transistor has three leads on it: the base, the collector, and the emitter. When wiring the circuit, make sure that you have correctly identified the leads on your transistor.

To test the shutter glasses interface, I refer you to Appendix A which discusses the software on the enclosed disk. Follow the instructions given for the program in Chapter 16 called PARK.

Writing Your Own Software

Now that we have an interface, it's time to look at generating the two different images that we need to produce an effective three-dimensional image. One of the most useful resources for stereoscopic image generation is the *Stereo Graphics Hardware and Software Info Pak* available from 3DTV. Let's begin our lessons by looking at a concept called parallax.

Parallax

When we look at the world, we are really seeing two different images. If we were to look at some object in our environment, take a picture of the image on our retinae, and compare the images from both eyes, we would find that they overlap each other. This is the result of *disparity* (see Figure 6.7). Disparity is the horizontal distance between any two points on the images projected on our retinae. It is this distance that produces binocular stereopsis. If you focus on something very close and measure the disparity in that instance and then compare it to the disparity created when you focus on something very far away, you would find that the distances are different. This is logical because if disparity produces stereopsis, then the distance must be different because you are focusing on objects at different distances from you.

Parallax, on the other hand, is the horizontal distance between any two points on the images projected on the monitor we are viewing (see Figure 6.8). When we generate stereo pairs and display them on the monitor, they will be flickering so fast that it will appear as if both images in the stereo pair were on the monitor screen. Parallax is important because the amount of it in our stereo pairs will determine the amount of disparity at the retinae and thus the amount of

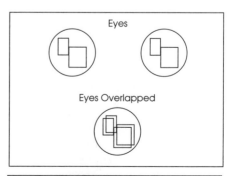

FIGURE 6.7 **Disparity**

stereopsis. Luckily, measuring parallax is a simple task. There are basically
four types of parallax we are going to
talk about: zero, positive, negative,
and divergence parallax.

Zero Parallax

As you might have already guessed,
when stereo pairs have zero parallax,
there is no gap between the separate
images. Figure 6.9 is an example of a
cube with zero parallax. If we were to
display the stereo pairs that make up
the cube on the monitor, it would
appear that the cube lies in the plane
of the monitor. When you are using
your favorite word processor, the
image on the monitor could be produced with stereo pairs that have zero
parallax. This would be a complete
waste of CPU time, but it is possible.

We should note that for the purposes of most of the terms and examples in this chapter, we are assuming
that the eyes are spaced 64 millimeters apart. This distance between the
eyes, or *interocular spacing*, is an
established average for the U.S. population.

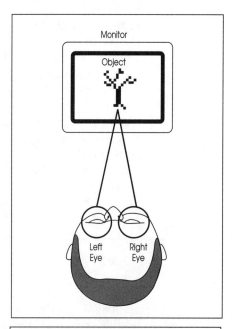

FIGURE 6.8 **Parallax**

FIGURE 6.9 **Examples of zero parallax**

Positive Parallax

Figure 6.10 shows an example of positive parallax. Once the computer displays
stereo pairs with parallax greater than zero, we begin to see depth. Positive parallax occurs when the distance between the images is greater than zero and less
than or equal to our defined interocular spacing. When positive parallax is
occuring, a three-dimensional object appears because the brain is able to fuse
the two images. Furthermore, the image will appear to be in the space from the
plane of the monitor screen and back. The more the parallax, the greater the distance the object will appear from you as a viewer. If you focus on an object at a
very great distance, the parallax of the images will be very close to or at your
interocular spacing. Your eyes will have a line of sight parallel to each other.

From a programmer's point of view, let's look at the value of parallax by means of an example. Imagine that we are designing the park scene we saw in Chapter 1. We have a bunch of trees in the background and a sidewalk that comes right under our feet. Let's add a few clouds in the sky as well. If we were to create stereo pairs for this scene, we would want the part of the sidewalk that comes right up to the bottom of the monitor to have zero parallax. As the sidewalk extends into the scene, the parallax should increase. The clouds are obviously very far away and should have a maximum parallax. The trees are in the middle of the scene and will have parallax values between zero and the maximum. Literature in the stereoscopic field suggests that the maximum parallax should be 8 millimeters when the monitor is viewed from a distance of 2 to 4 feet.

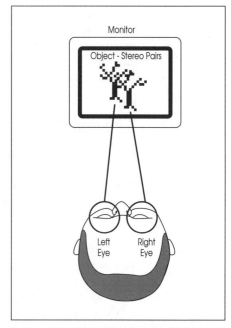

FIGURE 6.10 **Example of positive parallax**

Focus

Viewing stereoscopic images on a monitor is not a natural practice. When you are looking at a monitor, you are focusing on the monitor screen itself. Because all images, whether or not they have depth cues in them, are drawn on the monitor plane, your eyes do not have a choice as to where to focus. In the real world, if we are looking at something up close, our eyes focus on the object. If we suddenly change and look at a faraway object, our eyes refocus on the new object. This type of reflex cannot occur in our computer-generated stereo pairs. The result is possible discomfort caused by eye strain. Thus, when developing three-dimensional virtual environments, the main objects should be concentrated in the middle of the screen and as close to zero parallax as possible.

Negative Parallax

Negative parallax is the case where things start to get interesting—in other words, where ordinary computer graphics fail. Figure 6.11 shows an example of what negative parallax looks like. Negative parallax occurs when the lines of sight are crossed. When this occurs, the object being viewed will appear to be floating in the space between your eyes and the monitor. This type of imagery cannot be produced without the aid of stereoscopic techniques such as shutter

glasses. When this type of parallax can
be created, the effects are dramatic,
but there are a number of important
pitfalls of which software designers
have to be aware.

What we are dealing with here is
a situation where we are able to "pull"
objects out of the monitor. We have to
be careful about the border of the monitor itself. For instance, the example in
Figure 6.12 shows what can happen if
you're not careful. In the figure, the ball
is coming out of the monitor but over
to the side. When this happens, part of
the ball will be cut off because of the
border. This will produce a conflict of
depth cues. Our brains expect the ball
to occlude the border of the monitor,
but because the ball is not real, this
cannot occur. Our brains will probably
conclude that the ball is behind the
plane of the monitor, ruining the
desired effect. Of course, the reaction
of each viewer will vary.

There is a second problem—the
human optical system is able to see
around corners and edges. If you were
to look outside a window, your right
eye would see around the left edge,
whereas your left eye is blocked by the
edge itself. In the case of negative parallax and the monitor sides, the opposite will be true. The left eye will see

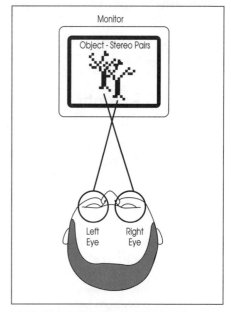

FIGURE 6.11 **Example of negative parallax**

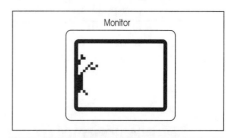

FIGURE 6.12 **Example of negative parallax problem**

more of the image, and the right eye will be blocked because there is nothing
behind the monitor. This situation is more noticeable with objects that are stationary or slow moving. If the object is moving at a high speed, the brain will
not be able to see the conflict as much.

Divergence Parallax

In the divergence example shown in Figure 6.13, the parallax value is greater
than the interocular spacing value of our eyes. This is a situation that never
occurs in the real world because it would force the eyes into a position that

would cause great discomfort if held for any length of time. Divergence should be avoided in stereo pairs.

Potential Problems

But there are other problems that can occur in addition to the ones we have already talked about. One of these is *crosstalk*, which occurs when the left eye is not totally blocked during the displaying of the right image. This can occur when the shutter glasses are not made of a material that is fully transparent or the switching mechanism triggers the shutters a bit too slowly or too soon. These problems typically occur in lower-end equipment because of cost-saving practices such as using cheaper materials or less-sophisticated

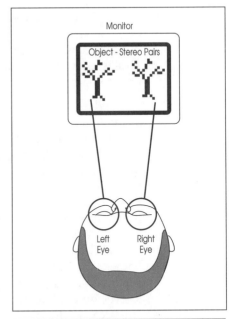

FIGURE 6.13 *Example of divergence*

electronics. Another potential snag is *ghosting*, which occurs when an image disappears incompletely from the monitor; the phosphors in the picture tube still retain some of the old picture when the new one is displayed. This is particularly true of the green phosphors, which tend to ghost more than the red and blue phospors. Changes in the colors of the objects and background in the environment can help to elimnate this problem.

Rotational Images

Now that we know some of the things that make up the stereo pairs, let's look at one way to produce the two different images that we need. One very common method is to perform a rotation on the image. The sequence for creating stereo pairs using rotation is

1. *Rotate (pan) the entire scene 4˚ from left to right to produce the left image*
2. *Rotate (pan) the entire scene 4˚ from right to left to produce the right image*
3. *Perform perspective projection*
4. *Display the images*

The literature that discusses using rotation for stereo pair generation warns that the resulting images may be difficult for some people to view, thus causing discomfort. One reason for this is that the rotation method introduces vertical parallax in the images. Because vertical parallax has no depth cue value, the brain is confused by its presence. Therefore, rotation should not be used for stereo pair generation.

Off-Axis or Camera Model Projection

What should be used is a technique called off-axis or camera model projection. Figure 6.14 shows an example of what the camera model should look like.

In the camera model, we are assumed to have two cameras with parallel line of sights and short focal lengths that are horizontally separated by some spacing value designated by the variable E and are located $-D$ units from the origin along the x axis. We will call the camera on the left cam1 and the other camera, cam2. Cam1 is spaced $-E/2$ from the x axis, and cam2 is spaced $E/2$ from the x axis.

During the rendering process, each of the points on our objects have to be converteted to actual x,y screen coordinates. The following equations are simply an additional step in the rendering process. Normally, we would calculate

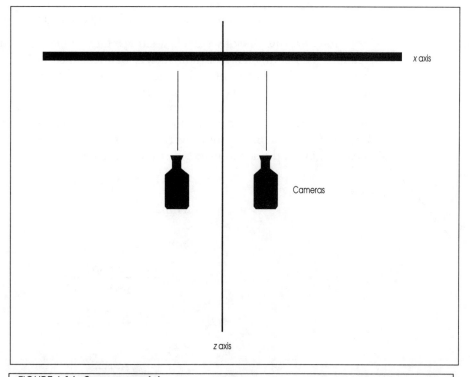

FIGURE 6.14 *Camera model*

the position of the screen pixel using just one camera. Now that we have two, we have double the calculations. The formulas for the two screen pixels are

$$X_{cam1} = \frac{xD-(zE/2)}{(D+z)} \qquad Y_{cam1} = \frac{(yD)}{(D+z)}$$

$$X_{cam2} = \frac{(xD+(zE/2)}{(D+z)} \qquad Y_{cam2} = \frac{(yD)}{(D+z)}$$

Recall that D is the distance the camera is from the origin along the x axis, E is the total distance separating the cameras, and the x,y,z coordinates are for the current point we are working on in some object. Now let's look at things again.

For every object in our environment, we have to determine where on the monitor the object should be drawn. The rendering software will normally determine the position of the vertices (the corners) of the object using the calculations above and then fill in the entire polygon. When the renderer performs those calculations, it is finding out where to place the object for the left camera or eye *and* the right camera or eye. The system will have to keep track of two entire graphics scenes if it does the calculations at the same time. Some systems will calculate the left eye and then come back and calculate the right eye.

However, this type of system is wasting a lot of time. Notice that in the calculations the Y component for the screen is identical in both views. As previously mentioned, we do not want to introduce any vertical parallax into our stereo pairs. By using the same value for each image, we are guaranteed to be free of it. Turning our attention to the X component, we see that there are also some similar terms between the two calculations. By simplifing the equations and making the use of a couple of temporary variables, we can save a considerable amount of calculation in the stereo pairs generation. The new equations become

$$temp1 = x * D$$

$$temp2 = \frac{Z * E}{2}$$

$$temp3 = (D+z)$$

$$X_{cam1} = \frac{temp1-temp2}{temp3}$$

$$X_{cam2} = \frac{temp1+temp2}{temp3}$$

$$Y_{cam1} = Y_{cam2} = \frac{y * D}{temp3}$$

By doing the "pre-math", we save three additions, three multiplications, and two divisions. This is a considerable savings when spread over several tens of thousands of pixel calculations.

Parallax D and E

In the calculations above, D and E have not been defined. We need to do so. Larry F. Hodges, a professor at Georgia Institute of Technology, explained in his paper "Basic Principles of Stereographic Software Development" that our parallax for any point can be easily calculated as

$$\text{parallax} = X_{cam2} - X_{cam1}$$

We know from our previous discussion on parallax that an object at infinity causes the eye's line of sight to be parallel. Thus the parallax value for these objects will be the value of our interocular spacing, parallax = E. We also know that objects at a distance D from the cameras will have a parallax value of 0. An object that is $2D$ centimeters from the cameras will have a parallax of $E \div 2$, and so on. These numbers are important because we always want to keep the parallax at or under 8 millimeters. Let's do some more calculations.

We know that the typical interocular spacing is 64 millimeters. This will be our value for E. When using shutter glasses, we will be somewhere around 600 millimeters, or 2 feet, from the monitor. Now let's assume that we are working with the point $(1,1,100)$. Substituting into X equations above, we get

$$X_{cam1} = 0 \quad \text{and} \quad X_{cam2} = 1$$

and the parallax value will be 1. Now try the point $(1,1,1000)$ for the values

$$X_{cam1} = -19 \quad \text{and} \quad X_{cam2} = 20$$

and the parallax value is 39. If this object was to be displayed, the positions of the object points would have to be scaled so that the parallax value will be 8 or less. The main reason for all of this is if the object was displayed with a parallax of 39, there is a good chance that people would not be able to fuse the images, thus causing discomfort. In his paper, Hodges and others recommend a value for E of $0.028D$.

On-Axis Model

Now let's look at a second type of model for calculating stereo pairs. On-axis projection is accomplished by using a single camera centered on the x axis and performing a manual horizontal translation of the calculated data. The algorithm from Hodges is

```
Loop for every point
        left_x = left_x + e/2
        perform perspective projection
        pan by -e/2

        right_x = right_x - e/2
        perform perspective projection
        pan by e/2
endloop
```

For each point, we will move it over to the desired location, perform a standard perspective projection calculation, and then pan the points by a certain amount. The advantage of doing on-axis projection is that some of the necessary calculations (perspective projection and pan) are sometimes available as hardware functions, giving them a considerable speed advantage over the off-axis projection where all functions are software-based.

Software

With the ugly calculations behind us, let's look at writing software that performs the calculations necessary for creating stereo pairs and driving our shutter glasses interface. There are three different examples we are going to look at: a simple interface driver, use of the previously discussed equations, and REND386.

A Simple Example

The program SHUTTER1.C on the enclosed disk is an example of code that will trigger the shutter glasses and display appropriate images. Credit for this code goes to F. van der Hulst. The algorithm used is

```
set graphics active page to 0
draw the left eye image
set graphics active page to 1
draw the right eye image
Loop
     wait for vertical retrace
     set graphics visual page to 0
     switch glasses
     wait for vertical retrace
     set graphics visual page to 1
     switch glasses
EndLoop
```

This program is very basic in that you must already have the stereo image pairs created when you execute it. Each of the images of the stereo pair is put into a separate graphics buffer. The program enters a loop that keeps a watch for the vertical retrace to occur on the monitor, which means the monitor has finished displaying a complete image on the display tube. At this point we want to put up a new image and change the shutter glasses. A program can determine when a retrace has occurred by watching the VGA graphics card register at location 0x3DA. When the fifth bit from the left has changed from a 0 to a 1, a retrace has occurred.

PCVR Renderer

During the course of publication of *PCVR Magazine*, we developed a simple ren-derer using code from the "Graphics" column in *Dr. Dobb's Journal*. One of the features of the renderer is its ability to do stereo image pairs and drive the shut-ter glasses interface. The stereo pairs are generated using the off-axis technique and the shutter glasses interface code. Although it's still under development, let's take a look at some actual code for producing stereo pairs. The first step in our generation of the images is to do preprocessing. You'll remember from our discussion of the off-axis equations that many of the calculations are duplicated in both images. After studying the equations, I have come up with four values that can be calculated before we do anything else.

```
x_d= FixedMul ( XformedPoints->X, view->stereo_d );
x_e = FixedMul ( XformedPoints->Z, view->stereo_e );
z_eby2 = FixedDiv(z_e, FIXED2);
dplusZ = view->stereo_d+XformedPoints->Z;
```

This rendering system relies on using fixed point instead of floating point for calculations, which is why we have routines called FixedDiv and FixedMul instead of using ordinary math instructions. Once we have this data, we are ready to proceed.

Whether the system is in stereo mode or in monoscopic mode, we always calculate the right eye position. We use the equation for the *x* and *y* coordinates:

```
ProjectedPoints->X = FixedDiv ( x_d - Z_eby2, dplusZ );
ProjectedPoints->Y = FixedDiv ( FixedMul (XformedPoints->y, view-
>stereo_d), dplusZ );
        or
ProjectedPoints->X = (x_d - Z_eby2) / dplusZ );
ProjectedPoints->Y = (XformedPoints->y * view->stereo_d) / dplusZ;
```

Then we convert these points to screen pixel values:

```
ScreenPointsRight->X = ((int) ((ProjectedPoints->X + FIXED05) >> 16)) +
SCREEN_WIDTHby2;
ScreenPointsRight->Y = (-((int)((ProjectedPoints->Y + FIXED05) >> 16)) +
SCREEN_WIDTHby2;
```

Now we have the screen *x,y* coordinate for the right image stored. A simple test is made of the variable stereo to determine if we must do the left eye image calculations:

```
if ( stereo )
{
 ProjectedPoints->X = FixedDiv(x_d + x_eby2, dplusZ);
 ScreenPointsRight->X = ((int) ((ProjectedPoints->X + FIXED05) >> 16))
+ SCREEN_WIDTHby2;
 ScreenPointsLeft->Y = ScreenPointsRight->Y;
}
```

Notice how few calculations were needed for the left image—just one division, two additions, a shift, and three assignments. It could be a lot worse. The system creates all of the screen locations for the object vertices and later displays them using an interrupt system for the shutter glasses interface that will be explained in the next section.

REND386

REND386 provides shutter glasses support as well. The majority of the actual code for doing the stereo pairs is embedded in the system code for REND386, but some of it has to be handled by us. The majority of REND386 programs will have configuration files supplied with them. This is where, if the programmer has provided internal support, you put specifics about your shutter glasses system. There are four lines that control everything:

```
switchedev SEGA
segaport 3FC 3 3 1 0
stereoset 600 250 320 64 600
stereotype SWITCH
```

The first line, `switchdev`, is followed by the name of the routine that the system will use to control your interface. In the case of the REND system, the word `sega` should follow. This indicates that you want to use the internal routine. The next line, `segaport`, describes the memory location where the interface is attached to the computer. It is followed by six values:

1. *Memory location for interface—* `0x3FC` *is COM1 and* `0x2FC` *is COM2.*
2. *This is a mask byte and determines which of the bytes at the memory address given in the first position can be used by the driver routine. The driver routine and interface uses just the first and second bits, so we enter a value of 3.*
3. *This is the value to write to the address given by the first value to clear the left shutter. A value of 3 is used.*
4. *This is the value to write to the address given by the first value to clear the right shutter. A value of 1 is used.*

5. *This is the value to write to the address given by the first value to clear both lenses.*
6. *This is the value to write to the other bits at the address given by the first value but not specified in the mask value.*

The third line, `stereoset`, describes the parallax and convergence values. The value are

1. *Physical distance—distance in millimeters between the viewer and the monitor*
2. *Screen width—the width of the screen*
3. *Pixel width—the width of the screen in pixels*
4. *Eye spacing—the interocular spacing of the viewer in millimeters*
5. *Convergence—the convergence distance. This is the distance from your eyes where the objects should have zero parallax (typically the same as physical distance).*

The fourth line, `stereotype`, is followed by a word indicating what type of stereo system you are using. The REND system can support several different systems, so for the shutter glasses interface, use the word `Switch`.

Program

Once these values have been set, it is time to look inside a program and see what it takes to support the shutter glasses. Here we have to set some things up if we are using the shutter glasses, so we must first determine if we are in stereo mode. We can do this by looking at the variable `stereo_type`. If this variable is set to `Switch`, we are in shutter glasses mode. When this is true, we perform the following routines:

Initialize the shutter glasses interface driver
Precompute stereo data for the left eye
Precompute stereo data for the right eye
Set up the interrupt system

The first three simply get the system ready to compute stereo data. The fourth, however, is worth investigating.

Every time the monitor displays a new picture, a vertical retrace occurs and the system must put up a different eye image and shutter the shutter glasses. If this does not occur on every retrace or the system is slow in performing the task, the three-dimensional effect will be lost. For this reason, REND is set up to use an interrupt when the vertical retrace occurs. When the initialization routine for the interrupt is called, the system determines the amount of time that passes between retraces. A timer interrupt is set to this time. Therefore, whenever the interrupt occurs, the system knows a vertical retrace has occurred, and it changes the image and triggers the shutter glasses.

This is very important because virtual environments can become so large that they take quite a long time to render completely. If the system were to trigger the shutter glasses after it rendered a scene, there would be times when the shutters changed very quickly and other times when the shutters would change slowly. This change in speed would be very noticeable to the wearer and would cause a breakdown in the three-dimensional effect.

Once all of the routines have been called, the program is ready to begin displaying stereo pairs. The actual generation of the images occurs in the renderer. Let's take a look inside to see what is going on.

Internal

Each time something changes in a virtual environment, the entire scene has to be recalculated and displayed again. In REND, this is called a *screen refresh*. Located in a library within the REND system, the routine `screen_refresh` has to determine how to redo the scene. If the program is executing in `mono-scopic` mode, there is much less work to be done. In the configuration file, we told the system we were in `switched` mode. The routine follows the algorithm:

```
setup left eye view
wait for the left eye's turn
prepare left image display buffer
render objects
setup right eye view
wait for right eye's turn
prepare right image display buffer
render objects
let shutter glasses driver know about new images.
```

If you look at this algorithm, you will probably say something like, "According to the calculations above, we can save a great deal of time if we do the stereo image generation at the same time." When REND386 performs its rendering loop, it stores a considerable number of precomputed values in each object. When we execute a program for stereo viewing, the system will generate first the right image and then the left image. No speed is lost because the left image is able to take advantage of the stored values from the right image.

The Limitations of Shutter Glasses

As you've seen in this chapter, a reasonably good 3-D image can be created by using shutter glasses. But the sense of immersion into a virtual world depends on the degree to which the world mimics our real senses and allows us to act in a familiar way. In addition to seeing in 3-D in the real world, we are accustomed to tilting and turning our heads from one side to another, all of which changes our point of view.

One of the main problems with shutter glasses is that you have to look at the monitor constantly. This causes problems because you know that you are not in a virtual environment. Not only do you have to keep your head fairly immobile, but you can also see the monitor's border and your surroundings. These problems can be solved with the use of a head-mounted display (HMD). Instead of looking at a monitor on your desk, we put two of them in front of your eyes. HMDs are much more expensive than shutter glasses, but the effect is much more realistic.

7

Connecting the StuntMaster Head-Mounted Display to Your PC

R ecently, VictorMaxx released a head-mounted display (HMD) called the StuntMaster. This is a great break for us garage-level VR people because the StuntMaster HMD sells for $200 and is available at stores like Software Etc. and the Electronics Boutique.

The main purpose of the StuntMaster is to provide a personal viewing system for either the Sega Genesis System or the Super Nintendo Home Entertainment systems. This HMD marks the first attempt by any company to enter the VR mass market arena.

 ## Specifications

The HMD consists of a single 2.2-inch color LCD with a resolution of 240 x 86 color triads. The total field of view is 17° according to VictorMaxx. When wearing the unit, you feel like you are viewing a movie screen some distance in front of you. It doesn't provide as much of a feeling of immersion as the HMD you will learn how to build in the next chapter, but the interface for the Stuntmaster is much easier to put together, and overall this is a less expensive project.

If you were to open the unit, you would find a very simple optical system. Directly in front of the user's eyes are two *fresnel lenses* (pronounced "FREH-nel"). The lenses are similar to the sheet magnifiers available from Walmart. The center of the fresnel lenses is placed in the area between the wearer's eyes. The concentric circles that form the lenses provide equal amounts of magnification for each eye.

The HMD also has built-in stereo headphones and a very simple form of head tracking that uses a potentiomenter mounted on the side. Because this first HMD was designed for the Nintendo and Sega machines, the head tracking had to be kept to a minimum. Therefore, the system is basically able to tell when the user is looking straight ahead, to the left, and to the right. We will be able to take advantage of this head tracking through our interface cable.

Before constructing the StuntMaster interface, you should put the HMD on your head and get an idea of what the field of view is like. Attach one of the two cables supplied with the StuntMaster to the end of the black cable coming out of the unit. Plug the power supply into the appropriate jack on the end of the cable. Now plug the power supply into an electrical socket. If you look inside the StuntMaster, you will see a white bar at the top of the visible screen. This bar will give you an indication as to the size of the LCD. Make sure this LCD size is not too small before you build the interface cable.

Building the StuntMaster Interface !

The interface that we are going to build allows the StuntMaster to be used as a virtual reality HMD using the PC as the host system. There are a total of four connections that have to be made:

1. *Video—The Stuntmaster accepts a standard NTSC signal as video input. (A NTSC signal is the Western Hemisphere protocol for transmission of a video signal.) This means that we will need a way to supply such a signal. The PC outputs a VGA signal to the monitor. We can produce a NTSC signal from the VGA signal by using a VGA-to-NTSC converter card; the NTSC signal can then be viewed in the StuntMaster or any ordinary television.*

2. *Audio—The StuntMaster has a pair of stereo headphones attached to it that we will use. The connection will be a stereo plug that can be used with any Soundblaster-type card or a home stereo system.*

3. *Power—We will need to put a jack on our interface cable in order to use the power supply pack that comes with the unit.*

4. *Head tracking—The head tracking of the StuntMaster requires two input lines to the computer. We are going to use one of the joystick ports as the input line. We have chosen this method because the parallel port has the Power Glove; the serial port has the Global 3-D Controller, CyberMan, or mouse; and the PC can accept two joysticks. Therefore, we haven't lost anything.*

StuntMaster Parts List

- ❏ VGA-to-NSCT converter card (available from Boffin Limited—see Appendix B for more information)
- ❏ 10–11 feet of conductor cable
- ❏ 1 RCA plug (Radio Shack: 274-451)
- ❏ 1 stereo ⅛" plug (Radio Shack: 274-284)
- ❏ 1 3.5-mm barrel jack, with 2.1-mm pin
- ❏ 2 male DB15 connectors
- ❏ joystick card
- ❏ 6-volt power supply included with VictorMaxx StuntMaster

Note: You can purchase an assembled interface for the StuntMaster through *PCVR Magazine* for $29.95 + $3.50 shipping/handling. See Appendix E for ordering instructions.

Figure 7.1 shows a completed interface with all the connections between the StuntMaster and your PC.

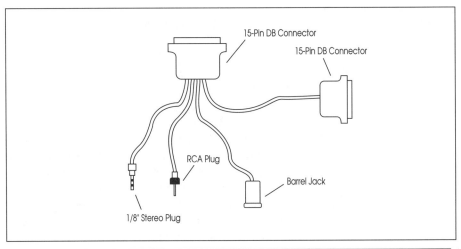

FIGURE 7.1 **Completed StuntMaster/PC interface**

Pinouts

Attached to the StuntMaster is a 15-pin connector that provides all of the signals necessary for using the unit. The pinouts are shown in Table 7.1.

Table 7.1. **StuntMaster Pinouts**

Pin #	Nintendo Mode	Sega Mode
1	+6V	+6V
2	GND	GND
3	Data	Sega Right In
4	Clock	n/a
5	Latch	Sega Left In
6	GND	GND
7	+5V	n/a
8	n/a	n/a
9	GND	GND
10	Video In	Video In
11	Data	Sega Right Out
12	Latch	Sega Left Out
13	GND	GND
14	Audio Left	Audio Left
15	Audio Right	Audio Right

The pinout descriptions were provided by the VictorMaxx Corporation. The pins we are going to use are shown in Table 7.2.

Because 11 pins are needed, we will be using an 11-conductor cable. Before we begin the actual constuction of the cable, however, we need to label the 11 different wires in the cable. For every pin number in Table 7.2, pick a colored wire and write down the color and number you're associating it with on a piece of paper. We will use this chart in making the interface.

The first step is to attach all 11 wires to their appropriate pins in one of the DB15 male connectors. Once all of the wires are in place, we can begin adding the individual connections.

Video

The video connection is made using an RCA plug. One that works well is 274-451 from Radio Shack. We will be using the two wires that you picked for pins 9 and 10. Take the RCA plug and remove the plastic housing (slide the plastic housing over the wire used for the video). You will see two connection points. The wire you picked for pin 9 should be attached to the large connection point, and the wire you picked for pin 10 should be attached to the small connection point. Once the two wires are attached, you can reassemble the plastic housing.

Audio

The audio connection is made using a 0.125-inch stereo audio plug. Radio Shack model 274-284 works well. We will be using the three wires that you picked for pins 13, 14, and 15. Remove the plastic housing from the plug and look at the back of it. You will see one large connection point and two small ones. The wire for pin 13 should be attached to the large connection point. Because we are using a stereo plug, we have to select the correct connection points for the left and right side. If you are looking at the plug from the back

Table 7.2. *StuntMaster Pins Used for the PC*	
Pin	**Sega Mode**
Pins 9 and 10	Video
Pins 13, 14, and 15	Audio
Pins 3, 5, 11, and 12	Head tracking
Pins 1 and 2	Power

side, then pin 15 should be attached to the small connection in the center of the plug. The wire associated with pin 14 should be attached to the remaining small connection point that is off to the right side of the plug.

Head Tracking

The head-tracking portion of the connection requires four connection points. Refer to Table 7.3 for the connections from the cable to the head-tracking DB15.

Power

Finally, we must attach the power supply that comes with the unit to our interface cable. We will need the 3.5-mm barrel jack for this connection. The wire associated with pin 1 should be attatched to the center connection point on the barrel jack. The wire for pin 2 should be attached to the outside connection point on the barrel jack. Once the connections are made, you should test the power connection by plugging in the power supply and measuring the voltage across pins 1 and 2 of the interface cable's DB15. If you get 6V using pin 2 as the ground, then the connection has been correctly made, and we are ready to hook up the system.

 ## Hook-Up

The interface cable is very simple to hook up. Just plug the DB15 end of the cable into the DB15 connector on the VictorMaxx Stuntmaster's cable. Plug the power supply into the appropriate connector on the cable and then into a wall socket. Attach the RCA plug to a video source and voilà—a virtual reality head-

Table 7.3. *StuntMaster-to-Joystick Connections for Head Tracking*	
StuntMaster Pin...	**Goes to Joystick DB15 Pin**
3	1
5	1
11	3
12	6

mounted display! Make sure that switch 2 on the Stuntmaster's DIP switch is in the ON position and switches 1 and 3 are OFF.

Software Interface

Now we have to consider the software needed to take advantage of head track-ing. When VictorMaxx released the information about the pinouts of the HMD, they also discussed the head tracking. Their comments were as follows:

> There are two modes—scroll mode and scan mode. In scroll mode, the StuntMaster will issue a directional signal as long as your head is turned off of center. In scan mode, a signal is issued as long as you are turning your head. When you stop turning, the directional signal stops. E.G. if you are in scan mode and you turn your head 30 degrees to the left, a left signal will be issued all the while that you turn through those 30 degrees, but will stop signaling when you stop turning. When you then turn back to the right, right signals will be issued, even though your head is to the left of center. SEGA only sup-ports scan mode, but Nintendo supports either mode (use dip switch 3 to control mode—on is scan, off is scroll).

When I read this paragraph initially, I was very excited because I thought we might have a true head tracker, but as I studied it more, I realized that we do not have such a beast. What we really have is *head positioning*, not head tracking.

The system can determine when the head is looking straight ahead—a reset position—and it can determine when the head is either to the left or to the right. It can in no way tell us exactly how *much* to the left or right. All we have is a directional signal. Therefore, I chose to use the simplest form of communi-cating with the HMD, which is the Sega mode.

The software interface we discuss here can be used with any software package. Once the program that is using the head-positioning ability of the StuntMaster begins executing, we have to initialize several internal variables and reset the HMD. The routine that performs this initialization is called `get_stuntmaster` and is

```
void get_stuntmaster()
  {
  int x1, x2, x3, x4, y1, y2, y3, y4;
  char *stunt_text[] = {
                      "",
                      "Please put Stuntmaster on your head.",
```

```
                     "Look straight ahead and press the",
                     "reset button.",
                     "",
                     NULL
                  };

joystick_init (&stunt_data, use_stuntmaster-1);
poptext ( stunt_text );
delay(10000);

joystick_read ( &stunt_data ); x1 = stunt_data.x; y1 = stunt_data.y;
delay(150);
joystick_read ( &stunt_data ); x2 = stunt_data.x; y2 = stunt_data.y;
delay(150);
joystick_read ( &stunt_data ); x3 = stunt_data.x; y3 = stunt_data.y;
delay(150);
joystick_read ( &stunt_data ); x4 = stunt_data.x; y4 = stunt_data.y;
delay(150);

x_stunt_value = (x1+x2+x3+x4)/4;
y_stunt_value = (y1+y2+y3+y4)/4;

stunt_position = 0;
}
```

The steps involved are as follows:

1. *Tell the user to put the HMD on his or her head, look straight ahead, and press the RESET button on the underside of the HMD. This causes the StuntMaster to read the current state of the potentiometer and record the current values as the center position.*
2. *Next we take four readings from the joystick port to which the Stuntmaster is attached. The values are averaged, and we have a record of the center position of the potentiometer. The value for the left Sega signal is kept in the variable* x_stunt_value, *and the right Sega signal is kept in the variable* y_stunt_value.
3. *The last statement in the function sets the variable* stunt_position *equal to 0. This variable* stunt_position *is used to indicate where the user is looking. If it is 0, then he or she is looking straight ahead. If the variable is set to 1, then the user is looking to the right, and if the variable is* − 1, *then the user is looking to the left.*

We are now set to read the StuntMaster while the program is executing. This reading is performed in the main loop of the program. The function is as follows:

```
void check_stunt() {
 int x1, x2, x3, x4, y1, y2, y3, y4, x, y;

 joystick_read(&stunt_data); x1 = stunt_data.x; y1 = stunt_data.y;
 joystick_read(&stunt_data); x2 = stunt_data.x; y2 = stunt_data.y;
 joystick_read(&stunt_data); x3 = stunt_data.x; y3 = stunt_data.y;
 joystick_read(&stunt_data); x4 = stunt_data.x; y4 = stunt_data.y;

 x = (x1+x2+x3+x4)/4; y = (y1+y2+y3+y4)/4;

  if ((x > x_stunt_value) && (stunt_position != -1) &&
(y<y_stunt_value))
  {
  if (stunt_position == 0)
   current_view->pan -= stunt_angle*65536L;
  else
   current_view->pan -= 2*stunt_angle*65536L;
  stunt_position = -1;
  }
 else if ((y > y_stunt_value) && (stunt_position !=
1)&&(x<x_stunt_value))
  {
  if (stunt_position == 0)
   current_view->pan += stunt_angle*65536L;
  else
   current_view->pan += 2*stunt_angle*65536L;
  stunt_position = 1;
  }
 else if ((x == x_stunt_value)&&(y == y_stunt_value))
  {
  if (stunt_position == -1)
   {
   stunt_position = 0;
   current_view->pan += stunt_angle*65536L;
   }
  else if (stunt_position == 1)
   {
   stunt_position = 0;
   current_view->pan -= stunt_angle*65536L;
   }
  }
 redraw =1;
}
```

These are the steps:

1. *Get a current reading from the StuntMaster's left and right signals.*
2. *Compare the new readings to the center values we recorded during the initialization of the HMD.*

3. *If the left reading is greater than the value in the variable* `x_stunt_value` *and the right reading is less than the value in the variable* `y_stunt_value`, *then we know the user has moved his or her head to the left. Once we have determined that the user has indeed looked to the left, we find out where he or she is currently looking by examining the value in the variable* `stunt_position` *and pan the viewpoint accordingly.*

Precision

The head-positioning mode is *very* sensitive and can be nauseating at times. To help combat this condition, there is a sensitivity wheel on the underside of the HMD. Adjust this wheel until you are able to look forward, left, and right and the image on the screen stays fairly constant.

 # Conclusion

As noted before, VictorMaxx's StuntMaster does not come close to the true virtual reality effects that we would like to have. However, this outfit was the first to market an inexpensive HMD that at least gives the user a general idea of what VR is all about.

Building a Head-Mounted Display

*T*he head-mounted display is the most expensive piece of virtual reality equipment except for the computer itself, but it is arguably the most essential for providing a true virtual reality experience. The shutter glasses introduced in Chapter 6 certainly allow the user to see three-dimensional objects, but nothing prepares a person for the feeling of immersion into a virtual world that the HMD can make possible.

So, what do we mean by *immersion?* Immersion can be defined as our sense of presence in a virtual environment. This feeling is not a product of sight alone; however, most of us are visually oriented, so when we build and use a head-mounted display, we have incorporated the sense most needed for immersion. Sightless people rely more on sound, so an elaborate 3-D sound system would probably be the most important element to create immersion for them.

In this chapter we'll look at the current HMD technology from various companies. Then we'll look at all the issues involved in deciding what kind of HMD you should build. Finally, we'll go step by step through the process of building an HMD.

Current HMD Technology

Before we begin building a HMD, let's look at the current state-of-the-art technology in head mounts from both the high and low ends. Figure 8.1 shows a picture of the Kaiser Electro-Optics Sim Eye head-mounted display.

The Sim Eye is a CRT-based head mount designed for the military. The cost of the unit is $95,000, which is just a bit out of the budget for the average hobbyist. However, the HMD provides very high resolution of 1,280 × 1,024 pixels and has a field of view 60° horizontal × 40° vertical.

Once we leave the high end, there are a number of different head mounts. I have chosen a few to show you to give you an idea of what the manufacturers have come up with. Keep in mind that we will need an enclosure for our HMD.

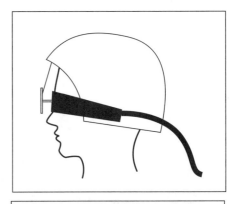

FIGURE 8.1 *The Kaiser Electro-Optics Sim Eye HMD*

Figure 8.2 shows the MRG2 from Liquid Image Corporation. The MRG2 has a field of view 110° horizontal × 37° vertical. The cost is $6,400. The MRG2 is a monoscopic system only. It was designed for the arcade industry.

Figure 8.3 shows the Flight Helmet from Virtual Research. It had a field of view 100° horizontal × 67° vertical. The cost was $6,000. It is no longer available; I include it here to show an example of a helmet HMD.

Figure 8.4 is an example of open HMD:1 the Tier 1 from VRontier Worlds of Stoughton, Inc. The field of view is 112° horizontal × 89° vertical. The cost is $3,800.

Each manufacturer has a different idea about what they want their HMD to look like. The helmet designs have a very nice natural look to them. Most of us are used to putting some kind of helmet or cap on our heads. However, the air inside helmet HMDs gets stuffy and unpleasantly warm. The open HMDs are more hygienic and do not suffer from the heat problem, but the new look takes some getting used to.

As a developer of virtual applications and environments, I prefer to use just the front part of the Tier 1. When I am creating a world, I can just pick up the HMD, look in it for a bit, and then put it back down. I have never found myself in the environment for more than a few minutes.

Well, now that we have talked about displays, optics, and what some

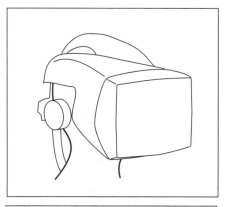

FIGURE 8.2 **Liquid Image Corporation's MRG2**

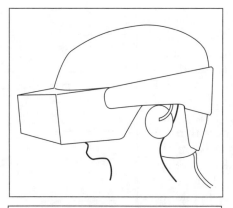

FIGURE 8.3 **Virtual Research's Flight Helmet**

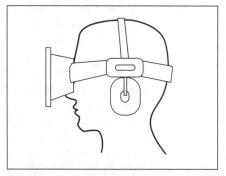

FIGURE 8.4 **VRontier World's Tier 1**

of the current technology looks like, we should begin actually building an HMD. We will outline the construction of both stereo and mono HMDs step by step. But first, let's look at some general information about HMDs.

 ## How HMDs Work

Before we can build HMDs, we need to know how they work and what goes into their design. As we stated before, the HMD's purpose is to create a sense of immersion by placing an image in front of our eyes. The image will typically be generated by a computer, but as we will see later, there are other methods. A head-mounted display consists of three components, as shown in Figure 8.5.

The first component is the *displays*. These are responsible for presenting the graphical images output by the computer. The second component is the *optics*. To see the importance of optics, take two small pieces of paper about 3 inches square and write the word *hi* on them in your normal writing style. Now take one of the pieces of paper in each hand and place them about 3 inches from your eyes. Can you read what is on the paper? Did your eyes begin to strain and hurt when trying to look at something that close? The images that we are going to display in the HMD are going to be about 3 inches from your eyes. The optics are required to allow your eyes to focus on something that close. They also have the ability to create an immersive effect if desired. The third component is the *enclosure*. Its main purpose is to hold the LCDs and optics, block out our view of the real world, and to keep the HMD firmly positioned on the head. Let's look at each of the components in detail.

Displays

When the first head-mounted display was created by Ivan Sutherland, his only choice for a display was a CRT (cathode ray tube). This is the type of tube that is used in television sets. Just imagine putting two of those things 3 inches away from your eyes! In the Sutherland design, the CRTs were not placed directly in front of the eyes; instead, mirrors were used to fold the image into the eyes. An example of this type of folding using mirrors is shown in Figure 8.6.

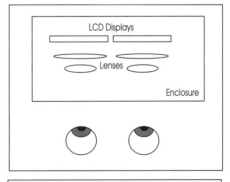

FIGURE 8.5 *Main components of a head-mounted display*

The main reason for using CRTs is their resolution. In the past, CRTs were ruled out for HMD use because of their weight and the safety concerns about radiation. But as technology has advanced, so have CRTs. You can now purchase very small CRTs (about 1 inch diagonal) that have upwards of 1,000 lines of resolution. However, the majority of these CRTs are monochromatic. To solve this problem, a number of companies have developed a technique that uses a monochromatic display and a three-color (red, green,

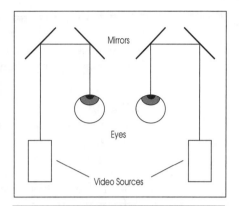

FIGURE 8.6 *Example of mirror folding*

and blue) wheel. This way, the computer can display very accurate images. It begins by displaying the red parts of an image, then quickly changing to the green parts and then the blue parts. As each of the different colored scenes appears on the CRT, the color wheel would change to the appropriate color. If done quickly enough (on the order of 90 times a second), the image appears in full color. Monochromatic CRTs offer the advantages of very high resolution and relatively low cost. Although this is an option, most HMD manufacturers are still using LCDs.

Liquid Crystal Display (LCD)

LCDs use tiny crystals and light to produce color images. When HMDs first gained popularity those that wanted to have a system for themselves would run down to the local Radio Shack or Walmart and purchase a hand-held television set containing a small (2.2 to 3 inches diagonal) LCD display. These units cost only about $100 or so. People simply removed the casing and extended the wires between the electronics and the LCD. In fact, one major manufacturer sold HMDs for thousands of dollars and used off-the-shelf Sony Watchmans for the LCDs. As things turned out, Sony pulled the Watchman as bigger LCD displays became feasible.

Resolution

One of the problems with LCDs is their resolution or lack thereof. A typical 2.7-inch LCD will have 360 horizontal and 250 vertical elements. This isn't bad when you consider that REND uses the 300 × 200 pixels display mode. However, because these LCDs are color, it takes three elements to make a single color pixel. This causes the resolution to be affected severely. Even if we step up to a 4-inch diagonal LCD, the element count is not much better: 479 × 234. As we will see later, as the LCD display grows in size, it becomes harder and harder to construct an HMD.

In its intended use, watching TV, you would normally view the LCD from a foot or more away. This distance causes the elements to blend together, producing a full, clear image, but at 3 inches from your face, problems develop that have to be fixed by means of optics.

Diffusion

In order to give you an example of what it is like to view the LCD at a 3-inch distance, go up to any screen door or window and position yourself so that you focus right on the screen itself. Now focus your eyes on the background. You can still see the mesh of the screen, and at times your eyes will focus on it instead of the background. This is what it is like for LCDs at a distance of 3 inches; you can see the individual elements of the display. To counter this, a diffuser has to be placed on the LCD screen or somewhere between the LCD and the optics. A diffuser is some type of material that causes the individual elements of the LCD to be blended together and therefore less distinguishable. HMD manufacturer VPL experimented with a piece of wax paper that had a dot pattern applied to it. By applying this wax paper to the LCD, the dots are smeared just enough to keep the eye from focusing on the individual elements.

When you use a hand-held television as it was meant to be used (as a TV, that is), the elements that make up the screen are so small and far away that the eye is unable to see them. In the case of the HMD, we apply a diffuser so that when the LCD is magnified up against our eyes, we have the same effect as when the TV is used in its normal application.

Screen Size

Most of the early-model commercial head mounts use an optical system called LEEP, which will be discussed in more detail a little later. These optics were not designed for use in HMDs, so fitting LCDs to them became a problem. It turned out that the optimal choice was to use LCDs from the Sony Watchman, as mentioned above. This LCD was 3 inches diagonal. When determining the size of an LCD to use in an HMD, we have to take into consideration that we must be able to put two of them side by side in front of our eyes. Figure 8.7 shows the optimal situation. The displays fit directly in front of the eyes, each of which is centered on an LCD. As manufacturers started to discontinue the small LCDs in favor of larger ones, HMD designers were faced with yet another problem. Figure 8.8 shows what happens when two 4-inch LCDs are placed in front of the eyes. As you can see, the eyes are no longer centered on their LCDs. If an image were to be displayed on the LCDs, each eye would be looking at a

FIGURE 8.7 *Optimal eye-LCD placement*

4" Displays

Eyes

FIGURE 8.8 *4-inch displays and eye configuration*

completely different part of it. Even though designers want bigger LCDs for better resolution, they have to do more work to get them in front of the eyes correctly.

Housing

If we do as the early designers did and use off-the-shelf components, we have to be concerned with the housing that makes the mini television look like a mini television. There is quite a bit of plastic holding all of the components together. Figure 8.9 shows how two 2.2-inch LCDs fit in front of the eyes, and Figure 8.10 shows how they fit if we leave the plastic on them. As the figure shows, the housing around the LCDs is usually not even, with more plastic on the right side than the left. If

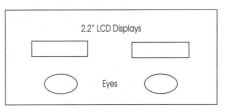

2.2" LCD Displays

Eyes

FIGURE 8.9 *2.2-inch displays and eye configuration*

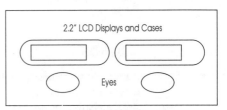

2.2" LCD Displays and Cases

Eyes

FIGURE 8.10 *2.2-inch LCD displays, their cases, and eye configuration*

this were not the case, we could leave the housing on and still use the LCDs directly in front of the eyes.

There is a second reason why the housing is such a concern: weight. If you combine all of the electronics, the LCDs, and the plastic for two televisions, you end up with a heavy load. This means that we would have to construct a good-sized weight on the back of our HMD to counter the heavy front. So it looks like the housing has to come off to use the LCDs effectively.

Price

Cost is always a determining factor in choosing any component. The average cost of a mini television is $100. This can fluctuate depending on where and when you get one and on LCD size. If you were to purchase the LCDs separately, you would probably pay considerably more than the price for the entire television itself because you would be getting your LCD at a resale price, rather than the wholesale price paid by large manufacturers who use millions of LCDs at a time.

Circuitry

If you decide to buy a separate LCD (rather than take one from a mini television), you need to be aware that all LCDs need some sort of driver circuitry to operate. The circuitry has to handle the input signal as well as the power requirements of the LCD and, typically, the backlight module. LCDs are by far the way to go for the VR experimenter because of their weight, price, and ease of use. However, there is one other option we should at least consider.

We have all heard about the wonderful things that fiber optics are going to do for us in the near future, and HMD designers are already putting this technology to good use. Images from a computer are projected into one end of a cablelike structure consisting of hundreds of thousands of tiny fiber optics by means of a special light device. The image is transferred to the other end of the cable, where mirrors reflect it into the user's eyes. The result is an image with very high resolution, but these displays usually cost around $100,000.

Optics

Once we have displays to work with, it's time to look at optics, which is probably a most confusing time for most experimenters. How many of us actually had a course in designing optics or have used them to any degree? All that most of us know is that we can purchase magnifying glasses that will make a small object look big, so let's start there. If we look at a word on a piece of paper, that word occupies a certain portion of our *eye space*, which is the area seen by the eye when it has a steady line of sight. If we place a magnifying glass between our eye and that word, it will occupy an even larger space than it did without the magnifying glass. At the same time, we are able to see the word in much greater detail. If there is a section of the word that has less ink than another part, we will be able to see the difference more clearly. We can apply all of this to the study of optics and head-mounted displays.

Field of View (FOV)

This is one of the most popular measurements of how well the optics are doing. In simplistic terms, the field of view is the measurement of how much we see. If you extend your arms out to each side and hold up a finger, you will be able to see both fingers when looking straight ahead. This means that your field of view measures 180° from left to right. Head-mounted display manufacturers aim for the largest possible field of view in order to mimic the view our eyes normally have. Currently, the largest field of view in commercial head mounts runs in the 110° range.

Immersion

Once we have a large field of view, we have to turn our attention to the question of immersion. How do we create the immersion effect using optics? First, let's talk about what immersion isn't. When you sit in a movie theater and watch a movie, do you ever feel as though you're up there with the actors, or do things always look faraway? In most cases, unless the movie is 3-D, the screen appears to be off in the distance and surrounded by a bunch of black space. This is a picture window or letterbox view of the world. It leaves you feeling left out. To create the immersive effect, we have to bring the screen up to your eyes and eliminate the black part around the screen. This isn't as easy as it sounds because removing the black part means sacrificing resolution.

We need to place the LCD display in front of our eyes, and there are ways to calculate just where exactly to put them. Figure 8.11 illustrates the ideal set-up. The placement of the lenses is based on a finding by Eric Howlett of LEEP Optics, Inc., whom we will discuss shortly. He states that an opening placed 1 inch in front of your eye would need to have a 2-inch diameter to provide an optimum field of view. If you wear glasses, you can prove this by measuring the diameter of your lenses and the distance of your eyes from them. We can express this statement in the following equation:

$$diameter = 2 * distance$$

Because our eyes can rotate and the lenses are round, the approximate viewing area of our eye is really a cone and not a triangle, as it appears in Figure 8.11. Using the diagram in that figure, we can measure along the triangle until the width matches the width of our display. Figure 8.12 shows the proper placement of 2.2-inch, 3-inch, and 4-inch diagonal LCD displays.

Now let's go back to immersion. The lens that we place in front of the LCD must be powerful enough that the magnified screen fills the entire field-of-view cone. If we were to place the display appropriately but without the lens, it would certainly not fill the field of view, but as we insert increasingly powerful lenses, the display appears to grow. This is exactly like the situation we had at the opening of this chapter. If you look at a word printed

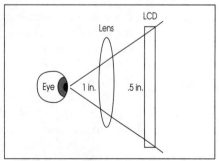

FIGURE 8.11 *Eye cone and positions of lens and LCD display*

on paper with a magnifying glass, it will fill more of your view than without the magnifier.

The lens has a second purpose in addition to providing immersion. If you hold a piece of paper with a word on it too close to your eye, you won't be able to read it, but if you place a magnifying glass between it and your eye, you can. Simply increasing the size of the word allows the eye to focus on it.

However, increased magnitude creates resolution problems. We al-

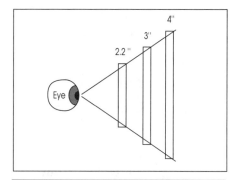

FIGURE 8.12 **Placement of 2.2-inch, 3-inch, and 4-inch displays**

ready know that the resolution for current LCDs is not great. As you increase the magnification, the individual elements of the display screen become very noticeable. Therefore, if you want to have an immersion system, you are more than likely going to need some type of diffuser, as previously mentioned. If you do not want to sacrifice your limited resolution for total immersion, you can experiment with different lens powers to determine which is most suitable for your application.

It should be noted that not all applications require the same type of head mount. If you are doing experiments in medicine or data visualization, you will probably want a very clear display. Under those circumstances, immersion would probably not be a big concern, so you could use a low-power lens to create an adequate display for this purpose. If your application is intended for entertainment, you will be less concerned with clarity and more concerned about immersion.

Divergence and Interocular Spacing

Once we have our magnification lens set up, we need to look at the placing of the LCD display. In the section on Housing, we talked about how different-sized displays, with or without the plastic housing around them, can cause problems. Figure 8.9 shows what the optimum configuration of the display and the eyes is. We want the center of the display directly in front of the eye. In some cases, though, this is just not possible. Figure 8.8 shows a situation where two large displays are used for an HMD. The displays are so big that there is no way that we can get them directly in front of each eye. If we were to simply put the screens together as much as possible and display an image in them, the eyes would have to diverge to see them correctly. Because our eyes are not designed to do much diverging, we have to come up with a way to solve this problem. Figure 8.13 shows what we're up against. We will discuss the solution later in this chapter.

Convergence

Once we have two displays in front of
our eyes with images in them, we have
to perform an operation called convergence. When our eyes converge on an
image, they each send a representation to our brains, which take both
pieces and form a single, fused image.

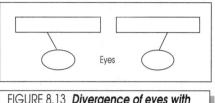

FIGURE 8.13 **Divergence of eyes with 4-inch displays**

In order to converge the images on the LCD displays, we may have to shift them
using either the displays or our software. When you look at the displays, you see
two very distinct images. In the software we can manually move the displayed
images so that they come together to form a single image. Once we have built
our HMD, we will have to go through this step to get an acceptable image.

Mono/Stereo

One of the last things that we need to talk about in this section on optics is the difference between stereo and mono HMDs. In a stereo system, we have two displays, each of which can accept a different image. This is required to provide
stereoscopic views to the user. In addition to the two displays, we have two complete sets of lenses that provide some degree of divergence and magnification,
depending on whether or not the HMD is to be immersive. The only reason to
have a stereo HMD is to provide the stereoscopic images. Now we have to worry
about how to create two images at once. Normally, the computer system to which
the HMD is connected would provide both signals. However, a great deal of head
mounts are connected to PCs. An IBM PC is unable to generate stereo images very
effectively because it is not designed to accept two VGA display cards. There are
certain boards available that will give you two VGA signals in a single PC, but they
are both expensive and not directly supported by any of the rendering packages.

With all of this in mind, we need to look at whether stereo is truly necessary. Stereopsis is just one of many depth cues that the brain uses. If enough
software depth cues are provided to the user, then adding stereo images to the
mix does not improve the outcome a great deal—at least that's how it looks to
my eyes and brain. Apparently, not all people benefit from stereopsis. I personally have a real hard time seeing the difference between the same scene displayed in mono and then in stereo. Maybe I just haven't seen software that produces really good stereo. In any case, if an HMD is designed for stereo, we have
to double our efforts in regards to the lenses and displays as well as be concerned with convergence and divergence. A mono HMD has a single display
screen and typically a single lens, the purpose of which is to allow us to focus
on the display, as well as to create some degree of immersion. In our quest to
build an HMD, we will look at both the stereo and mono options and describe
how to build both types.

LEEP

Before we end our discussion on optics, we have to touch on LEEP Optics, Inc., and Eric Howlett. Several years ago, Eric developed a system of lenses called LEEP that performs a decompression algorithm on pairs of stereo slides that are produced by special cameras that execute a compression algorithm on the scene they are shooting. This compression allows for a larger field of view to be put on normal 35-mm film. In order to view the slides correctly, the compression must be decoded. The LEEP optics perform this decompression, thus allowing the user to enjoy a wide field of view from the slides. When the first HMDs were being produced, someone came upon these optics and experimented with them. As it turned out, placing an LCD display about 3 inches in front of the optics caused the field of view to expand. This was just what the HMD developers wanted. The only problem was the decompression algorithm that had been designed into the lenses. When an image appeared in the displays, the outside edges were affected by the algorithm; straight lines turned into curves, and curved lines became straight. Because this only occurred at the edges, concern was minimal. As time passed, developers were able to change the rendering software so that the compression algorithm used for the photograph was applied to the computer graphics, which cleared up the problem. However, the computational cost of the compression on every single image coming out of the computer was so high that it was determined that this procedure was not needed. Since that time, HMD manufacturers have designed their own optics to overcome this problem.

Building Your Own HMD !!!!!

The first thing that we have to do in our quest for an HMD is to obtain the displays. As we discussed earlier, if you just purchase an LCD display, you are going to have to build a driver circuit for it. Although not a hard task for some, this is beyond the scope of most garage-level VR people. If you are interested in this method, you should purchase the LCD from a distributor and ask for the complete datasheet and all tech notes that they can get from its original manufacturer. Many times, the manufacturer will include all the information about driving its displays; in fact, some will even include a simple circuit that does the job. They want you to use their displays, so they will more than likely help you as much as possible. If the tech notes do not hold the answer, just call the manufacturer and ask to speak with a field engineer, who will probably be able to point you to a schematic for the display. If all else fails, you can find a friend or hire someone to design the driver board from the datasheet. It is not an enormously complex circuit.

I'm going to show you a simpler method. We will take the LCD displays out of something completely unrelated to VR—a hand-held TV. For the remainder of the chapter I will assume that we are working with small LCD displays in the range of 2.2 to 4 inches. The following list gives you a good idea of what is needed to complete this HMD, but what you need will vary depending on the choices you make throughout this chapter. My advice is to read this entire project, make some notes, and then go out and buy the parts.

Parts List for a Head-Mounted Display

- ❏ 2 Casio model 470 color LCD mini televisions or other mini televisions
- ❏ 1 prism lens (if necessary)
- ❏ 1 magnification lens
- ❏ 1 large piece of balsa or other soft wood

A Warning About Using CRTs

Recall that Ivan Sutherland developed one of the first HMDs using CRT displays. In order to keep from looking directly into the CRTs, he folded the image into the user's eyes. However, the CRTs were still very close to the user's head. There are questions concerning the safety of using CRTs in HMDs. Therefore, I can neither recommend nor frown on the use of CRTs. Just be aware that there are concerns.

Locating Good LCDs

The easiest place to find the LCDs are in mini televisions. These can be purchased with displays from 1.6 to 4 inches, depending on the price you want to pay. Radio Shack sells two different models, Casio has 2.2- and 2.7-inch systems, and Sony's models have larger displays than the Radio Shack models. Any of these will work; it's just a matter of taking the system apart and extending a few wires.

Places to look for these TVs include discount stores such as Wal-mart or Kmart or the numerous stores in your area that carry consumer electronic products. One very important source is pawn shops, where I have been able to find black-and-white TVs for under $20. I wouldn't discourage the use of black-and-white TVs because not having to split the elements up into red, green, and blue means a much better picture. You can typically find color TVs for $50 or so in pawn shops. Because we are going to be ripping them up, the appearance of the case is immaterial. Just make sure that the picture on the LCD is working correctly and that there are no scratches on the surface of the displays because we will be magnifying the image and any defects on the glass will show up. One last place to consider is liquidators. At times, these companies will purchase large quantities of discontinued merchandise and sell it quite cheap.

For my HMD, I am using the Casio model 470 color TV. This product has a 2.2-inch LCD display. I will show you pictures and discuss the progression from destruction to construction. If you are willing to spend a little more money, you can purchase the Memorex 2.7-inch Pocket TV from Radio Shack. Not only does it provide a larger screen to work with, but it also has direct video inputs that will eliminate the need to purchase the video modulator discussed later in this chapter.

Disassembling a Portable TV

We begin our disassembly by taking off the back cover:

1. *Unscrew the screw in the upper right-hand corner.*
2. *Remove the battery face plate and remove the screw in the lower right corner.*
3. *Carefully pull the two pieces apart. They are connected by a ribbon cable, so be careful.*
4. *Remove the front part by pulling the ribbon cable out of the back electronics board. Note the orientation of the connection.*
5. *Remove the screw in the lower right-hand corner of the board in the back part of the TV.*
6. *Turn the bottom part over and gently pry the top left battery connection off the ledge on which it is hooked.*
7. *On the left-hand side of the bottom part is a little wheel for adjusting the picture; gently pry this off with a screwdriver.*
8. *The board will now lift out of the bottom enclosure very easily. Be very careful not to create static electricity or touch the electronic parts of the board. You can unsolder or cut off the two battery connectors; they are of no use to us. We will now empty the front part of the TV.*
9. *Remove the four screws in each of the four corners of the printed circuit board (PCB).*
10. *Gently pry the assembly out of the enclosure. There is a bit of glue holding it in, so pull on each side until it unsticks.*
11. *Cut the wires that run from the speaker to the board as close as you can to the PCB or unsolder them.*

On the piece that you just removed, you will see a metal framing around the LCD itself. If you remove this by unsoldering the three connections that hold it to the other metal pieces, you will find that the LCD is attached to the circuit board by three very tiny ribbon connectors. You can see that the entire LCD-and-backlighting mechanism is in a plastic case of its own. For our purposes, the metal framing can remain.

At this point, you are finished with the disassembly. To use the system, you would attach the two PCBs together using plastic risers, as shown in Figure

8.14. Each end of the risers would be attached to one of the PCBs. You could also extend the cable between the PCB and move the second one to the back of your enclosure, as shown in Figure 8.15.

The other option is to try to remove the LCD from the PCB. This is a good idea because it lets you center the LCD in front of each eye. However, the connections for the LCD and PCB are very thin. I would practice my soldering technique before attempting this step.

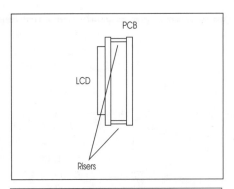

FIGURE 8.14 **PCB separated by risers**

Selecting Optics for Your LCDs

After the disassembly of the LCD displays, we have to look at the optics. I will cover several different situations for those using displays other than the 2.2-inch display we're working with. Figure 8.16 shows the exact measurements for placing the 2.2-inch LCD screens in the proper position relative to my eyes.

The screens should fit perfectly in front of my eyes, with 2 mm of space between them. To determine where your displays should be placed, measure horizontally from their edges to their very centers. If this measurement is greater than 16 mm, then we know that placing them directly in front of your eyes isn't an option. We are going to use standard 64 mm interocular spacing so that a wide range of people will be able to try your HMD. Because the screens are bigger than the area we have available, we are going to have to solve a divergence problem.

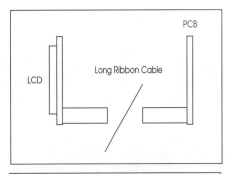

FIGURE 8.15 **LCD and PCB separated by long ribbon cable**

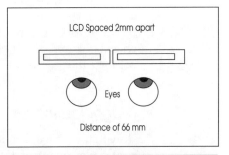

FIGURE 8.16 **Relative placement of 2.2-inch LCD displays and the eyes**

If the measurement is less than 16 mm, then you will need to have a space that is 64 mm minus 2 times the horizontal measurement of the screens. If your screens are 20 mm horizontally, then you will need a spacing of $64 - 2(20) = 24$ mm.

Divergence

If your displays were less than 16 mm, you can skip this section. If your displays have a center measurement greater than 16 mm, however, they will have to be placed in such a way that we can easily bend the line of sight into the centers of the displays. This sounds easy, but it's not every day that we force our eyes to diverge. We're going to use prisms to bend the light that exits the LCD displays so that it enters our eyes at the correct angle.

Now we cannot simply put our displays as close as possible to each other and just use some prism to bend the line of sight. Off-the-shelf prisms do not come in every angle imaginable. First we need to discover the smallest possible angle sufficient to bend the line of sight. This angle will be measured with the displays as close as possible to each other. Figure 8.17 shows an example of how to draw the line-of-sight lines from your eyes to the center of the displays with a representation of a prism in their path.

If we measure the angle between our normal line of sight and the angled line of sight with a protractor, we will have the lowest possible angle necessary to get the job done. We must now find a prism that comes as close as possible to the angle we have measured above. It must be the exact angle measured or larger. If you have to purchase a larger-angle prism than measured, you will have to move your screens farther apart to compensate for the larger angle. One of the best sources for optics is Edmund Scientific (check Appendix C for their address), which has a specific catalog for optics that is available upon request. (Be sure to keep a close eye on your checkbook and credit card when you get the catalog.)

Magnification

Now that we have positioned the horizontal placement of the displays, we need to look at the vertical placement. As we stated earlier, the eye's field of view is shaped like a cone. We can place the LCD approximately one-half the diagonal measurement of the LCD itself from the eye. Therefore, if we are using a 3-inch display, it should be

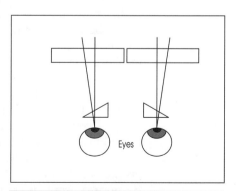

FIGURE 8.17 *Illustration of line-of-sight paths for divergence*

placed approximately 1.5 inches from the eye; a 2.2-inch display would be placed at 1.1 inches from the eye, and so on. This placement will vary, however, because of the focusing distance required for the magnification lens.

The magnification lens should be placed 1 inch from the eye, which is just about where glasses wearers have their lenses. As we pick our lens, we have to keep the size approximately 2 inches in diameter, as we discussed several sections ago. Home-based work by Dr. Suding, a new virtual reality researcher, resulted in some interesting findings for an LCD with a 2.7-inch diagonal measurement. He found that a plano convex lens provided the necessary magnification in three different possible powers:

A 45-mm diameter × 78-mm focal length created a 60˚ field of view
A 57-mm diameter × 110-mm focal length created a 35˚ field of view
A 40-mm diameter × 92-mm focal length created a 45˚ field of view

Obviously these numbers will vary depending on the display that you use. Now comes the experimentation part. Lenses are not cheap. They average $8 apiece, and we need two of them. There is no good way to experiment without purchasing several sets and building the cost into the HMD. Another hitch is that you are going to magnify the LCD so much that the individual elements will be visible. We will talk about how to reduce this next, but we will still have to make a compromise shared by all HMD manufacturers. To have a wide field of view and a feeling of immersion, you must sacrifice clarity. The smaller the field of view, the more the image will become *letter boxed*—that is, the image will seem to be out in front of you, with black space around it. So how you handle this situation will be a personal choice.

Placing Your Optics

When placing the magnification lens, it should be between the prism and the LCD display. We will need some sort of carrier to hold the displays and our one or two lenses. One option is to use a balsa wood frame. It is lightweight and relatively strong. Other options include a cardboard frame or a frame made of sheet metal. (Be *very careful* with the metal frame because you have some voltage around!) If you are using a wood enclosure or something made out of cardboard, you can secure all the components with glue from a glue gun. The glue will cool very quickly after it comes out of the gun, so you can assemble the entire unit very quickly. The idea here is to create a compact unit that you can attach to some type of enclosure like a baseball helmet.

Selecting a Diffuser

Everything is all set to go with the optics except for two things, the first of which is diffusion. If you have purchased lenses that create a relatively wide field of view, you are probably able to see the individual elements of the LCD. We can help things out by diffusing the elements. As we mentioned earlier, VPL used a wax paper–like substance, so try it and see if you like the effects. Another option is to use halftone paper from a printer. This is sticky-backed paper with a bunch of dots on it. The higher the halftone paper line count, such as 100 line, the more and smaller the dots. The paper is placed directly in front of or on one of the LCD screens. Try various different line counts and find one that gives you the best image.

Adjusting for Convergence

The last thing we have to mess with is convergence. What we want to do is determine if the two images in the displays become one image when we look at them together. We can do this by providing the same input signal to each display and looking in our HMD. If you see a single image, then the displays are converged. If you see two images side by side, you will need to move one of the displays either left or right horizontally. As you are looking into the HMD, have someone very slowly move one of the LCD displays in one direction or the other until you see a single image. Be aware that some people will not be able to converge the images that you provide them in the HMD. The HMD is optimized for the roughly 90 percent of the general population that have an interocular spacing from 60 to 80 mm, so people that have less or more spacing will have problems.

Building an Enclosure

Now it's creativity time. What are you going to put your displays and lens in so that you can wear them on your head? The main thing you are going to have to be concerned with is a counterweight to offset the weight of the displays. Usually the best place for the weight is in the back of your enclosure, directly opposite the displays. One of the easiest enclosures to make is based on the helmet. In sporting goods stores, you can purchase baseball helmets that are very durable. Using nylon ties, you can fasten the balsa wood enclosure that houses the displays and lenses to the bill of the helmet. Figure 8.18 shows an example of how to attach the lens/LCD assembly to a helmet. A counterweight can then be bolted or attached using the nylon ties as shown in Figure 8.19. For whatever enclosure

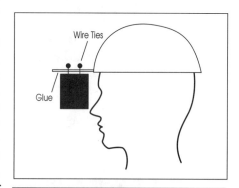

FIGURE 8.18 *Mounting lens/LCD to enclosure*

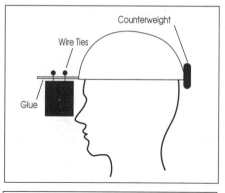

FIGURE 8.19 **Counterweight attachment**

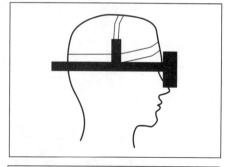

FIGURE 8.20 **Example of an open design HMD**

you come up with, you will want to provide some type of mask that fits up against and around the eyes so that light is not able to shine on the displays.

An alternative to the helmet is the open design. Figure 8.20 shows an example. This type of HMD has several components. The first is the band that holds the entire unit to the user's head. Almost all HMDs use the type of headband found in hard hats, which is made of hard plastic and shown in Figure 8.21. Attached to the headband is a plastic cage that appears in Figure 8.22. The cage is made of ¼" thick ABS plastic, which can be purchased from plastic companies in sheets.

To build the cage, you will need to cut two pieces of this plastic; one piece should be 2" × 37" × ¼", and the other should measure 2" × 15½" × ¼". The long piece of plastic is bent as shown in Figure 8.23. (The easiest way to bend the plastic is to use a heat

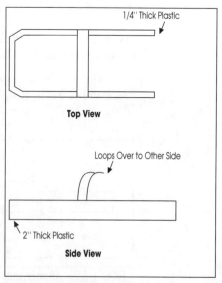

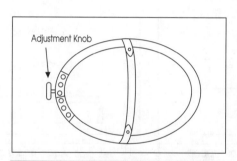

FIGURE 8.21 **Headband used in most HMDs**

FIGURE 8.22 **An open design plastic cage**

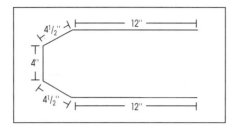

FIGURE 8.23 **Dimensions for plastic cage**

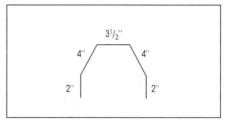

FIGURE 8.24 **Dimensions for support plastic**

gun.) Once the plastic is pliable, bend it to the desired position and blow on the heated area to cool it. The second piece of plastic should be bent in the shape shown in Figure 8.24, and the second piece of plastic is attached to the first as shown in Figure 8.25. The next step is to attach the top of the headband to the inside top of the cage, as seen in Figure 8.26. As in the first enclosure, we need to attach a counterweight. Bolt a piece of metal directly to the back of the cage for this purpose.

In both enclosures, the LCDs and optics are contained in a box. The front of the box appears as in Figure 8.27. The first step in creating the display box is to cut out holes big enough but not too big for your magnification lenses—they should fit snugly into the holes. Secure them using a glue gun. The optics should be placed on the bottom side of the box, and the LCDs should be mounted on the lid of the box. Each LCD has a hole in it that is ideal for this purpose. You can adjust the distance from the lenses to the LCDs by using spacers between the lid of the box and the back side of the LCDs. Figure 8.28 is a cutaway view of the whole display box.

The box is mounted at the front of the plastic cage and attached to the baseball helmet as previously discussed.

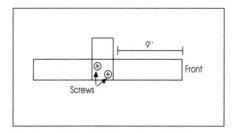

FIGURE 8.25 **Attachment of support plastic to cage**

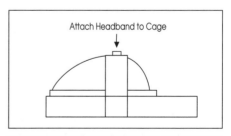

FIGURE 8.26 **Attachment of headband to support plastic**

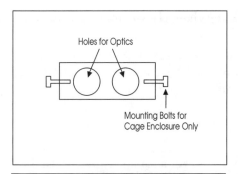

FIGURE 8.27 *Front view of LCD/optic enclosure*

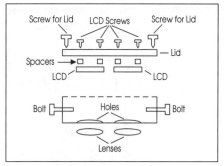

FIGURE 8.28 *Exploded view of LCD/optic enclosure*

Getting a Good Video Signal to Your HMD

To use the HMD effectively, we need to supply it with video. Because we are using parts from a television for our displays, we have to follow the needs of the unit. Normally, these TVs bring in their signals from the antenna. All of the units have a separate jack that allows a separate, usually better, antenna to be used for reception. For our purposes, we will have to use the antenna jack. This means that we have to convert our video signals, whatever they are going to be, to a normal television signal and further convert it to a form that the antenna jack will accept.

Modulator

Radio Shack to the rescue! They sell a small unit called an *RF modulator* that accepts composite video, an NTSC signal, and converts it to a frequency compatible with channel 3 or 4 on the television tuner. Figure 8.29 shows a block diagram of what we have to do to get a signal to our HMD.

As far as the antenna jack is concerned, you can either use a 0.125-inch plug and keep the original jack, or you can cut it off and hardwire a better cable to it. When the signal is supplied to the RF modulator, it will be displayed on the television somewhere around channel 3 or 4. There is usually a switch on the RF modulator that will let you pick one of two channels to try. If your local television sta-

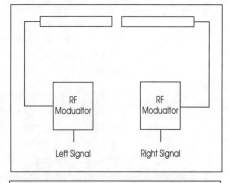

FIGURE 8.29 *Signal path to displays*

tions broadcast on one of the channels, you may get some interference. Try the other channel and see if it clears up.

If you used the mini television from Radio Shack mentioned earlier, you will not need the RF Modulator. The television accepts the NTSC signal coming from the NTSC converter discussed in the next section.

Computer

Now that we have the ability to get a signal to the television, we have to think about a source. In most cases, we have built the HMD for use with the computer. Depending on the computer that you have, this can be a simple operation or one that requires yet more hardware. What we have to do is take the video format of the computer system and produce an NTSC signal. If you own an Amiga, this is very simple because these have an output port for NTSC. Simply connect a cable from the Amiga to the RF Modulator's input port, and you can skip the next section.

VGA to NTSC

If you own an IBM personal computer, the situation is a bit more complicated. If you wish to use CGA graphics, the original graphics standard for the IBM PC, you can use the composite port on the CGA card to give you the necessary signal to input to the RF modulator. If you are going to use VGA graphics, which I will assume is the case, you will have to purchase a VGA-to-NTSC converter. This card takes the VGA signals from the graphics card and splits them, sending one set back to the monitor and converting the other set to the NTSC signal. There are a number of different converters available. A good source is Boffin Limited; their address is listed in Appendix C. They sell an external converter for $99. You simply connect a couple of cables and install some driver software. When you activate the driver software, it does a few things to the VGA card, and we have an NTSC signal.

If you have a multisync monitor, you will get a picture on the monitor as well. It will be smaller than the original picture and not as clear. You can now run any software that uses the text modes as well as a number of the graphics modes up to usually 640×480×256.

If you are running REND386 with the video driver vd256.rvd you will have a problem. The original driver made changes to the graphics card as well. Now we have a second piece of software that is playing with the VGA registers. To combat this, someone wrote a new driver called vd256y.rvd that I have supplied on the enclosed disk. Just replace the file vd256.rvd with the file vd256y.rvd; you will have to call it vd256.rvd to work with current compiled REND software. The original driver put a large black hole in the middle of the picture; the new one corrects this problem.

Boffin also carries other converters for a variety of other purposes. If you want VHS-S support, they have a card for it. I am using an internal card that they sold for $199 a couple of years ago. Now for the problems: Because the converter software for the cards actually makes changes to the VGA registers, some commercial software cannot be used with them. For instance, the VREAM development system causes the inexpensive converter software to really have problems. In this case, you will have to go to a better converter. These are available from many computer companies that supply computer equipment and usually cost over $500.

The last computer option that you have is to purchase a separate video card that outputs NTSC directly. A company called Visionetics International sells a TSENG-4000 chip-based VGA card that has built-in NTSC. This is a very nice option. The card can also be used in a multi-VGA mode where multiple cards can be put into the computer. This is certainly the way to go if you want to do stereo.

Stereo/Mono

If you are going to use stereo signals in your HMD, you will need two computer sources. Most computers do not output two separate signals. You will have to separately purchase cards like the one just mentioned or dedicated graphics cards. Another option is to use two separate computers that are connected by a cable allowing them to communicate with each other about the virtual scene.

VCR

You can also watch movies in your new HMD. All VCRs have composite video input and output signals. You can attach a cable to the VCR output line and to your HMD for very private viewing of your videos. The quality isn't too good, but it works.

Camcorder

Finally, this is something you should all try. Hook your HMD up to a camcorder. Most if not all camcorders have a video output as well so that you can bypass recording on the tape. Use this as input to your HMD and have someone point the camcorder at the back of your head. By having them turn it around, you can have eyes in the back of your head! Tell them to move the camcorder slowly though—you can really get sick.

Cyber Sickness

This brings me to the point of cyber sickness. A good majority of the people who use HMDs will experience some negative side effects after the experience, such as headaches, nausea, and dizziness. If you spent a great deal of time in an HMD, these effects can last as long as 24 hours.

Also be aware that you are blind in an HMD. It is best to use one sitting down. It would not be a good situation to trip with all of that electricity and glass right next to your eyes.

Trying Out Your HMD

The HMD we have just completed, as well as the StuntMaster and the monoscopic HMD to come, can be used with the software provided on the enclosed disk. In fact, you can use all of the HMDs with any software that will execute on your computer. This is possible because a head-mounted display is just a monitor strapped to your face that blocks out the outside world. In the case of the stereo HMD, you will need two separate signals to produce the desired image. You can get around this by either building a mono HMD or using a Y-connector to put the same image into both eyes of the stereo HMD. The only problem with doing this is that you will lose one of the depth cues available in stereoscopic viewing. However, most computers cannot output stereo anyway, so not much is lost.

Building a Mono HMD

Well, we have just completed the construction of and video input to a stereo HMD. We are now going to look at some of the things to consider when building a monoscopic HMD, which is much like building a stereo HMD except we only have a single display and lens. In addition, we only have a single image coming from the computer. In the case of stereo, the computer must be able to output two separate video signals, one for the right eye and one for the left. The brain uses the two signals to create one of the depth cues. In a monoscopic system, we are relying on the programmers to provide the necessary depth cues.

Because we have a single display, we do not have the divergence problem. The display should be centered between the eyes as shown in Figure 8.30.

We will now place a square lens in front of the display at the 1-inch position. The lens has to be long enough to allow both of our eyes to see through it, as shown in Figure 8.31.

My recommendations for the lens and displays are

> ***Use a display that is at least 3 inches diagonal***
>
> ***Use a lens from one of the handheld magnifiers available at department and discount stores***

If you use a small display, it will have to be magnified so much that the elements will be very noticeable and distracting. Again, consider using a diffuser to blend in the elements. The VictorMaxx StuntMaster is an example of a monoscopic HMD that does not provide immersion. As we saw in the previous chapter, we were able to hook up the StuntMaster to any device that provided a video signal. There was no need to have two separate signals. This is what makes the monoscopic HMD so attractive.

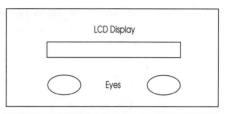

FIGURE 8.30 *Monoscopic system with one LCD display*

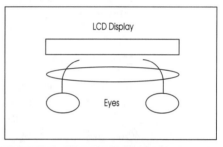

FIGURE 8.31 *Monoscopic system with display and lens*

In addition, because we only need a single video signal, the computer does not have to generate two separate images. This translates into more speed. The computer can simply generate a single image with all of the necessary depth information included in it and output it to the HMD.

A Few Notes for Programmers

Writing software for an HMD is very different than writing software for the monitor. It really wouldn't seem that way, but there are a great many problems with HMDs. We will look at several techniques.

Center Only

Because of the way the optics work in the head mounts, the clearest part of the displayed image will be the center. What this means to software designers is that they will want to keep the majority of the scene in the middle if possible.

Because we give the users a great deal of control over their movement in the virtual environments, this is not always possible—just keep it in mind.

Colors

Not all colors show up well on HMDs. This is due to the low resolution of the LCDs themselves. If you were to use the LCDs as TVs, you would see that they do not look nearly as colorful as normal televisions do. This means that you will more than likely have to play with the colors in order to get a pleasing image. Bright colors can also be a problem because the screens are so close to the eyes. They tend to create eye strain.

Depth Cues

Whether you are using a stereo HMD or a mono one, you will want to create as many depth cues as possible. This is especially true in HMDs because the eyes and the brain are more aware of the images. They do not have anything else to concentrate on. If depth cues break down, the depth illusion can be lost.

Text

Text and an HMD are bad news. As an example, if you create text messages using the font provided with REND386, you will be abe to read about two words if they are in the direct center of the screens. As the words move out to the sides, they become blurred. You should use either blocky or thin fonts. Any kind of fancy font will be very hard to read.

Speed

The last concern is speed. If the image is moving very fast, sickness can occur. Try playing Wolfenstein 3-D in your HMD on an IBM 80486 computer. Just stay in one position and spin around. My head already hurts thinking about it.

 # Conclusion

Building your own head-mounted display is not nearly as complicated as one would initially think. The actual technology, outside of the LCDs, can be found in books dating back to the 1920s and probably earlier. Although there is some cost involved, building an HMD will be worth the effort.

3-D
Sound
Theory

9

The most common type of virtual world built today incorporates only visual cues. All of the projects we have discussed so far deal with interaction in the visual world. We will now extend the complexity of the worlds by adding auditory cues. If we were in a world where our task was to shoot an opponent and to keep from being shot, we would want to be able to tell where the opponent was from the sound of his or her gun. Every time the other person fired at us, we would hear it. This really isn't anything new because most computer and arcade games provide auditory feedback. However, if we are immersed in a virtual world and we hear a gun, we will want to know exactly where our opponent is, and very quickly. With a normal stereo sound system, we can't pinpoint where the sound is coming from; all that can be distinguished is whether it's on the right, left, or in front of us. What is needed is a system that will allow us to hear a sound from the precise direction of the opponent. If they are behind us, we should hear the gunshot behind us.

This type of sound is called *three-dimensional sound*. It is how we normally hear in the real world. If we hear footsteps behind us, we know that someone is there. When we hear an ambulance siren, we are able to locate the vehicle with little trouble. This chapter is for programmers and other people interested in the theory behind the complex systems necessary to reproduce a sound so that our auditory system can accurately find its source.

Introduction to 3-D Sound

In order to create three-dimensional sound, we must understand how a human determines the position of a sound source. In the late nineteenth century, Lord Rayleigh, one of the first scientists to explore how the human auditory system works, studied this phenomenon. His findings, combined with others', have led to the theory that the ability to locate sound sources is strongly dependent on *interaural time differences* (ITDs) and *interaural level* or *pressure differences* (ILDs or IPDs) for the horizontal plane and *spectral cues* for the vertical plane.

Interaural Time Differences

Interaural time differences are the least complex of the directional cues that the human auditory system uses to determine the placement of a sound. Figure 9.1 shows what happens to sound waves presented to the right side of a listener. The interaural time difference, as depicted in the figure, is the time between sound wave W1 and sound wave W2 reaching the listener. Depending on the location of the sound, there will be a specific time difference between when one ear hears W1 and the other ear hears W2. In the example figure, wave W1 wil reach the right ear of the listener long before wave W2 reaches the left ear. The difference in time accounts for the localization of the source to the right of the listener. If we move the sound to a different location, we can observe the waves again.

In Figure 9.2 the sound generates waves that reach each of the ears at the same time; therefore, the time difference is zero. This causes the listener to hear the sound directly in front of him or her. You should be thinking to yourself about the problem caused if the sound is directly behind the listener, because the time difference will also be zero. This is a case there interaural time difference does not provide the necessary cues for localization, and we'll talk more about that issue later.

Reproducing Sounds

In our virtual world we could represent the placement of sound by just having a speaker at some particular location in space for each object. However, several problems occur with this idea. If we had a world as shown in Figure 9.3, we

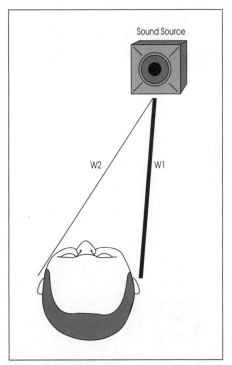

FIGURE 9.1 *Sound waves from a source*

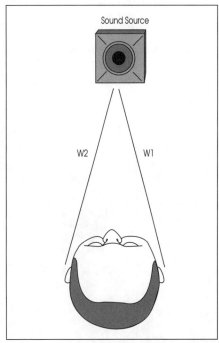

FIGURE 9.2 *Sound waves from a frontal source*

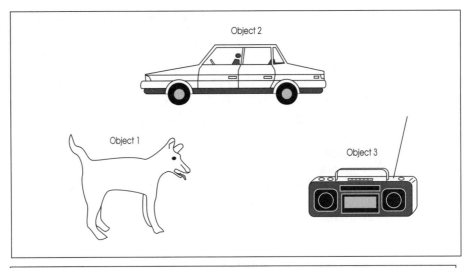

FIGURE 9.3 **Sample world with three audible objects**

would end up with a contraption like Figure 9.4. In most cases, we expect users to be able to move around in the world. If we were to supply a speaker for each object, the speakers would have to move relative to the user. This is obviously not a practical solution to the problem of creating three-dimensional sound. Instead, the solution is to artificially create the time difference necessary to place the sound. We can do this by causing a delay between the time the right ear hears a sound and the time the left ear hears it. If we use two speakers, one for each ear, we can tell the computer to make a sound in the left speaker and,

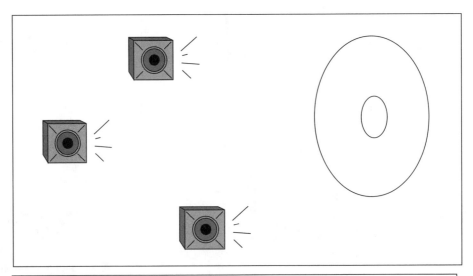

FIGURE 9.4 **Speaker placement for sample world**

after a specific delay period, make a sound in the right speaker. Because the sound started in the left speaker first, the sound will be perceived as coming from the left. The length of the delay determines exactly how far to the left the sound will be located.

Stereo

Figure 9.5 shows the typical stereo set-up—the listener hears the sound at the same time from both of the speakers. This causes the auditory sytem to perceive the sound as coming from directly in front of the listener. Take a moment to sit in front of your stereo system. If you have a speaker to the left and right of where you are, you will perceive the sound to be coming from a point between the speakers.

You have probably heard songs in which the recording engineers have played with the "locations" of the sounds. At times, you will hear music coming from the left speaker seem to move through space and end up coming from the right speaker. The engineer is simply playing with the delay.

Secondary Waves
If you look back at Figure 9.1 you will see that we represented the sound as two different waves that travel to the ears separately. You could have also drawn this

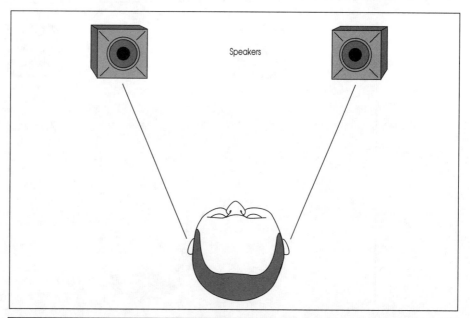

FIGURE 9.5 *Typical stereo sound set-up*

conclusion from the discussion of stereo sound. It would appear that the sound from the left speaker would be heard just by the left ear. This is not an accurate representation of sound waves. Figure 9.6 presents a more realistic view.

As you can see, there are secondary waves that emanate from the sound sources. These secondary waves are heard by the ear opposite to the sources. However, because there are two sound sources and, therefore, two secondary waves, our auditory systems are able to cancel out the secondary waves. This is very important because without the cancellation, the auditory system would hear the sound from a different location than where it was actually coming from.

Sound Levels

Further research has shown that the sound's frequency level plays an important part in determining the location of sound using interaural time differences. At high frequencies, the head of the listener creates a "shadow" effect on the sound waves, which is depicted in Figure 9.7.

Sounds with a frequency of 4,000 Hz and greater suffer from the shadowing effect more than those of lesser frequencies. The reason is that high-frequency wavelengths are relatively short. This allows more of the waves to hit the listener's head and be shadowed from the ears. Placing these sounds' origins relies more on interaural pressure differences, but we'll discuss that later.

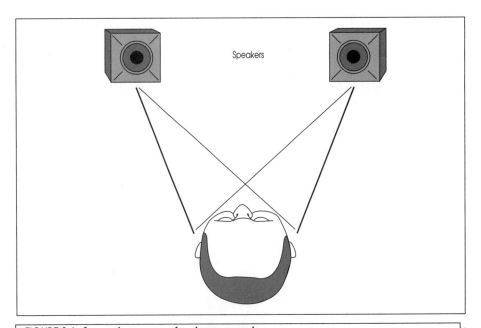

FIGURE 9.6 *Secondary waves for stereo sound*

Sounds below 1,000 Hz are not subject to much of a shadowing effect because the wavelengths are very long and thus able to circumvent the listener's head. It has been shown that between 1,000 and 4,000 Hz, the shadowing effect is listener-dependent— that is, it depends on the listener's perceptual threshold.

Equations

Tremendous research has gone into determining the exact delays necessary to reproduce the interaural time difference cues. One set of equations can be broken down as follows:

For frequencies less than or equal to 4,000 Hz, the ITD is

$$\frac{3 \times radius}{speed\ of\ sound} * \sin (angle)$$

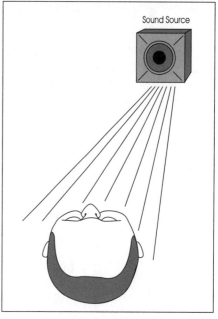

FIGURE 9.7 **Shadow effect of waves and head**

For frequencies greater than 4,000 Hz, the equation becomes

$$\frac{2 \times radius}{speed\ of\ sound} * \sin (angle)$$

Angle (often expressed by the lowercase Greek letter theta, θ) is the angular position of the sound we are placing, assuming that 0° is directly behind us. This means that our left ear is at 90° and our right ear is at 270°. The radius of the listener's head is expressed in centimeters.

How are these equations used? Let's consider the equation for low frequencies. Given that the speed of sound is 343 meters per second and the radius of the listener's head is 9 centimeters, we obtain

$$ITD = 0.052478 * \sin (angle)$$

If we place a sound source at an angle of 45° to the right of the listener, we would get an ITD value of 0.037107 seconds. This tells us that there must be an interaural time difference of 37.1 milliseconds between when a sound wave reaches the left ear and when it reaches the right ear. To simulate this situation in our virtual environment, we would generate a sound in the right speaker and, 37.1 milliseconds later, generate the same sound in the left speaker.

If we were to move the sound source to 45° to the left of the listener, or 315° to the right, we would get the same value except reversed.

In two pieces of literaure, the ITD equations were slightly different. The first is from **R.S. Woodworth** and **H. Schlosberg**, *Experimental Psychology* (New York: Holt, Rinehart, and Winston, 1962), in which the equation is stated as

$$ITD = radius (\theta + \sin \theta)$$

In Kendall and Rogers (1981), the ITD equation is given as

$$ITD = .0008 \sin \theta$$

Kendall and Rogers state that this equation is an approximation derived from many different actual interaural time difference measurements. Using data from Kendal, Rogers, and Woodworth, the plot in Figure 9.8 shows the interaural time differences in milliseconds for different azimuth angles.

Interaural time differences aid in identifying the location of sound on the horizontal plane for low frequencies. ITDs are also used for high frequencies, but interaural pressure differences are the primary cues used in that range.

Interaural Pressure Differences

Simply put, interaural pressure difference is the difference in volume of the sound source. If a sound source is closer to one ear than the other, there will be

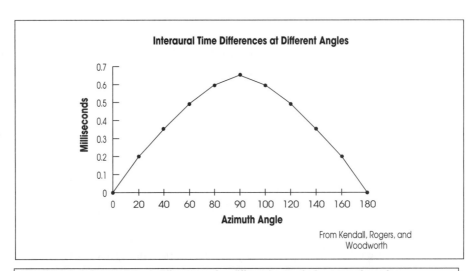

FIGURE 9.8 *Interaural time differences for different sound placement angles*

a difference in the intensity of the sound waves arriving at the closer ear. Our auditory system uses these differences to figure out where sounds are coming from. Over the years, many different researchers have measured the pressures generated at the ears when a sound source is present.

These findings show that interaural pressure difference begins to come into play when the sound frequency reaches 3 kHz. Once the frequency of the sound reaches 5 kHz, IPD is the primary cue for locating sound. Using data from Kendall and Rogers and various other sources, we can plot the IPD for a given frequency in the form of a chart. Figures 9.9 and 9.10 are some examples.

From the figures we see that the IPD in the 6,000 Hz range is much greater than in the 500 Hz range.

The pressure differences are basically caused by two different conditions. The first is the arrival time. If a sound reaches your right ear before the left, it will be more intense in the right. This creates a small IPD. The second and more useful condition is the shadowing effect of the head that we talked about ear-

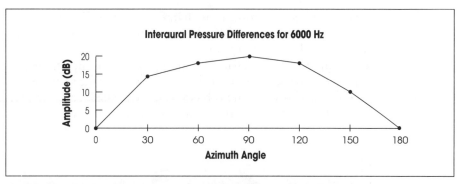

FIGURE 9.9 *Chart showing interaural pressure differences for 6,000 Hz*

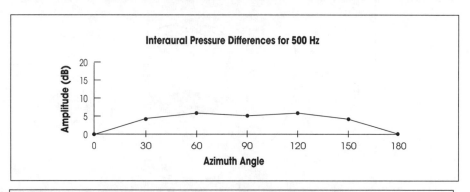

FIGURE 9.10 *Chart showing interaural pressure differences for 500 Hz*

lier. Because of the shadowing, fewer waves will reach the farther ear than the closer ear. This causes a significant difference in the IPD.

Equations

Kendall and Rogers (1981) gives the following interaural pressure difference equation:

$$IPD = 1.0 + (f/1{,}000)^{0.8} * \sin \theta$$

where the frequency (f) is given in kHz.

Both interaural time difference and interaural pressure difference cues are used by our auditory systems to locate the origins of sounds in the horizontal planes around our heads. A different set of cues are used for the vertical plane.

Spectral Cues

One of the biggest problems with interaural time difference and interaural pressure difference is that the values they produce will be the same whether the sound is in front of or behind the listener. Figure 9.11 illustrates this dilemma. If a sound is produced with the appropriate delay and intensity values such that it is placed at location L1, the listener may think the sound is at location L2, and vice versa. This is a real problem when we consider adding three-dimensional sound to a virtual environment. We have to be able to simulate directional

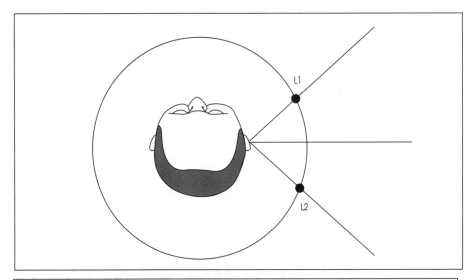

FIGURE 9.11 **Sound sources L1 and L2 have the same ITD and IPD values**

sound to the point where the user can correctly determine where the source is. It would be pretty disappointing to have an object emitting a sound in front of the user only to have him or her turn around 180° and look for it. A great deal of research has gone into finding the missing pieces of the puzzle, which are also know as spectral cues.

The major spectral cues for locating sound in the vertical plane are head scattering, torso scattering, and pinna scattering. (The pinna is the outer part of the ear.) When a sound hits any of these three body parts, it will be reflected and diffracted simultaneously toward and away from the ear canal. Only recently has research begun to reveal exacltly how the pinna affects sound waves. In Blauert (1983), an equation is given for the alterations that a sound undergoes once it hits the outer ear—an extremely complex equation that is not really worth reproducing here. A series of fast Fourier transforms are used to appropriately modify the original signal. This goes beyond the scope of this introduction to the theory of 3-D sound. I direct you to the publications in the "3-D Audio" section of the Bibliography for a more detailed explanation of pinna-related cues.

Head-Related Transfer Functions

Since the early years of this century, scientists have performed experiments to determine how we locate sound sources. Out of these experiments have come the head-related transfer functions (HRTFs). Scientists introduce sounds from loudspeakers to the listener at precise angles. As the frequency of a sound changes, microphones located in the listener's ears pick up changes in the original tone. The total change for a range of frequencies is called a *transfer function*. Figure 9.12 shows what a transfer function might look like.

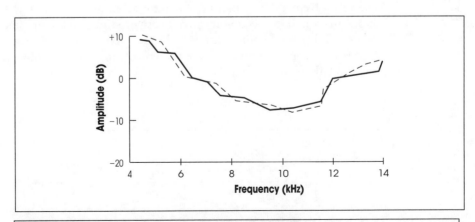

FIGURE 9.12 *Example of a head-related transfer function*

The solid black line represents one ear and the dashed line represents the other. This line graph shows how the amplitude of the sound source changes as the frequency changes. Each angular position around the head will have a different transfer function. Using these transfer functions, a system can be developed that accurately places sound around the user.

Technique

In order to create a head-related transfer function for use in three-dimensional sound reproduction, researchers gathered results from experiments, like the above, on many different subjects. By performing this type of experiment with many different people and many different placements of sound, the researchers were able to come up with HRTFs that mimicked the way a sound changed once it entered the ear canals.

By using a technique called *convolving*, the HRTFs can be used to change the characteristics of a sound before it leaves the computer, causing it to seem to originate from somewhere other than where it really did. Convolving a signal involves multiplying the discrete Fourier transform (DFT) of the original signal by the discrete Fourier transform of the transfer function. Figure 9.13 shows an example of a convolving DFT sample with a unit sample. The convolving DFT sample in our example had the effect of decreasing each of the original signal samples by one-half of its original amplitude.

Power Requirements

There is a tremendous amount of computation involved in a system that produces 3-D sound in this manner. There are products on the market that are able to place four sounds in real time (and space) using convolving and 128 parallel processors. One such product, the Convolvotron, costs $14,000 and consists of two full-length IBM PC cards.

DFT Sample × Unit Sample = Result

FIGURE 9.13 *Convolving a DFT sample with a unit sample*

Systems such as the Convolvotron work well in placing 3-D sounds. However, each person has a different transfer function for each of the possible angular positions around the head. It would be ideal to take measurements for each person who wanted to use a virtual reality system with 3-D sound in order to personalize placement of the sound. However, this is not realistic, so the designers had to find a person who placed sound almost perfectly when presented with the sound experiments we talked about in relation to head-related transfer function. The HRTF for this person would provide accurate placement for most people using the system.

 # Conclusion

We have looked at interaural time differences; interaural pressure differences; head scattering, torso scattering, and pinna cues, and head-related transfer functions. Each of these components is essential for the human auditory system to locate the origin of a sound. However, they are not the only cues; research over the last couple of years has found many others.

The procedures for reproducing three-dimensional sound are extremely mathematically oriented. In addition to this chapter, I would strongly recommend the three articles by Richard Moore listed in the Bibliography that explain the fundamentals of digital signal processing.

We must now look at how to produce three-dimensional sound on a garage-level budget. There are basically three options. The first is to use the new Gravis Ultrasound 3-D sound card. The second is to build an inexpensive sound system using digital-to-analog converters. The third is to use a mixer.

10

Building a 3-D Sound System

In the previous chapter we discussed the techniques necessary for reproducing three-dimensional sound. The majority of the commercial products available to virtual reality developers are very expensive, but the cost of these systems is offset by the quality and quantity of sound that they produce. In this chapter, we will present two separate systems—one inexpensive and one downright cheap. The first is the Gravis Ultrasound 3-D sound card. This is a SoundBlaster-compatible card that is able to place a single sound in limited three-dimensional space. The second system is based on two digitial-to-analog converters that are used in such a way as to place a sound in the horizontal plane around the user.

Gravis Ultrasound

What makes the Gravis Ultrasound 3-D card special is that by using a pre-processor program based on algorithms from Focal Point, the user can convert a normal sound file into a sound that can be placed anywhere around the listener. Focal Point is a company that markets a three-dimensional sound card for the PC and the Macintosh that costs over fourteen hundred dollars. The filtering allows sounds to be placed above, behind, in front of, in back of, to the left of, and to the right of the user. However, Focal Point does recommend that listeners use headphones.

In this chapter we will look at what's involved in creating a 3-D sound file and adding 3-D sound capabilities to our programs using the Gravis Ultrasound system. The second half of this chapter shows you how to build and program your own 3-D sound system for even less money.

Building a 3-D Sound System
with the Gravis Ultrasound 3-D Card !

Parts List for the Gravis 3-D Sound System
❑ Gravis Ultrasound 3-D soundcard
❑ Software Development Kit from Gravis

Step 1—Recording the Sound

Obviously, the first step in placing three-dimensional sounds is to obtain sounds. There are two ways this can be accomplished: capturing sounds on your own or using prerecorded sounds. Before we look at these options, we should define the requirements for our sounds.

Sound Requirements

All sounds that are going to be used for 3-D placement must satisfy the following requirements:

- ❑ *Mono*
- ❑ *8- or 16-bit quality*
- ❑ *11,025 Hz, 22,050 Hz, or 44,100 Hz*

The documentation that comes with the software development kit points out that the resulting file for the 3-D sound will be of 16-bit quality regardless of whether the sound was initially 8 or 16 bits.

Sound Capture

An easy way to obtain a sound is to record one. The Ultrasound card provides the capability to record an 8-bit sound using either its PLAYFILE or ULTRASOUND STUDIO program. I will direct you to the card's documentation for descriptions of these programs. There are also a number of other sound-capturing programs on the market that can be used, including the multimedia extensions to Microsoft Windows and those provided with the SoundBlaster card.

Prerecorded Sounds

As more and more sound cards have hit the market, the number of available prerecorded sounds has risen. You can purchase these sounds, which come on diskette, at many computer software stores. In addition, there are numerous sites on the Internet such as 128.252.135.4 that provide sound. You will probably need some type of sound conversion program to get the sound file into .SND form, the sound format for the Gravis Ultrasound.

Step 2—Preparing the Sound

We are ready to convert the sound to a 3-D sound file. This is accomplished using a utility called FP3D.EXE that is provided on the software development kit diskettes. This is a program provided by Focal Point that performs convolving algorithms on the sound. Convolving algorithms are a type of sophisticated filtering system that converts the sound into four to six different tracks, one for each location around the head. During playback, each of the tracks is played at the same time with their volumes and balances adjusted in such a way that the sound appears to be coming from the place you specified. The FP3D.EXE program accepts a number of parameters on its command line:

```
fp3d.exe  INPUT-SOUND  OUTPUT-SOUND  [switches]
```

```
Switches:

/i8     =   Input file is 8-bit, default is 16-bit
/i1     =   Input file is binary offset, default is two's complement
/f44    =   Input file is 44,100 Hz; default is 22,050 Hz
/f11    =   Input file is 11,025 Hz; default is 22,050 Hz
/n6     =   Generate 6-track file; default is 4
/012345 =   Tracks to generate:
                             0 = Front
                             1 = Right
                             2 = Rear
                             3 = Left
                             4 = Above
                             5 = Below
/m      =   Swap bytes on 16-bit file; default is NO
/h      =   Help screen
```

It should be noted that if you use the Ultrasound Studio to produce your sound files, both switches /i8 and /i1 are necessary because that program produces an 8-bit binary offset sound. We should now talk about the /n switch.

Placement and /n

When you are creating your 3-D sound file, you have to remember that it will be up to six times larger than the original file. Therefore, some thought has to go into what tracks are to be produced. If you are going to place your sound only in the space around the user, then you will only need to produce a four-track sound file—one track each for front, rear, left, and right. If you decide that you also want to be able to place the sound above or below the user, you will need a six-track file.

Step 3—Header

After the 3-D sound file has been created, we have to attach a header to it that describes the file. The header is created with the program HEADER3D.EXE and is 256 bytes in length. HEADER3D.EXE is provided on the Gravis Ultrasound software development kit diskettes. It contains the following information:

❑ *A 10-character tag*
❑ *A major and minor version number*
❑ *An 80-character description*
❑ *The type of 3-D sound file (Currently only binaural is supported. It appears, however, that they are prepared to use the 3-D sound file format for sur-round and Q sound in the future.)*
❑ *The tracks used in the file (This is a field created through bit definitions.)*
❑ *Twenty-four* int *spaces for reserved use*
❑ *The volume of the file*
❑ *Ten* int *spaces for reserved use*
❑ *Number of bytes in blocked data*
❑ *Loop offset*
❑ *Nine long spaces for reserved use*
❑ *Playback frequency*

When you run the HEADER3D program, you will be asked the following questions:

1. *Description:*
2. *Do you want this file to be in blocked mode?*

If a sound is put into *blocked mode*, it is assumed that the entire sound file will be brought into the sound card's DRAM memory. Blocked sounds are usu-ally short sound effects that are played frequently. They are also called *looped* or *one shots*, depending on whether they are played a number of times or just once.

If you answer no to question 2, then the program assumes that the sound file is *interleaved*. An interleaved file is usually a large sound that cannot be brought into the card's memory all at once. These types of sounds are used for background sound effects such as music coming from a jukebox.

3. *Is this a looped 3-D sample?*

A loop in a sound file is a section of the sound that is repeated a number of times. This can be useful when you want a number of sounds for every play. For instance, if you want a machine gun sound, you could loop a single gun shot ten times to create the sound.

4. *What is the initial frequency?*
5. *What is the maximum volume?*

Be kind to your virtual world participants.

6. *Which tracks will be used?*
7. *What is the loop offset?*

A new 3-D sound file will be created with the name TEMP3D.F3D. You will need to rename it as you see fit.

Step 4—Testing the Sound

We are now ready to test our new 3-D sound. The program PLAY3D.EXE in the development files on the software development kit diskettes will play your sound. The format of the program is

```
play3d  -d  SOUND-NAME
```

The program assumes that the front, rear, left, and right tracks were created for the sound. It places the sound behind you and slowly moves it all the way around you. It will continue to do this until you press any key. You can also use a joystick with the PLAY3D program using a different keyboard switch:

```
play3d  -j  SOUND-NAME
```

Once you execute this program, the sound will begin to circle around your head. Move the joystick in a circle a couple of times to calibrate it. Once you have done this, the sound will follow the movement of the joystick. If you press the joystick button, the sound will restart. You will need to do this if your sound does not have a loop in it.

If you are using an interleaved sound file, the program PLAY3DI.EXE will perform the same functions as above but with the interleaved file.

Step 5—Adding the Sound to Our Programs

We have seen how to use the 3-D sound tools provided in the development kit for the Ultrasound card. Let's now look at adding 3-D sounds to our own programs. The development kit comes with a number of example programs and a manual with all of the 3-D functions described above. This makes adding the sound a little easier, but it is sometimes confusing.

Earlier we mentioned that our sound file could be either blocked or interleaved. It is important to know which it is, because the two different types are programmed differently. We will begin with blocked data.

Blocked Sounds—Sound Effects

The first step in adding sound to our programs is to find out whether or not a sound card is available. We do this with the function `UltraGetCfg`, which accepts a pointer to a variable of type `ULTRA_CFG`. We will use the name `CONFIG_DATA` as our pointer. Once this function returns, we verify that a card is in the machine by probing it with the function `UltraProbe(CONFIG_DATA.base_port)`, which will either return `ULTRA_OK`, or `NO_ULTRA`.

Once a card has been found, we have to initialize it with the function `UltraOpen(CONFIG_DATA, Num_Voice)`. `Num_Voice` is the number of voices that you will be requiring, which can range from 14 to 32—the fewer the voices, the better the sound quality. The function will return one of the following error codes: ULTRA_OK, NO_ULTRA, BAD_NUM_OF_VOICES.

After the card has been initialized, we will set it up to output sounds using the function UltraEnableOutput();.

Step 6—3-D Sound Loading

The Ultrasound card is now ready to operate. We will load our 3-D sound file into the card's memory with the function UltraLoad3dEffect(SOUND, FILENAME, BUFFER, BUFFER_SIZE);. The parameter SOUND is of type SOUND_3D and is the handle for the 3-D sound we are loading. It will be passed to all of the 3-D sound routines. filename is the name of the file for the 3-D sound. BUFFER is a pointer to memory allocated using the malloc function in C. This is a section of memory that the card will use to transfer the sound from the disk to its own memory. The larger the buffer, the faster the sound will load. BUFFER_SIZE is the size of BUFFER in bytes. This function can return a number of different error codes, but the easiest to test for is ULTRA_OK. If the function returns any other code, then you know there has been an error in loading the 3-D sound file.

Step 7—Positioning

We are now ready to play our sound. Because we are using a 3-D sound, we will want to place it somewhere around the listener. We accomplish this by using one of three functions: UltraAbsPosition3d, UltraAngPosition3d, or UltraAngFltPosition3d.

UltraAbsPosition3d (SOUND, x, y, z); positions the sound SOUND at the Cartesian coordinate specified by the *x*, *y*, and *z* values. The values allowed for positioning are −511 to +511 in all three cases. These break down as follows:

> *x = −511 (left) to 511 (right)*
> *y = −511 (below) to 511 (above)*
> *z = −511 (front) to 511 (rear)*

All other values will be clipped.

We can also place a sound using the function UltraAngPosition3d (SOUND, azimuth, elevation, volume);. This function places the sound SOUND using angular measurements. The values are

> *Azimuth—0˚ is directly in front of you, 180˚ is all the way to the right, and −180˚ is all the way to the left.*

Elevation—0˚ is self-explanatory, 90˚ is straight above your head, and −90˚ is directly beneath you.
Volume—the volume at which the sound is to be played.

The last positioning function is `UltraAngFltPosition3d (SOUND, azimuth, elevation, volume);`. This function is similar to `UltraAngPosition` but uses real values for azimuth and elevation.

Volume

We will notice that the function `UltraAbsPosition3D` did not provide us with a method of specifying the volume of the sound. The reason for this is that we were given the ability to specify the z coordinate. If we place a sound very far away, the volume will be less than if we placed the sound very close. The system will automatically determine the volume based on our z value and the maximum volume value we specified when we created the 3-D header.

Step 8—Start/Stop

Once the sound is placed, we can start it playing with the command `Ultra Start3d(SOUND);`. The sound will begin to play at the position you specified earlier. To stop a sound, we use the function `UltraStop3d(SOUND, FAST);`, which will stop the sound immediately if the variable `FAST` is true. The sound will be ramped down if the variable is false.

Once we are finished with the sound or exiting the program, we free our 3-D sound resources with the function `UltraUnLoad3dEffect(SOUND);`. We shut down the Ultrasound card with the function `UltraClose();`.

That's all there is to playing a blocked 3-D sound anywhere we want. If we have some background or very long samples, we need to look at a different approach.

Interleaved Samples

Playing interleaved 3-D sound samples involves basically the same procedure as the blocked samples except we have to constantly ask the system if more of the sample needs to be read from the disk. The Ultrasound card is initialized just as it was in Step 5 for blocked data. After the initialization, we need to begin reading the interleaved sound file with the function `UltraSetup3DInterleave (SOUND, FILENAME, BUFFER);`. As is the case with the blocked sound file, `SOUND` is a handle for the sound we are reading, `FILENAME` is the name of the file on the disk for the sound, and `BUFFER` is the number of bytes that the card should allocate in its own memory for the sound. The function returns a num-

ber of different error codes. Look for ULTRA_OK and produce an error message on anything else.

Step 9—File Initialization

After the card has been set up, we need to do some work with the sound file. We begin by pulling the header of the 3-D sound file into the buffer. According to the example programs in the kit, we have to find the position of the very first track in the sound file. This is done by looking at each of the voices in the file, determining which is first, and storing a point in FIRST_VOICE. Once that is determined, we determine the middle point of the file by taking the overall size of our buffer and dividing it by two. Next, we actually load in the first part of the sound file with the function load_dram(HANDLE, SOUND, FIRST_MEM, BUFFER, SYS_BUF_SIZE, SYS_BUF);. HANDLE is the file handle for our sound file. SOUND is the handle allocated when we initialized the 3-D sound. FIRST_MEM is the location of the first track in the sound file. BUFFER is the number of bytes reserved in the card's memory. SYS_BUF_SIZE is the size of the buffer we have allocated for temporary storage between the disk and the card. SYS_BUF is the actual storage space.

We now start the sound as we did in Step 8 for the blocked sound using the function UltraStart3d(SOUND);. As the sound is being played, our program has to constantly monitor where the card is in its memory. We do this with the function UltraReadVoice(FIRST_VOICE);, which will return a long value. We compare the current position in the card's memory with the middle of the sound file. If we are past the middle, we fill in the rest of the buffer and set variables to indicate that we are now onto the second half of the file. We continue this throughout the entire sound file. When the sound is finished, we simply start back all over again if we are playing a looped file.

After the sound has been played or when the program ends, we release everything as we did in Step 8 for the blocked version. This is a very simple introduction to interleaved sound programming for the Ultrasound. I refer you to the card's documentation for further information.

 # Building and Programming Your Own 3-D Sound System ‼️

In the first half of this chapter, we talked about a system that provides relatively good three-dimensional sound by means of a sound card. The only costs of this system come from the purchase of the card itself and the disk space necessary to hold the different sound files. Remember that any sound file will be four to six times its original size once prepared for use with the sound card.

In this half of the chapter, we will build a simple 3-D sound system that can also be used to place sounds in the horizontal plane and that can also be used with a number of sound programs to play music. Constructing it will involve developing a circuit that interfaces with the bus of the IBM PC computer, learning the correct way to produce sound, and developing programs that use the sound system.

Parts List for a 3-D Sound System
❏ 1 Intel 8255 Peripheral Interface Adapter
❏ 1 74LS138
❏ 2 741C op-amp
❏ 2 DAC0800
❏ 6 5K resistors
❏ 2 0.01 capacitors
❏ 1 IBM PC Breadboard

Sound is made up of waves that strike the ear drum, causing it to vibrate. The longer the length of the wave, the lower the sound. This means that sound is an analog, not digital, process. Because computers are digital, we have to have a way to convert a series of 0s and 1s to a recognizable form. We do this by using a digital-to-analog converter (DAC).

Building the Digital-to-Analog Convertor

The simplest kind of digital-to-analog converter is shown in Figure 10.1.

This circuit works by supplying a reference voltage, Vin, which is the voltage into the circuit. We will use 5 V as an example for this discussion. If none of the switches are closed, the voltage Vout (the voltage out of the circuit) should be 0 V because there is no

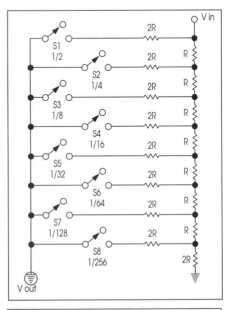

FIGURE 10.1 **Simple DAC**

path for the Vin voltage to get to the output. We can achieve maximum Vout by closing all of the switches. When this happens, all of the Vin current runs through each of the resistors. The voltage at Vout is Vin / R after solving for the equivalent resistance. The circuit in Figure 10.1 shows the fractions of Vin that will be obtained at Vout when any switch is thrown and the others are left open. We will receive a specific fraction of the full voltage available at Vin.

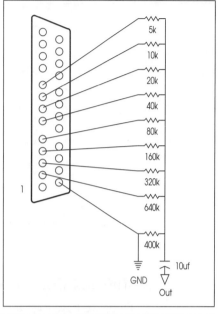

We can express this relationship in a digital format because each combination of switches forms a distinct binary value from 0 to 255. Therefore, this circuit provides a conversion from digital to analog for an 8-bit byte. Each value from 0 to 255 will be represented by a specific voltage output from Vout. Figure 10.2 shows how this digital-to-analog converter called a resistor ladder can be attached to a parallel port.

FIGURE 10.2 *Parallel port digital-to-analog converter*

The actual values for the resistors are given as well. For every value that you output from the parallel port, a voltage will be generated. Now you can see your data without a printer. This circuit works just fine for our application and is very inexpensive. We can take the next step up in quality by purchasing an inexpensive integrated circuit.

IC DACs

Many different companies make integrated circuits that do what the resistor ladder does. ICs differ from resistor ladders in that the voltage output is provided on two pins and the ladder is split into a high and low section. Each section is driven by separate Vin voltages in order to reduce noise that can build up in the resistor ladder. For these reasons, ICs are more precise and produce less error. Figure 10.3 shows the IC digital-to-analog converter that we are going to use.

The DAC0800 is an inexpensive 8-bit digital-to-analog converter that requires a very minimal number of external pieces to make it operational. Attached to its output is an op-amp that converts the current from the converter into a voltage that can drive an amplifier.

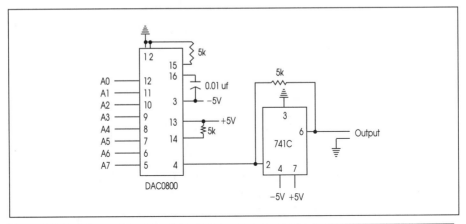

FIGURE 10.3 *Digital-to-analog converter for 3-D sound system*

Interfacing the Circuit

Once we have the DACs built, we have to interface them to the computer. One of the easiest ways to do this is through the computer bus where interface cards are usually plugged. Cards added to IBM personal computers distinguish themselves from the other cards by occupying some number of locations in the computer's I/O address space. The PC has a 64 K address space that is used by the parallel and serial ports, for example. We are going to add a card that can occupy several different spaces. Figure 10.4 shows the circuit necessary to access the PC's bus.

The 74LS138 integrated circuit in Figure 10.4 is a demultiplexer that we use to monitor the bus address lines until one of the following ranges of values is detected:

```
0x200-0x21F
0x220-0x23F
0x240-0x25F
0x260-0x27F
0x280-0x29F
0x2A0-0x2BF
0x2C0-0x2DF
0x2E0-0x2FF
```

If one of these values is on the address lines, it means that some program is wishing to communicate with a device that is using the bytes in one of the ranges. In the case of our circuit, we will attach our DACs to one of the lines associated with a group above. When a program wants to output data to the converters, it just uses the values in the appropriate range, and we receive the necessary information. If we were to put a value on the address line for any of the other value ranges above, we would not receive the information.

Unfortunately, we cannot connect our converters to the bus directly. What we need is an additional interface. The one we are going to use is based on the Intel 8255 Peripheral Interface Adapter. This chip attaches to the PC bus and the 74LS138 and gives us 24 input or output lines for our own use. Our entire interface circuit is shown in Figure 10.5.

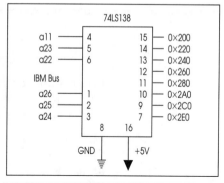

FIGURE 10.4 *Bus circuit for PC interface*

Chip Control

The Intel 8255 is a very versatile and easy-to-use interface between the PC bus and the real world. When connected to the bus, we can control the chip using four registers inside the chip that are in turn mapped to the PC I/O bus using the 74LS138. These registers are

control
port a
port b
port c

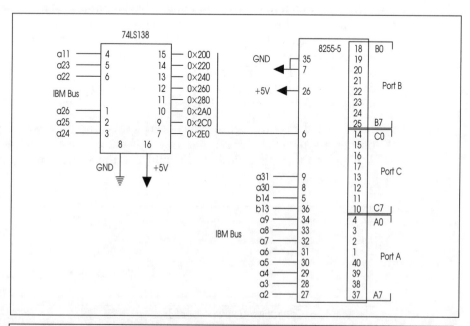

FIGURE 10.5 *Complete interface circuit for PC bus*

The `control` register is used to place the chip into different input and output patterns. The registers `porta`, `portb`, and `portc` each control 8 of our 24 total data lines. By placing a specific value in the `control` register, we can tell the chip which ports are input, which are output, and which are both.

Let's assume for the moment that we are going to use the 8255 at address location 0x200. We would do this by connecting pin 6 of the 8255 to pin 15 on the 74LS138. The registers of the 8255 would be defined as

0x200 = `Control Register`
0x201 = `Port A`
0x202 = `Port B`
0x203 = `Port C`

Control

Before we can actually use the data lines, we have to tell the chip what the data lines' functions will be. Figure 10.6 shows a chart of all possible control register values and their associated data line functions. For our purposes, we are going to want two of the ports for output because we will be outputting data to the digital-to-analog converters. We are not concerned with the third port at this time. We will set all three of the ports to output mode with the statement `outportb(0x200, 0xF0);`. Let's look at what happens when this statement is executed by the computer. The command tells the computer to put the value 0xF0, 128, in the I/O location 0x200. Now the computer assumes that there is some device attached to the memory location. So it sends the value 0x200 down the address lines to wake up the device. At the same time, it puts the byte to be sent on the data bus. If there is a device at the I/O memory location, the value on the data bus is actually stored somewhere. If there was not a device at the memory location, the data byte would be lost.

Once the control register has been set, we can now use the ports by outputting a byte to the port register. Say we wanted to make lines 0 and 1 of port A high and the others low. We would use the statement `outputb(0x201,`

```
Bit 0 - Port C (lower) 1 = Input, 0 = Output
Bit 1 - Port B 1= Input, 0 = Ouput
Bit 2 - Mode Selection 0 = Mode 0, 1 = Mode 1
Bit 3 - Port C (upper) 1 = Input, 0 = Output
Bit 4 - Port A 1 = Input, 0 = Output
Bit 5,6 - Mode Selection 00 = Mode 0, 01 = Mode 1, 1x = Mode 2
Bit 7 - 1 = Active
```

FIGURE 10.6 *Control word values for 8255*

0x03);. Each of the lines corresponds to a single bit of the register. After executing this statement, lines 0 and 1 would have a reading of 5 V on them and the others would be 0 V. The same is true if we were using any of the lines as inputs. We would read them with the statement val = inportb(0x201);. The variable val would tell us which of the lines had voltage and which did not.

That's all there is to programming the Intel 8255. We now have the ability to get data to our DACs. The final step is to attach them to the 8255. We will put them on ports A and B.

Assembly

The entire circuit must be built either on an external board or a PC board that can be plugged into one of the bus slots. Radio Shack sells a prototyping card that can be used for this purpose. The card provides the board space necessary for the chips and allows access to the IBM bus. If you build the circuit on an external board, you will still need the prototyping card or some other way to get the necessary bus signals to the card. Be aware that the further your lines are from the bus, the less reliable they will become.

Programming the Software Interface

We have a complete and operational 3-D sound system—at least, we think it is operational. We need to write software that will drive our new system. Creating sound through a DAC is not a simple task, and neither is there a great deal of information available about how to do it, so we will start from the beginning and hopefully in the end be able to produce sound.

In order to produce sound from our digital-to-analog converter, we have to understand what sound is. Sound is made up of waves that travel through air (or water). These waves are given off by vibrating objects. The *frequency* of sound refers to the number of waves that will pass by a given point each second. It is frequency that determines a sound's *pitch*. Certain pitches have been standardized into our familiar system of musical notes and octaves: C, C sharp, D, and so on. A sound created by a sine wave (Figure 10.7) will have a specific frequency and will be heard as a certain note. If we want to simulate the sounds from two different instruments, we simply change the shape of the sine wave for one of them; we end with a different sound, but of the same tone as the first. For a computer to create sound, all it has to do is specify the correct frequency, the proper duration, and certain tonal characteristics. A square wave is a rough approximation of a sine wave and can be produced very easily. However, the final sound quality of the square wave is far less pleasing than that produced by a sine wave.

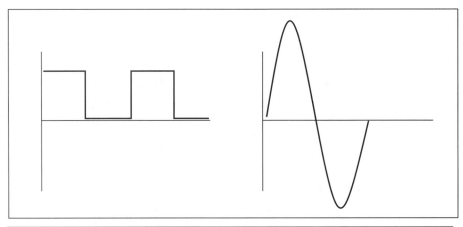

FIGURE 10.7 **Square and sine waves**

Frequencies

Figure 10.8 shows all of the notes in the chromatic scale and their associated frequencies. Let's begin by taking the case of middle C. If we wanted to produce a square wave that emitted this tone, we would have to turn our converter on for some amount of time and then off for some amount of time. Looking back at Figure 10.7 we see that that is exactly what a square wave looks like. The question we must answer is this: For what length of time do we turn the converter on and off?

Note	Frequency
Middle C	261.6 Hz
C Sharp	277.2
D	293.6
E Flat	311.1
E	329.6
F	349.2
F Sharp	370.0
G	392.0
A Flat	415.3
A	440.0
B Flat	466.2
B	493.6
Octave C	523.2

FIGURE 10.8 **Notes and their associated frequencies**

Figure 10.8 tells us that a middle C tone has a frequency of 261.6 Hz or cycles per second, which means that there must be 261.6 square waves each second in order to produce the middle C tone. To determine the times required for a single cycle, we divide a second by 261.6. This gives us 3.826 milliseconds. Therefore, each cycle in the middle C tone must be completed in 3.826 milliseconds. Because our square wave cycle has two parts, on and off, we divide 3.826 by 2 and obtain 1.913 milliseconds. We can use this value to produce a simple algorithm for producing the square wave middle c tone:

```
Loop 261 times
      Turn converter on
      Delay 1.913 milliseconds
      Turn converter off
      Delay 1.913 milliseconds
endloop
```

In terms of our digital-to-analog converter, we would code this algorithm as

```
for (i=0;i<261;i++)
{

        outportb(0x201, 0xFF);
        for (j=0;j<delay_value; j++) NULL;
        outportb(0x201, 0x00);
        for (j=0;j<delay_value;j++) NULL;
}
```

The variable `delay_value` would be calculated based on the machine on which the software is executing. Remember that different machines will be able to execute a loop more quickly than others. If we were to hardcode a delay value into the loops, we would generate a different tone depending on the speed of the machine.

Sine Wave

If you use the algorithm above, you will produce a fairly good tone except that it will sound tinny. This is a characteristic of the square wave. To produce a better tone, we have to switch to a sine wave. Figure 10.8 showed us what a sine wave looks like. Notice that instead of one giant step to the top of the wave like the square wave, the sine wave gradually increases to the top and then gradually decreases. Figure 10.9 shows the values and timings we could use to create a very crude sine wave.

We can do better than the crude sine wave in Figure 10.9 by placing more values in the wave and less delays between them. To play a middle C sine wave, we have to adjust the delays so that we are able to get all of the values in Figure 10.9 within 1.913 milliseconds. A possible algorithm is

```
Loop 261 times
        Put value to converter
        Increment index in table
        Delay;
endloop
```

This would be coded in C as

```
for(i=0;i<261;i++)
{
        outportb(0x201,
lookup[index++]);
        for(j=0;j<delay_value;j++)
NULL;
}
```

This time our `delay_value` variable has to be calculated based on the middle C tone requirements as well

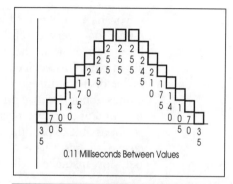

FIGURE 10.9 *Sine wave with lookup values and delays*

as the time it takes to do the retrieval of the given value. We are now able to produce any tone necessary as long as we have the frequency requirements. There are several other things that we have to take into consideration when outputting tones: duration, tone, and delay.

Duration

The duration of a sound is the amount of time it is audible. Typically, a quarter note gets one complete second of play time. This would translate to 60 tones per minute. At this rate, a middle C note would have the following cycles:

> **Whole note middle C = 1046.4 cycles**
> **Half note middle C = 523.2 cycles**
> **Quarter note middle C = 216.6 cycles**
> **Eighth note middle C = 130.8 cycles**
> **Sixteenth note middle C = 65.4 cycles**

Each of these values would be used in place of 261, which we used in the previous algorithms. Note that we are simply using multipliers in order to obtain the duration of the desired note.

The sine wave we produced above creates a pure tone, a tone that is created using the exact cycle/second values given above. When we listen to the radio, we are constantly hearing the middle C tone; however, the sine wave that makes up the tone is changed in a specific way based upon the instrument that the note is coming from. We can do the same thing to the sine waves we are working with by simply changing them. Figure 10.10 is an example of a sine wave that has been altered to give a slightly different sound than the pure sine wave.

Note Delay

If you have ever played music (or listened to it very carefully), you may have noticed that there is usually a slight pause between each note on the order of 10 milliseconds or so. This comes about because on almost every instrument there is a position where it is impossible to produce a note. In the case of drums, this is obvious. A trumpet, for instance, will have a point

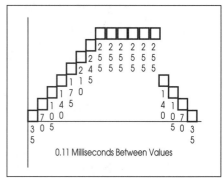

FIGURE 10.10 **Sine wave for tone other than pure**

where the musician is either taking a breath or has closed all pathways for a note to escape. Therefore, we should include a single pause after each note.

Outputting a Tone

Using the information above, we can create a number of routines that will output a tone in either of the DACs. Here's what the routine PLAY_NOTE (DAC1, DAC2, DURATION, NOTE);, which outputs a middle C note to either or both of the DACs, looks like:

```
VOID PLAY_NOTE (DAC1, DAC2, DURATION, NOTE)
{

 int  note_delay = ceil(0.5*(1/note));
 int i;

 for (i=0;i<duration;i++)
 {
   outportb (DAC1_LOCATION, 255);
   outportb (DAC2_LOCATION, 255);
   for (j=0;j<note_delay*delay_val;j++) NULL;

   outportb (DAC1_LOCATION, 0);
   outportb (DAC2_LOCATION, 0);
   for (j=0;j<note_delay*delay_val;j++) NULL;
 }
}
```

The parameters DAC1 and DAC2 accept a value of either 0 or 1; a value of 1 indicates that the note should be produced for that converter, and a value of 0 indicates no tone. The parameter DURATION is the length and NOTE is the frequency of the sound we are going to play. The routine uses all of these values to play the note based on a square wave. The procedure is basically the same for the sine wave except we have a lookup table (Figure 10.9).

Placing a Tone

Once we are able to play a tone, we want to be able to place it. The technique we are using to place our tone is interaural time delay. Therefore, we need to be able to start the tone in one DAC before starting it in the other. The routine to place a tone is called PLACE_NOTE (ANGLE, DURATION, NOTE); and looks like this:

```
void PLACE_NOTE (ANGLE, DURATION, NOTE)
{
  int note_delay = ceil(0.5*(1/note));
  int angle_delay = angle_delays[angle];
  int DAC1, DAC2;

  if ( angle < 180 )
  {
    DAC1 = LEFT_DAC_LOCATION;
    DAC2 = RIGHT_DAC_LOCATION;
  }
  else
  {
    DAC2 = LEFT_DAC_LOCATION;
    DAC1 = RIGHT_DAC_LOCATION;
  }

  if (angle != 180)
  {
    for (i=0;i<=duration;i++)
    {
      outportb (DAC1_LOCATION, 255);
      for (j=0;j<angle_delay;j++) NULL;

      outportb (DAC2_LOCATION, 255);
      for (j=0;j<note_delay-angle_delay;j++) NULL;

      outportb (DAC1_LOCATION, 0);
      for (j=0;j<note_delay - note_delay - angle_delay;j++) NULL;

      outportb (DAC2_LOCATION, 0);
      for (j=0;j<note_delay-angle_delay;j++) NULL;
    }
    delay(10);
  }
  else
  {
    for(i=0;i<duration;i++)
    {
      outportb (DAC1_LOCATION, 255);
      outportb (DAC2_LOCATION, 255);
      for (j=0;j<note_delay*delay_val;j++) NULL;

      outportb (DAC1_LOCATION, 0);
      outportb (DAC2_LOCATION, 0);
      for (j=0;j<note_delay*delay_val;j++) NULL;
    }
    delay(10);
  }
```

The parameter ANGLE is the desired angle at which you wish to have the tone placed. A value of 90 or less will place the sound in the left ear only, whereas a value of 270 or greater will place the sound in the right ear only. All values between 90 and 270 will place the tone somewhere between the two ears. DURATION is the length of the tone, and NOTE is the frequency of the tone.

The algorithm for placing our sound is very simple:

```
Find values for the NOTE we are playing
Find value for ANGLE position

If (angle < 180)
        DAC1 = left_dac
        DAC2 = right_dac
Else
        DAC1 = right_dac
        DAC2 = left_dac
Endif
If (angle != 180)
        Loop for the desired DURATION
                Turn DAC1 on
                Delay angle_delay
                Turn DAC2 on
                Delay note_delay - angle_delay
                Turn DAC1 off
                Delay note_delay - note_delay - angle_delay
                Turn DAC2 off
                Delay note_delay - angle_delay
        Endloop
        Delay(10);
Else
        Loop for the desired DURATION
                Turn DAC1 on
                Turn DAC2 on
                Delay half;
                Turn DAC1 off
                Turn DAC2 off
                Delay other half;
        Endloop
        Delay(10);
Endif
```

The first thing we have to do is obtain the appropriate delay and loop values for the duration, note, and angle we are using. After we have the values, we have to determine which of the two digital-to-analog converters will be turned on first. If the angle we have specified is less than 180, then the note will be placed on the left side of the head, and the DAC associated with the left ear must be turned on first. The opposite is true if the note is placed at an angle greater than 180. Next we determine which of two ways we should play the note. If the note is placed directly in front of us at 180 degrees, then there will be no delays to determine the two DACs, so we can use a simpler play routine. If the sound is not placed directly in front of us, we have to use the appropriate delays based on the angle of placement.

Delays

We start the play routine by turning on the first DAC and delaying the angle_delay amount. The angle_delay value is the amount of time we need to delay before starting the second DAC; once the delay has expired, we start it. Now things start to get complicated. We know that we have to keep both of the DACs on for one-half the cycle times for this particular note. Because we have already turned on the first DAC and delayed the angle_delay value, we have to delay note_delay minus the angle_delay time which we have already used. Once this new delay has expired, it is time to turn off the first DAC. We now have to delay a little more in order to let DAC2 have its complete time. Once this time has expired, we turn DAC2 off and delay just a bit more to clear everything. We have now successfully placed the tone.

Using a Preexisting Sound

There are numerous ways to extend the capabilities of our 3-D sound system, the most useful of which is the capability to play preexisting sounds, which come in all different formats from MOD to VOC to SND. Each of the formats has a different way of representing the music or sound it holds. For simplicity's sake, we will talk about the technique involved in placing these sounds without presenting any routines.

A sound format is just a file that contains some number of 8-bit values that represent some position in a sound (the ones that handle stereo sounds are 16-bit). The original sound was recorded at a fixed sampling rate such as 22,050 Hz, which means that every 0.4 microseconds the recording hardware took a reading of the sound being recorded and placed it in the file. In order to correctly reproduce the sound that the sound file contains, we have to present the values in the file to our digital-to-analog converter at the same rate. So a simple algorithm would be

```
Read sample file and place in buffer
Loop to end of buffer
        Get buffer value
        Place value in DAC1
        Delay
        Place value in DAC2
        Delay
End loop
```

This algorithm would place the preexisting sound at the position desired based on the code we used to place our own tone.

Conclusion

Although our 3-D sound system may not be able to place multiple sounds all around us, it does provide the foundation necessary to add 3-D sound to a virtual environment inexpensively. The added realism that comes from three-dimensional sound is outstanding.

11

Voice Recognition and Speech Synthesis

Probably one of the most overlooked components that should go into a virtual environment is voice recognition. A great deal of effect has gone into creating better and more unique input devices, while all along the most powerful input device is carried with us everyday. At most VR trade shows, a number of demonstrations by companies in the industry are given in which participants have to put on a head-mounted display and then manipulate a joystick or other devices. They fumble to grip the device and use their fingertips to explore the different buttons.

By using voice recognition, we can interact with the virtual environment as if it were reality. After all, this is exactly what we are trying to accomplish. At the same time, certain objects in our environment should be able to talk back to us. Just think how real the virtual environment would be if you could talk to a robot and it could talk back. This capability is available to us today.

Covox Voice Blaster

One of the easiest ways to add voice recognition to a virtual environment is to use the Voice Blaster from Covox. This is a software package that allows the SoundBlaster card to recognize words.

How It Works

The software is a Terminate And Stay Resident program that resides in memory once it is installed, constantly listening for you to say a word or a phrase. Once you begin talking, a series of events is set in action. Figure 11.1 shows the algorithm the Voice Blaster uses for voice recognition.

First, the Voice Blaster software buffers, or "records," our command somewhere in its memory. After the software system determines that you have finished speaking the command, typically by a significant pause in your speech, it will run the buffer through a set of filters to remove any background noise that may interfere in its pattern-matching process. Before we continue, we should discuss the data that the software recorded. Figure 11.2 shows what the word *hello* looks like when recorded using the SoundBlaster card.

```
Loop
 Record voice
 Filter voice
 Loop
  match voice against pre-recorded
  score each voice
 Endloop
 Pick pre-recorded with highest score
 Execute macro
Endloop
```

FIGURE 11.1 *Algorithm for voice recognition*

The technique used to convert our voice into this pattern is called *analog-to-digital conversion*. This is exactly the opposite of the digital-to-analog process we used for sound reproduction. As we speak into the microphone of the SoundBlaster, our voice waves are converted to a voltage—the higher the frequency, the higher the voltage. Using an analog-to-digital converter (ADC), the voltages are converted to a digital form typically in the range -127 to 128 for an 8-bit ADC or $-32,767$ to $-32,768$ for a 16-bit ADC. Each of the values represents the position of the sound wave at a given moment.

There are other ways that the voice can be digitized, including spectral analysis and Fourier transforms. However, the easiest to use and least computational is the analog-to-digital conversion. The Voice Blaster software converts voices into a purely digital form and saves the resulting byte stream in its mem-

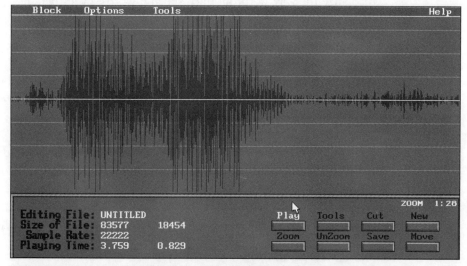

FIGURE 11.2 *Digital representation of the word hello as spoken by the author*

ory. During the filtering process, the software applies a specific function to each of the bytes and possibly changes the values to eliminate background noise and interference caused by the microphone.

After the filtering process, the software begins a pattern-matching algorithm. The stream of bytes just recorded by the software will be matched with all of the templates available, which are byte streams that the system had previously recorded when we trained it to recognize a series of spoken commands. These words were recorded and filtered as above and saved for future reference. The pattern-matching algorithm that the Voice Blaster uses performs an exhaustive template search. During each comparison, a score is calculated based on how close the given word matches the template. Once all of the templates have been scored, the software selects the one or ones with the highest score. If that score falls within some allowable tolerance, the system will execute a macro associated with that template. This macro execution only occurs if one template is selected by the software; if more than one is selected, the system assumes that it cannot match the spoken word to any of its templates and simply ignores the command.

Multiple Voices

The Voice Blaster software works well for research and experimentation but is not usable for demonstration purposes. Because we have to train the system to recognize the way we pronounce specific words, every person who was to use the system would have to train the system as well. This would take a tremendous amount of time and is really not useful. The reason for this can be seen in Figures 11.3 and 11.4. Figure 11.3 is an example of the author saying the word *forward*. Figure 11.4 is an example of the author's wife saying the same word. Notice how the wave forms are distinctly different. The Voice Blaster software would not be able to recognize my wife's version of *forward* without her having trained it to do so.

Speech recognition is still a very active area for research. IBM has recently introduced a system with a vocabulary around one hundred thousand words that can be used without training, but its cost is still quite high.

Adding Voice Support to Your Virtual Environments

Adding voice support to our virtual environments can be very simple using the Voice Blaster system; however, we have to structure the program and its inputs correctly. As briefly mentioned above, when the system has found a single template that matches the word just spoken, it executes a macro, which is a series of characters that the program will output to the computer as if we had typed

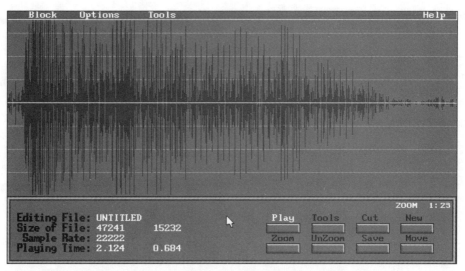

FIGURE 11.3 *Digital representation of the word forward as spoken by the author*

them from the keyboard. We could train the Voice Blaster to recognize the word *directory* and use a macro to type the word DIR followed by RETURN.

This means that if we want to add voice support to our virtual environments, we have to write the interface such that for every action we allow a voice command to initiate, there must be a corresponding key on the keyboard that

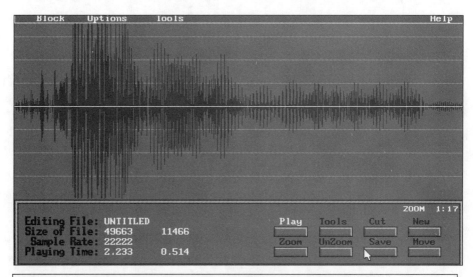

FIGURE 11.4 *Digital representation of the word forward as spoken by the author's wife*

initiates the action as well. For instance, if we want the user to be able to walk forward in our world by just saying the word *walk*, we would have to have a key that performed the same function such as the letter *w*. If the user pressed the *w* key, he or she would begin walking forward. When training the user's voice for the *walk* command, we would enter the letter *w* as our macro. When the system recognizes the user saying *walk*, it would type the letter *w*, and the virtual environment would react accordingly.

If we analyze this situation, we see that although we have a limited number of keys available on the keyboard, we can take advantage of the CONTROL and ALT keys as well as SHIFT to extend the key combinations to a point where we would probably have a tough time remembering what key does what. The Voice Blaster system has a theoretical limit of recognizing 1,024 words, which is probably more than we will ever use. So given these two facts, we have the power to add significant levels of voice recognition to our virtual environments using an inexpensive software and hardware system.

Speech Synthesis

The last feature of the Voice Blaster system I would like to talk about is its ability to respond verbally to our commands. Using a program supplied with the system, we can have a macro that outputs a sound file based on a trained command. This would provide a great deal of surprise to a user who thinks the objects in the environment cannot talk back.

For example, in Chapter 17, we develop a shoot-'em-up game that pits users against an opponent. We could add some sort of dummy robot as a second opponent. It would wander around helplessly until it began getting in the way of the human players, who would be trying to shoot their opponent. If the voice recognition system was set up correctly, it could recognize the words *stupid* and *robot* in the sentence, "You stupid robot." (We would be anticipating that the human players might say something like that when the robot got in their way.) When the system recognized the two key words, it could play a sound file that sounded like the robot saying something like "Humans are more stupid than robots." You could also have the system choose a random phrase based on any key words the human says. This type of sound file selection would be a function of the system software, because the Voice Blaster software does not have this type of capability.

12

Building an Arm-Based Head Tracker

One of the strongest senses the human body has is its ability to know where it is in space. If we turn our heads to the left or right, we know that our surroundings will change. The same is true if we look up or down.

In the virtual environments and equipment we have discussed so far, we have not been able to provide this sense. To get an idea of how necessary this sense is, put on your HMD and play Castle Wolfenstein on an IBM 486-66 Mhz computer. There is a good chance that you will feel some ill effects after you are finished. This is called cyber sickness. You were in an environment that changed relative to the joystick, not your head or body. When you moved the joystick to the left, the scene changed. Your brain expects your head to be rotating to the left, but it isn't. This is confusing for the little neurons in the brain; they get sick, and then we get sick. This chapter and the next will present two projects that will give you the ability to track the position of the user's head. This is very useful when using the head-mounted display because you are able to change the environment based on a physical movement of your body.

In Chapters 3 and 4, we allowed the computer to track the movement of the hand in order to give us a more realistic interaction with the virtual world. This provided a much greater sense of being immersed *in* the world. Tracking the head will add to the realism even more.

 ## Head-Tracking Techniques

In this section we look at the various types of systems that are used for head tracking. In the cases where an inexpensive alternative can be found, we will present it for possible use. It can be argued that head tracking came about because of the U.S. military, which wanted pilots to be able to control certain parts of the plane with their heads. For example, if a pilot looked at a specific part of the cockpit, a computer would activate a switch. The only problem was determining where the pilot was looking. Head trackers solved this problem.

One of the first companies to create a head tracker was Polhemus Navigation Systems. Since that time, several companies have come up with different ways to track head movement. There are four basic categories of head trackers: mechanical, optical, ultrasonic, and magnetic.

Mechanical Head Trackers

The mechanical head trackers use means other than electronics to track the movement of a head. There are three varieties: arm-based, gyro, and string test systems.

Arm-Based Systems

An arm-based head tracker consists of a series of rods connected together with joints. Each of the joints has a potentiometer to measure the degree of flex. Figure 12.1 shows an illustration of an arm-based head tracker. As the user looks around the virtual environment, the potentiometers send analog signals to an analog-to-digital converter. The digitized information is fed to a computer to calculate where the user is looking. The arm-based head tracker restricts the user because it attaches directly to the head-mounted display. However, if built correctly, the user should experience minimum discomfort. In a later section we will discuss the construction of an arm-based head tracker.

Gyro Systems

In 1991 there was a discussion on the `Usenet` news group, sci. virtual-worlds, about using small gyros to determine the position of the head. Gyros are used in R/C (radio-controlled) airplanes to keep them stable by measuring the amount of rotation. Thus, if we mounted one on our head, we could measure the amount of pitch, roll, and yaw. One problem with these gyros is *continued rotation*. If you panned your head from left to right quickly and then tried to pan from right to left, the gyros would still have significant rotation remaining from the left to right yaw. The measured results would not be accurate.

String Test Systems

The string test is a restrictive system for measuring either head position or head movement. Three strings are attached to the user's head. One string is connected to the back, one to the immediate left, and another to the immediate right. Figure 12.2 illustrates this system. The opposite ends of the strings are connected to an auto-retrieving reel that is always trying to retract the string. As the user moves his or her head, each of the different reels either retracts or releases string. A computer measures the initial state of the system and subsequent movements, thereby determining the position of the user without delay. This type of head tracker can be duplicated fairly easily. I refer you to Issue 13 of

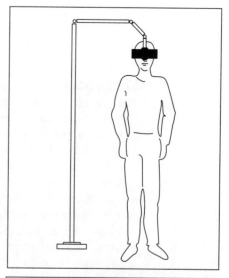

FIGURE 12.1 *Illustration of an arm-based head tracker*

PCVR Magazine for an article called "A simple 3D tracker" that discusses such a system.

Optical Head Trackers

Optical head trackers use a source of light to measure the degree of head movement. There are two kinds of optical head trackers: inward camera systems and outward camera systems.

Inward Camera

An obvious way to determine the gaze of a user is to look at him or her. A computer can look at an object using a camera and a digitizer, which are positioned toward the user. As the user moves his or her head, the computer digitizes the pictures from the camera and locates differences between the current picture and the previous picture. The computer can determine the new gaze of the user by analysis.

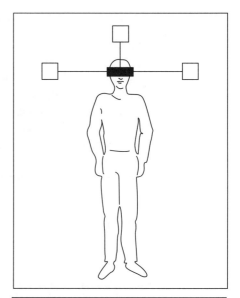

FIGURE 12.2 *Use of string for determining position*

In order for the computer to determine whether or not a change has occurred between two digitized images, there must be some reference point on the user's head. This reference point can be determined through two methods: visible source or edge detection.

Visible Source

The visible source option involves putting some sort of pattern on the head of the user that the computer can easily and quickly recognize and analyze. This form of head tracking is very closely related to computer vision and image processing. Several different schemes have been proposed. The first involves using a series of infrared LEDs arranged in a triangle on the user's head, which is illustrated in Figure 12.3.

When the user pans his or her head, the horizontal position of the

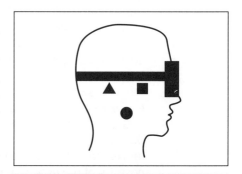

FIGURE 12.3 *LEDs on side of user's head*

three LEDs changes. When the user tilts his or her head, the LEDs roll forward or backward. When the user rolls his or her head, the vertical position of the LEDs changes. All of these shifts in position can be accurately detected by the computer once an image is digitized.

It may be obvious by now that the computer is doing a large amount of computation. The steps involved include

Digitizing the pictures
Locating the LEDs
Comparing their location to the previous picture
Performing calculations to determine x,y,z position
Performing calculations to determine gaze direction
Discarding the old picture and saving the current one

If the computer is doing all of these operations as well as rendering the scene, we will need a personal computer that is significantly more powerful than the Pentium. There are two ways to solve this problem. The first is to dedicate a second personal computer to perform all of the steps listed above and send the final data to the rendering system. The second solution is to design a hardware card to take care of these necessary functions.

Two other methods can be used that don't involve LEDs. Research has been performed using a series of patterns of triangles, squares, and circles on the head that basically take the place of the LEDs. The principle behind this method is this is more easily detected by the computer software. A second approach proposed putting lasers on the user's head and capturing the room on camera. The lasers would supply three points of light on the walls that the computer would use to determine position. It has been noted that the resolution of the camera and digitizing software is probably not yet good enough to pick up the laser-generated points of light.

Edge Detection

Edge detection is very much like the LED approach above. Instead of having LEDs or patterns on the head, however, the digitizing software picks out the edges of the user's face. This system was developed by three researchers at NTT Human Laboratories in Japan. It uses a fast algorithm that picks out the contrast between the user's hairline and face to recognize the face. The hardware consists of a video digitizer connected to a SUN Microsystems SUN4 workstation. The system operates at 10 frames per second. The researchers' application sent the face orientation to a Silicon Graphics IRIS workstation where a graphics face mimicked the movement of the human user. The system software is written in C and provides 6 DOF under limited conditions. The researchers pointed out in a paper they wrote that the person must have an acceptable amount of hair in order for the system to detect the hair-face demarcation properly.

Building an Inward Camera Tracker

Building an inward camera head tracker is easier than you might think. You need the following equipment:

> *Personal computer*
> *Digitizing card*
> *Camera*
> *Software*

It is assumed that you already have the personal computer. Digitizing cards are available from many different sources. The camera can be expensive. If you have a camcorder, you can use it. The algorithms for detecting the LEDs can be found in many books on computer vision and image processing.

Outward Camera

The opposite of the inward camera is the outward camera. This type of head tracker puts a number of cameras on the head of the user to track the location of LEDs on the ceiling. The best-known system of this type was developed at the University of North Carolina at Chapel Hill. Its structure is fairly simple. Three infrared sensors or cameras are placed on top of a head-mounted display. Each of the cameras is fitted with a wide-angle lens. On the ceiling are 30 suspended ceiling panels, each of which has a total of 32 infrared LEDs.

The system operates by scanning. A computer turns on one of the LEDs and records whether or not any of the sensors on the head of the user detected it. This sequence is continued for each of the 960 LEDs. Once this information is calculated, it is sent to other computer systems for processing. The collinearity system determines any change in detection from this set of information and the set calculated previously. Using the changes, the head position is sent to the graphics engine. The developers programmed several heuristics in the system to provide for faster recognition of head position changes.

The system suffers from several problems regarding LED detection. If the user moves to the edge of the paneled area's ceiling panels, the system will not be able to determine the position of the user's head. Because the user cannot see the edges, the user will become lost. The second problem is the degree of head tilt allowed by the system: a mere 45°.

Ultrasonic Head Trackers

A very inexpensive way to determine head movement is to use ultrasonics. This type of position tracking is the same used in the Mattel Power Glove. We will look at using ultrasonics in the next chapter.

Magnetic Head Trackers

The most common head trackers use a magnetic field to determine the location of the user's head. The Polhemus and Ascension head trackers are the industry standards. These systems consist of three components: a transmitting antenna, a receiving antenna, and associated electronics. Each of the antennae consists of three mutually orthogonal coils. To determine the position of the receiver, which is typically attached to the user, each of the transmitting antenna's coils is independently excited, and the receiver coils detect the magnetic field created by the transmitter. The controlling electronics use the resulting vectors to determine the $x,y,z,$ yaw, pitch, and roll of the receiver and then give this information to the computer.

Building an Arm-Based Head Tracker !!!

We want to build an arm-based head tracker that will be inexpensive yet hold up to the rigors of experimentation as well as demonstration to our family and friends. The electronics will measure the position of the angle created in the joints of the boom when we move our head in different directions. The computer will take this information from the electronics and accordingly change the scene we are viewing. Before we get into the actual construction of the tracker, we need to look at the computer interface.

Parts List for an Arm-Based Head Tracker
❑   3 5 Megaohm potentiometers
❑   4 ¼ wooden dowels
❑   1 1″ × 1″ × 2′ pine board
❑   1 camera tripod or
1 2″ × 4″ × 8′ pine board
❑   1 IBM bus interface from Chapter 10

Computer Interface

In Chapter 10 we constructed an interface to the computer using the Intel 8255 Peripheral Interface Adapter. For the sound system, we used two of the three ports available on the 8255. Unfortunately, our head tracker requires one complete port and three lines from another port, which leaves us in a bind. The solution is to add a second 8255 IC to the interface. Figure 12.4 shows the interfacing of the second 8255.

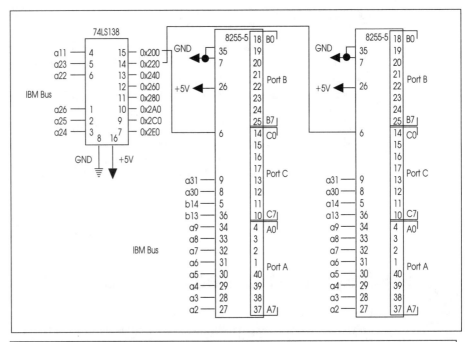

FIGURE 12.4 ***Second 8255 for head-tracking electronics***

If you did not build the 3-D sound system and you are going to build the head tracker, you can disregard the 8255 chip in the middle of Figure 12.4. You only need to add a second 8255 if you build the 3-D sound system.

You'll recall from the description of the interface in Chapter 10 that we used the 74LS138 to determine where the single 8255 was placed in memory. We simply picked the memory location we wanted and connected the pins of the 74LS138 to the chip select pin of the 8255. Thus, when a read/write access was made to any of the memory locations relating to the pin on the 74LS138, it would activate the 8255. In order to add the second 8255, all we have to do is piggyback all of the interface lines except for the chip select line, which will be connected to a different set of memory locations specified by the 74LS138. So, in theory, we could add up to eight 8255 interface chips to the original circuit. It should be noted that we would want to put a buffer chip in the address and data lines because we would be driving a large number of chips and the load might be too much for the lines.

The second 8255 is programmed in the same way as the first one, except that we use a different memory range. To set the 8255 appropriately, we have to look at what will be attached to it.

Converting Body Movement into Numbers

Our arm-based head tracker will use three potentiometers to determine the position of the user's head. The purpose of the potentiometers is to change the amount of voltage that flows through it based on how much it is turned. If the potentiometer is turned full on, it allows its input to be sent directly to its output. If the potentiometer is turned full off, it doesn't allow any of the input to reach its output. In our case, we are going to supply the potentiometers with a 5 V power source and determine how much voltage is getting to the output of the port using an analog-to-digital converter, which is shown in Figure 12.5.

Circuit

The ADC0804 analog-to-digital converter is an 8-bit chip. It will express the amount of voltage in the range − source (OV) to + source (5V) as a number from 0 to 255; therefore, each increment of one represents 0.01953 V. Input to the converter is through pin 6. We have attached the CD4051B chip, which is an 8-to-1 multiplexer, to this line input. Based on the value supplied to pins PB0–PB2, one of the eight inputs from Input Channels 0–7 will be directed to the output pin 3. In other words, if you want to look at the input coming in Channel 0, we set PB0–PB2 to 0. If you want to look at the input coming in

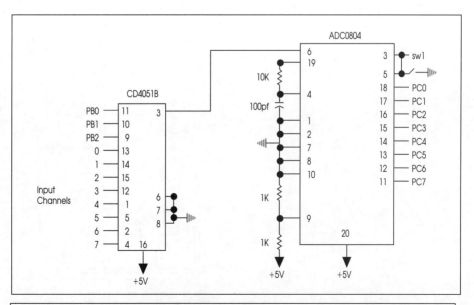

FIGURE 12.5 *Analog-to-digital converter circuit*

Channel 7, we set PB0–PB2 to 1. If you want to look at the input coming in Channel 4, we set PB0 and PB1 to 0 and PB2 to 1. This single converter chip is able to handle all three potentiometers.

The digital output from the ADC chip comes from PC0–PC7 on the 0804. PC0 is the least significant bit of the value. These pins will be attached to the ports of the 8255.

8255 interface

Figure 12.6 shows how the ADC circuit is attached to the second 8255 chip in our interface circuit. Because the output of the ADC0804 is input to the 8255, we have to designate port C of the 8255 as input. The three lines we are connecting to Port B determine from which channel we will obtain a reading, so we

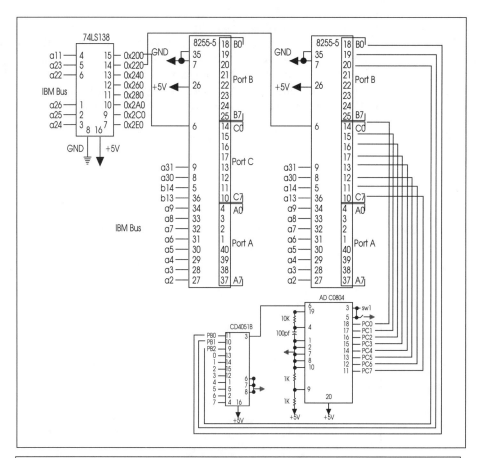

FIGURE 12.6 *Analog-to-digital converter and 8255 interface*

should set port B as output. This will allow us to assign a value to the CD4051B. The actual programming of the chips will be discussed later.

Building the Arm

Now that we have the electronics for the tracker, we need to look at construction. Figure 12.7 shows what the completed tracker will look like. It will allow us to detect all three of the principal movements: yaw, pitch, and roll.

The Pedestal

We will assume that people using the tracker will be sitting down, so its base will be some sort of pedestal. There are many different design choices. The first we'll consider is a solid base for the tracker like that shown in Figure 12.8.

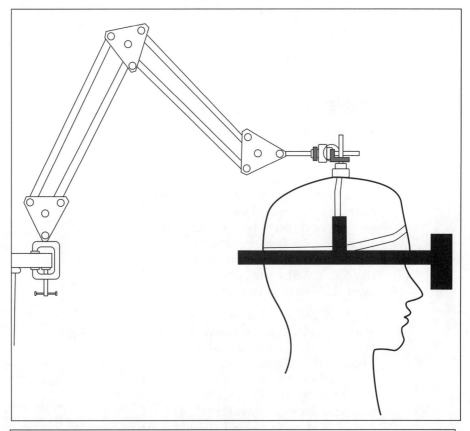

FIGURE 12.7 *Actual arm-based head tracker*

This base is simply a wooden box upon which the arm part of the tracker will be attached. The nice thing about this type of base is that it can be placed on any surface near where the person is using the head-mounted display. During demonstrations you will be able to have all of your equipment on a table right next to the user's chair.

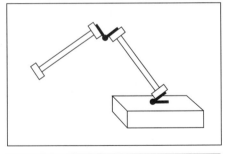

FIGURE 12.8 **Boxlike base for head tracker**

A pedestal could be made from an old camera tripod as well. Most tripods have holes in the top of their platforms through which the arm mechanism could be attached. Figure 12.9 illustrates this pedestal, which can be built for under $5.

The pedestal is just several two-by-fours attached to a plywood base. Each two-by-four has a series of holes drilled in it even with the other two-by-four. A third two-by-four has additional holes drilled in it. The arm mechanism is attached to the top of the third two-by-four and raised or lowered based on the user's preference. A rod runs through all three boards to hold the tracker in place.

Tracker Arms

The strength of the tracker comes from its two arms, which are shown in Figure 12.10. The length of the arms is not that important, but you should make them long enough to allow the pedestal to be some distance from the user. I found that if both of the arms are around 2.5 feet, the set-up is very stable and can be used in all circumstances. Lengths of 3 feet or more cause the system to be unstable.

The arms are made from two wooden rods, approximately ½" in diameter, that are attached to two wooden end pieces, which can be fashioned from a 1" × 2" board. For my system, I cut off four pieces from the end, each approximately ½" thick. Into each of these pieces I drilled two holes approximately ¼" deep to accept

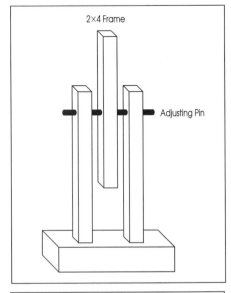

FIGURE 12.9 **Two-by-four base**

the wooden dowels (see Figure 12.11). Put some wood glue in the holes and insert the wooden dowels. Let the two arms sit overnight before using them.

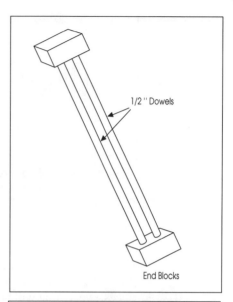

FIGURE 12.10 ***Head tracker arms***

The Head-Tracking Device

The next thing we have to do is create the actual component that performs the head tracking. Figure 12.12 illustrates the proper placement of the three potentiometers that we'll need to detect the three types of movement we're interested in.

The tricky part is mounting all of the potentiometers so that they look something like the set-up in Figure 12.13. (Remember that yaw corresponds to the x axis, pitch corresponds to the y axis, and roll corresponds to the z axis.) We will begin by looking at the yaw potentiometer. In order for a potentiometer to measure the amount of yaw, it must be positioned parallel to the y axis and perpendicular to the x axis. Figure 12.14 shows the potentiometer's placement.

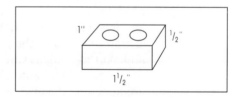

FIGURE 12.11 ***Wooden arm bend blocks with drill holes***

Attaching the Yaw Potentiometer

We need to have a way of attaching the potentiometer to the top of the head-mounted display. Because everybody will have different enclosures on their HMD, I present two different mounts in Figure 12.15. Either of the mounts will work. The main thing to be concerned about is the shaft of the potentiometer. The enclosure should attach to the potentiometer by means

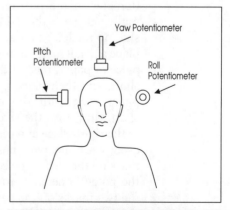

FIGURE 12.12 ***Placement of potentiometers for head tracking***

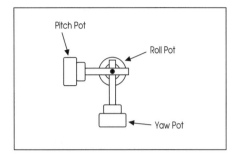

FIGURE 12.13 **Desired final placement of potentiometers**

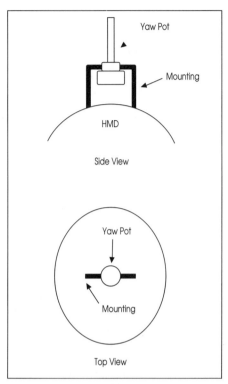

FIGURE 12.14 **Yaw potentiometer placement**

of its nut and threads. As long as the enclosure is mounted using these pieces, everything will be fine. So now we have a way to measure the yaw of the head. If this is all you will ever need from a head tracker, then you are finished. Just attach the end of the arm to the shaft of the potentiometer and skip to the software control section later in this chapter. Whether you are attaching the arm of the boom or the pitch potentiometer, you will need to find the center of the yaw potentiometer. To do this, place the potentiometer in the position it will normally have on the HMD. Turn the shaft to the left as far as it will go and place a small mark on top of it. Take a piece of paper, push it down over the shaft, and then place a mark on the paper even with the mark on the shaft. Now, turn the shaft all the way to the right. Place a mark on the paper even with the new position of the mark on the shaft. The center point of the potentiometer is exactly between the two marks on the paper. Turn the shaft until the mark on it is even with the middle point on the paper. The yaw potentiometer is now centered.

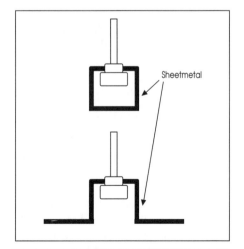

FIGURE 12.15 **Mounting for yaw potentiometer**

Attaching the Pitch Potentiometer

The next step is to attach the pitch potentiometer. It must be parallel to the x axis and perpendicular to the y axis. In order for everything to operate correctly, we need to be able to attach the base of the pitch potentiometer to the shaft of the yaw potentiometer. For stability's sake, however, we want to have the shaft of the yaw potentiometer positioned in the middle of the pitch potentiometer.

With this in mind, we can construct a simple attachment piece, shown in Figure 12.16. It is made from a small piece of wood with a hole drilled through it just a tad smaller than the diameter of the yaw potentiometer's shaft. This piece of wood fits on the shaft and slides down to the enclosure that attaches the yaw potentiometer to the HMD. The wood will be our foundation for the pitch mounting. We attach a small piece of either metal or wood to the pitch potentiometer using its threads and nut. This piece of metal or wood is attached to the piece of wood on the yaw potentiometer. When you are finished, you should have something that looks like Figure 12.17.

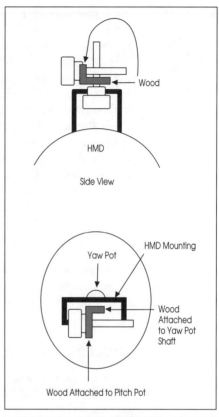

FIGURE 12.16 **Pitch potentiometer attached to yaw potentiometer**

Again, if you are only building a tracker to handle pan and pitch, then you are finished. The tracker arm would be attached to the shaft of the pitch potentiometer and then to the pedestal.

Attaching the Roll Potentiometer

The final potentiometer to be attached to the tracker is used to measure roll. This one is positioned so that it points out the back of the head, as in Figure 12.18. We are gong to attach the roll

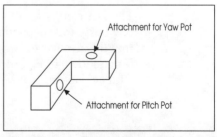

FIGURE 12.17 **Pitch attachment piece**

potentiometer in the center of the
pitch potentiometer just as we did with
the pitch-and-yaw combination above.
This is done for stability's sake. The
mounting system for the roll potentiometer is the same as for the
pitch/yaw system, except the first piece
of wood is attached to the pitch shaft
and the metal/wood piece is for the roll
potentiometer. Now when attaching
the wood foundation piece to the pitch
potentiometer we have to make sure
that the wood is positioned when the

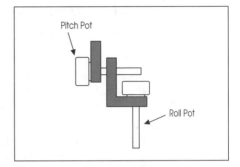

FIGURE 12.18 **Position of roll
potentiometer**

pitch potentiometer is at its center position. Recall from the discussion about
positioning the yaw potentiometer how marks on paper were used to place it
correctly. This same technique should be used on the pitch potentiometer
before pushing the wood piece on the shaft. You have now successfully completed the construction of the arm-based head tracker. The last two steps are to
attach the arm to the potentiometers and to the pedestal.

Attaching the Arm

The arm of our tracker is attached to the shaft of the roll potentiometer. Figure
12.19 shows what we are dealing with here. The arm is designed to ride above
the user in order to give it a certain degree of movement when the user moves
his or her head. This causes the end of the arm to be at an angle to the actual
head tracker. The easiest way to attach the arm is to put a piece of wood on the
shaft of the roll potentiometer as we did in the previous attachments and attach
a piece of angle metal to the wood. Move the arm up to the metal and bend the
metal until it is at the angle of the arm wood. Attach the metal to the arm, and
we are finished. Figure 12.20 shows what you should now have.

Securing the Arm Assembly to the Pedestal

The last step is to attach the arm to the pedestal. How this will be done will
obviously vary depending on the pedestal used, but the point to remember is
that the arm has to be attached to the pedestal using a flexible joint, such as the
hinge shown in Figure 12.21. It is best to use a very simple metal hinge and not
a fancy one because we need stability here at the base of the system.

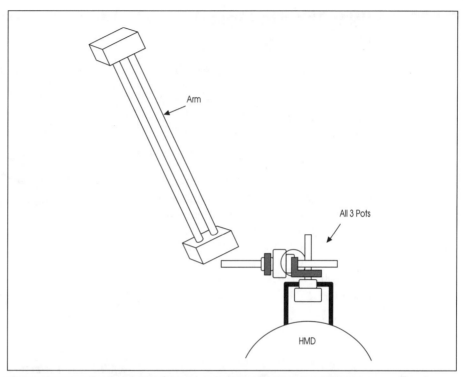

FIGURE 12.19 **Position of head tracker arm relative to potentiometer**

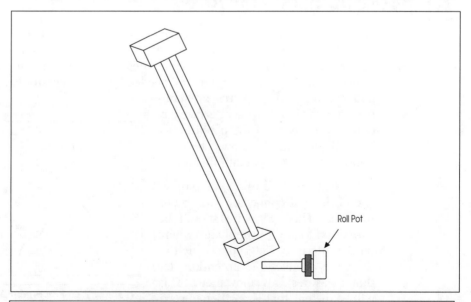

FIGURE 12.20 **Arm attachment for roll potentiometer**

Using the Arm-Based Head Tracker

Once you have the tracker assembled, you will want to make sure that you have a complete range of motion available. To do this, attach the tracker to your head or head-mounted display. Move your head in each of the yaw, pitch, and roll positions. If the tracker keeps your head from moving completely in any of the directions, the potentiometer that controls the movement is probably not centered correctly. Detach the tracker from the potentiometer and rotate it enough so that you will get the full range of motion.

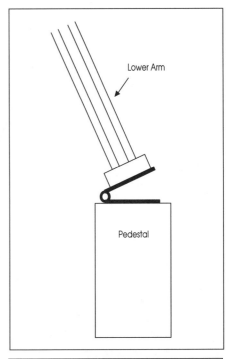

FIGURE 12.21 *Lower arm attachment to pedestal*

Programmer's Guide to Head-Tracking Software

Now it's time to use our system. Each of the potentiometers has to be attached to the CD4051 chip in our computer interface. Because we have a total of three potentiometers, we will need a four-connector wire running up the arm of the tracker. One of the wires is the +5V needed by our analog-to-digital converters and the other three wires are connected to the input of the interface circuit and one each of the potentiometers. Figure 12.22 shows how to hook-up one of the potentiometers.

Next, we need to hook the other end of the four-connector wire to our interface. The +5V wire should be connected to a +5V supply anywhere on the interface. Determine which of the wires handles the potentiometer that measures yaw movement. This will be the one that is positioned vertically on our arm assembly. Attach the

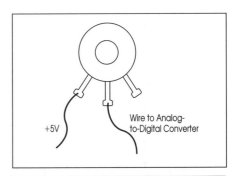

FIGURE 12.22 *Placement of wires on potentiometer*

wire to Channel 0 of the CD4051. Now determine which wire handles the potentiometer that measures tilt movement. Attach the wire to Channel 1 of the CD4051. Lastly, determine which wire handles the potentiometer that measures roll movement. Attach the wire to Channel 2 of the CD4051.

Now that we have the arm wired up, we can begin reading values from it. Plug the interface card into the PC and turn on the power. In order to access the tracker, we need to write a simple piece of software. The first thing that has to be done is to set the 8255 chip as we discussed earlier in Chapter 10. This can be done with the instruction `outportb(0X220, 137);`.

A value of 137 indicates to the 8255 chip that Port B should be output and Port C should be input. To read the potentiometers, we use the following algorithm:

```
Loop
        select Channel 0
        read Channel 0
        select Channel 1
        read Channel 1
        select Channel 2
        read Channel 2
Endloop
```

In C this would be:

```
while ( true )
{
        outportb (0x222, 0x00);
        yaw_value = inportb(0x223);
        outportb (0x222,0x01);
        pitch_value = inportb(0x223);
        outportb (0x222,0x02);
        roll_value = inportb(0x223);

        printf ( "%d %d %d \n", yaw_value, pitch_value, roll_value);
}
```

Upon each iteration of this loop, the variables `yaw_value`, `pitch_value`, and `roll_value` will contain some numeric value indicating the position of the potentiometers. What we have to do now is figure out exactly what the values mean.

Head Movements

To determine what these values mean, we need to consider all of the possible head movements. If you pan your head without moving your shoulders or your body, you will find that you are able to yaw in an arc of approximately 200°. You should be able to pitch and roll your head in arcs of roughly 180°. This means that the head tracker needs to be able to detect movement in these arcs only. In order for the system to work correctly, we have to determine how many degrees

our head has moved for each value the potentiometers return. We can do this very simply using the head tracker itself. Remember that when we put the potentiometer assembly together, we made sure that they were inserted into their cradles so as to be in the middle of their turn range. We did this so that we would have full use of each. Now when you put the head tracker on your head and look straight ahead, each of the potentiometers should be in its middle position. If you run the program above, the system will be printing values indicating the potentiometers' positions. Now have someone watch the yaw values on the screen as you turn as far left as possible. When you are at the farthest point, have that person record the value on the screen. Now turn your head as far right as possible and have that person record this value. Do this test for pitch and roll as well.

Now we have some numbers to play with. Working with the yaw numbers, take the smallest of the two values and subtract it from the largest. This is the total number of possible positions that the tracker can handle with you as a user. Now divide 200° by this value you have obtained. The result is the total number of degrees that *one* unit from the potentiometer represents. Let's look at an example. Say that the smallest value read from the pan potentiometer was 12 and the largest was 212. If we do the subtraction, we get a total range of 200 units. Dividing 200° by 200 units gives us 1° per unit. Now when you put the tracker on your head, the program will give you a reading somewhere around 106 or so. If you look to the left until the value is 100, we know that you have looked 6° to the left. If you look to the right until the value is 112, we know that you have looked 6° to the right.

This is true for the pitch and yaw values as well. Each of these values are given to our rendering software to change our point of view. Therefore, our final algorithm for the head tracker is

```
int YAW_DEGREES  1
int PITCH_DEGREES 0.85
int ROLL_DEGREES 0.9
Initialize head tracker electronics
Loop
        select Channel 0
        read Channel 0 to  yaw_value
        select Channel 1
        read Channel 1 to pitch_value
        select Channel 2
        read Channel 2 to roll_value

        current_view_YAW += (old_yaw_value - yaw_value) * YAW_DEGREES;
        current_view_PITCH += (old_pitch_value - pitch_value) *
        PITCH_DEGREES;
        current_view_ROLL += (old_roll_value - roll_value) *
ROLL_DEGREES;

        old_yaw_value = yaw_value;
        old_pitch_value = pitch_value;
```

```
        old_roll_value = roll_value;
end loop
```

The constants YAW_DEGREES, PITCH_DEGREES, and ROLL_DEGREES will be the values you calculate using your system. We begin by reading the current state of the potentiometers. The new point of view is calculated by determining the change from the previous readings we took, multiplying by the number of degrees each unit represents, and adding the resulting value to the current view's yaw value. This is repeated for pitch and roll. Once the new point of view is established, we throw out the old reading value and replace it with the current values.

Conclusion

The tracker we have constructed in this chapter does a good job of telling us where the user is looking. It can handle yaw, pitch, and roll. At times, this could be overkill because the majority of our head movements involve only yaw. Very rarely do we actually roll our heads. In the next chapter, we will look at making a simple modification to the Power Glove to give us an inexpensive tracker for determining the yaw movement of the head.

13

Using the Power Glove as a Head Tracker

The Power Glove provides us with more than just a simple input device for a video game. We can use the individual components of the glove to help us solve other problems. The design of the Power Glove's ultrasonic system allows it to track the x,y,z position of the glove as well as the roll. At first glance this doesn't really help us much, but if we look more closely at a commercial ultrasonic head tracker, we may get some ideas.

 ## Logitech Red Baron

In early 1993, Logitech introduced the Red Baron 3-D mouse/head tracker. This system, which is based on ultrasonics, consists of two major components: the receiver, a small triangle that contains three microphones, and another, larger triangle that contains three transmitters. The receiver is mounted on top of the head-mounted display, pointing toward the ceiling. The transmitter triangle is suspended from the ceiling in whatever manner is convenient and points toward the floor. The transmitter sends ultrasonic signals downward, and the receiver picks them up. A microprocessor takes this information and converts it into position and orientation information transmitted via RS-232 to a host computer. This system is very accurate and works well; however, it costs $1,495. We can build something like the Red Baron using the Power Glove.

 ## Using the Power Glove to Build a Head Tracker ‼

There's no reason you should pay $1,495 for a head tracker when you can use a $45 Power Glove instead.

Parts List for the Power Glove Head Tracker
❑ 1 Power Glove
❑ 1 Power Glove–to–parallel port interface from Chapter 2
❑ 1 head-mounted display

If you look at the Power Glove, you will see that there are basically two components to the ultrasonics. The first part is in the plastic marked by the word Power Glove; this is where the ultrasonic transmitters are located. The second part is the keypad, which contains the electronics for the system. Our goal is to mount the transmitter portion of the system on our head-mounted display as shown in Figure 13.1. The transmitters will need to be positioned so that they are parallel to our eyes. This will allow the system to detect when our heads are panning. This is important because with games like Wolfenstein 3D, you cannot tilt or roll your head, but you can yaw.

The first step in using the Power Glove as a head tracker is to eliminate the finger sensors and the plastic glove. Refer back to Chapter 3 and the instructions for building the 3-D Mouse. When you have removed the ultrasonic sensors and the electronic keypad from the glove, you are ready to begin using the electronics for the head tracker. You can discard the old glove and finger sensors.

Our next step is to attach the electronics to our HMD. (I will assume that you are using a baseball helmet for the HMD.) Figure 13.2 shows an attachment piece for the ultrasonic enclosure. Once the ultrasonic enclosure is attached to the helmet, the last step is to attach the keypad to the back. Figure 13.3 offers a possible solution.

You are now ready to use the Power Glove as a head tracker.

Tilt/Roll

But wait! If we have the Power Glove transmitters on top of the head-mounted display and we tilt our heads, won't the distance between the transmitters and receivers change? Figure 13.4 illustrates this situation.

Notice what happens when we tilt our heads: The transmitters follow a downward arc. This means that according to the set-up we have, the glove would appear to the system to be moving toward the floor along the *y* axis. If we were to tilt our heads backward, the glove would appear to be moving to-

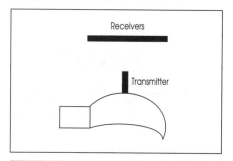

FIGURE 13.1 **Power Glove ultrasonics on HMD**

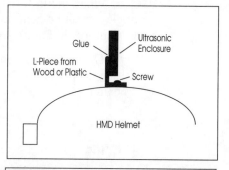

FIGURE 13.2 **Ultrasonic attachment**

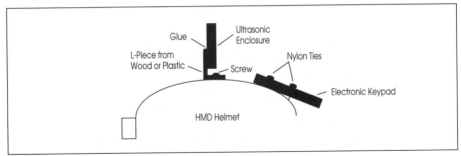

FIGURE 13.3 ***Electronic keypad attachment***

ward the ceiling along the y axis. Therefore, we can use the change in the y coordinate to indicate that we are tilting our heads. We can do the same thing for rolling motions—instead of the y axis, we can use the z axis.

Receivers

Once the transmitters are placed on the head-mounted display, we have to do something with the receiver triangle. Probably the most obvious place to put it is the ceiling. This will work unless you are using the head-mounted display sitting down, if that's the case, then the distance between the transmitters and receivers will be too much, and the electronics will have a difficult time tracking. What we need to build is a stationary arm upon which we can place the triangle. Figure 13.5 shows an example of such an arm.

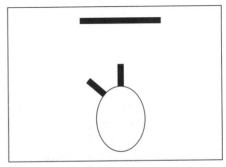

FIGURE 13.4 ***Tilting of Power Glove HMD***

When mounting the triangle on the arm, we have to be sure that the triangle cannot be bent or moved around. To keep this from happening, we need to reinforce it. Figure 13.6 shows how to do this.

The best set-up for the system is to have the receivers as close to the transmitters as possible. This will help avoid any interference and make for better tracking.

Pitfalls

The major problem with this system is that the glove isn't very good at detecting roll. There are only 12 different values for a total of 360°, which means each value represents 30°! So how can we compensate for this problem? One way

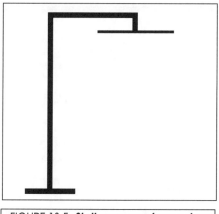

FIGURE 13.5 **Stationary arm for receiver triangle**

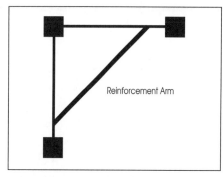

FIGURE 13.6 **Reinforcement of receiver triangle**

that works well—if your virtual world is not so complicated that the frame rate is tremendously small—is to split your movements into smaller pieces. In other words, if the user is looking straight ahead and the system registers a roll of 5 and then they yaw to the right and the system responds with a value of 6, we do not have to change the scene from straight ahead to straight ahead plus 30° all in one scene change. Instead, present a 15° change and then a 15° change immediately after. If your system is fast enough, it doesn't look too bad and certainly much better than instantly going to a 30° shift.

Another problem that can occur is that users don't turn their heads enough, which causes the system to report a value of 5, then a value of 6, and then back to 5. What you don't want to do is present the straight-ahead scene and the +30° scene in rapid succession. This will cause users to get very sick. Your software can be smart enough to determine when this flickering of values is occurring and present users with a scene shift of +15° and not change it until a good reading of some other value is obtained. It is tricky but can be done.

Software

The other side of the story is software. Thankfully, there isn't much construction needed. Because we are using the standard Power Glove components, we can use the drivers presented in Chapter 2. We simply use the values somewhat differently. The roll value will correspond to our yaw, the y value to pitch, and the x value to roll. Appendix A will give you the information needed to use the PARK and SHOOTER programs with the Power Glove head tracker.

14

Rendering Software

ver the last 13 chapters, we have seen how to attach a number of different components to our personal computers in order to add some degree of realism to a virtual world. Our next step is to program our computers to create virtual worlds as well as control all of the hardware. Software for a VR system is called a *rendering package*. This software takes numbers such as those in Figure 14.1 and converts them into a picture such as Figure 14.2.

The renderer does not simply convert the numbers into an object and then display it. The software must take into consideration where we are in the virtual world, after all, there is no sense in displaying objects that are behind us and therefore not in our field of vision. In addition to where we are, the renderer must know from what perspective we are looking into the world. Are we on the ground looking up, or are we in the air looking down? Once the renderer has all of this information, it determines which of the objects should be rendered and how they should be presented on the display.

The Renderer

Whether low-cost or high-cost, all renderers function in pretty much the same way. Figure 14.3 shows the loop that a simple renderer performs. In this section, we give a brief idea about what each of these steps entail.

```
8 6 0
0 0 0
0 2 0
2 2 0
2 0 0
2 0 -2
2 2 -2
0 2 -2
0 0 -2

4 1 2 3 4
4 4 3 6 5
4 5 6 7 8
4 8 7 2 1
4 2 7 6 3
4 8 1 4 5
```

FIGURE 14.1 **Cube object vertices and polygon definitions**

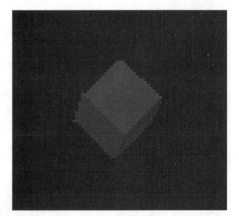

FIGURE 14.2 **Rendered cube**

User Input

User input is usually supplied via the keyboard and the mouse, so the renderer must have the capability to recognize a key press as well as a movement of the mouse. In a number of cases, the mouse is used to control a virtual hand in the world. In addition

```
Loop
      Get User Input
      Transform and Project Vertices
      Sort Objects
      Backface Removal
      Color
      Draw
Endloop
```

FIGURE 14.3 *Rendered loop*

to these input devices, we have to consider the Power Glove, the 3-D Mouse, the head tracker, and any voice recognition software. Because the Power Glove and the 3-D Mouse were built with the same basic interface, they can be considered at the same time. The renderer has to be able to communicate with the Power Glove electronics in order to read the x, y, z and roll position of the glove and how bent the fingers are. The Power Glove will more than likely be used to control a virtual hand, so the renderer must be able to determine where in the virtual world to place the hand. Obviously, this placement has to be in relation to where we are looking.

To determine where we are looking in the virtual world, the renderer must take input from the Head Tracker. If the head tracker indicates that we are looking to the left, the renderer must change the world it displays appropriately. For the voice recognition software, the renderer must simply be prepared to take keyboard input because our voice system activates the renderer through the keyboard.

Transform and Project Vertices

When an object is designed for a virtual world, the points of the objects are described in world coordinates that have $x,y,$ and z values based upon some origin 0,0,0. The renderer has to be able to convert the objects from world coordinates into x,y pixel values for the display screen. This conversion is called *projection* and requires only two steps, which are outlined in Figure 14.4.

The first step is to convert the vertices from world coordinates to view space coordinates. There are several different coordinate systems for view space, the most common of which is perspective. Figure 14.5 shows what a perspective view does to a cube drawn on the screen—it creates depth in the image. Figure 14.6 presents the formulas for converting world coordinates to perspective view coordinates. Notice that the z coordinate stays the same from world to view coordinates.

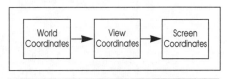

FIGURE 14.4 *Projection of object to computer screen*

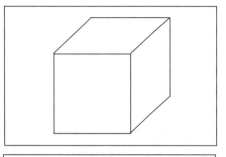

FIGURE 14.5 **Cube drawn with perspective view**

$$\text{Projected\_X} = \frac{(x*d)}{z}$$

$$\text{Projected\_Y} = \frac{(y*d)}{z}$$

FIGURE 14.6 **Perspective projection equations**

The second (and last) step in the projection is to convert the view coordinates to screen space coordinates, which are the actual *x,y* positions of the pixels that will make up the objects on the computer screen. Because there is no *z* coordinate for computer screens, it is simply discarded. The *x,y* values are obtained using the equations in Figure 14.7.

In addition to the projection of the object vertices, the computer must move objects in accordance to the user's interactions with the keyboard or other input devices. If the user wishes for a specific object to be moved some distance in the *x* coordinate direction, the computer must adjust the vertices of the object accordingly. This adjustment is usually performed using transformation matrices. Figure 14.8 shows the transformation matrices for translation (movement). All vertices of an object have to be transformed using matrix multiplication. These calculations are obviously very expensive timewise when considering that the renderer must work in real time.

In addition to translation, the renderer should be able to move the objects in any way the user wishes. To accomplish this, we must include rotation and scaling capabilities. Figure 14.9 shows the matrices necessary for rotation, and Figure 14.10 shows the matrix for scaling.

$$\text{Screen\_X} = \text{Projected\_X} + \frac{\text{Screen\_Width}}{2}$$

$$\text{Screen\_Y} = \text{Projected\_Y} + \frac{\text{Screen\_Height}}{2}$$

FIGURE 14.7 **Screen equations**

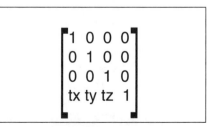

FIGURE 14.8 **Transformation matrix for translation**

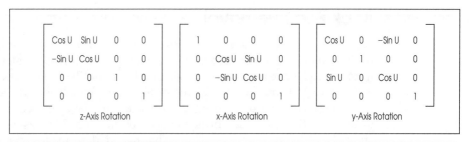

FIGURE 14.9 *Rotation matrices*

Sort Objects on *z* Depth

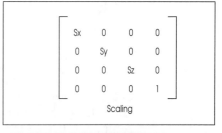

FIGURE 14.10 *Scaling matrices*

Once all of the objects have been given view and screen coordinates, we sort them based on their *z* coordinate. This is done to determine which objects are in front of other objects. If we have two objects and object A is in front of object B, we will want to draw object B first and then object A. The result would look like Figure 14.11. If we were to draw A and then B, we would get the reverse, as shown in Figure 14.12.

By sorting all of the objects, we can always draw from the back of the list forward. In practice, the list is kept sorted at all times. When an object is transformed using a translation or rotation matrix, it is located in the list and repositioned according to its new *z* coordinate.

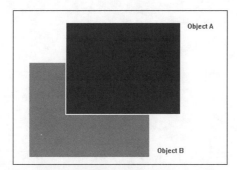

FIGURE 14.11 *Result of drawing object B, then A*

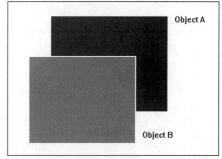

FIGURE 14.12 *Result of drawing object A, then B*

Back Face Removal

Back face, or hidden surface, removal is performed to save rendering time. If we have a cube in our world and we are looking at one of its sides, there is no need to render the opposite side because it will not be seen. Back face removal is determined from the normal vector to a specific polygon. If the normal vector is directed toward the user, the surface must be rendered. If it is directed away from the user, the surface can be eliminated. Figures 14.13 and 14.14 show the difference between a cube that has hidden surfaces removed and one that does not.

Color

For realism in a virtual world, color is very important. Most renderers have the ability to specify lights in the virtual world. Each light will have a direction and a color. As the renderer begins to draw a new screen, it will determine how much each of the lights affects objects based upon the angle between the light and each object. If the object is directly in front of the light, then the full intensity of the light is felt by the object and is colored accordingly. If the object is at some angle to the light source, then some fraction of the available intensity will be used. By employing a shading scheme, each of the objects can be different shades of the same color based upon the intensity of the lighting.

Drawing

The last step in the rendering process is the drawing. Significant time and energy is given to this subject by developers of rendering packages because of the amount of time spent drawing to the computer screen. The faster the line

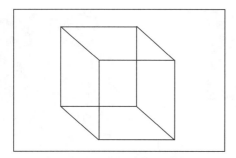

FIGURE 14.13 *Surfaces not removed from object*

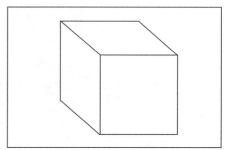

FIGURE 14.14 *Surfaces removed from object*

drawing routines, the faster the renderer can update the screen after some user input. The majority of this code is written in highly optimized assembly language.

REND386

The remaining chapters of the book will present several different applications built using a freeware PC rendering package called REND386. This renderer was written by Dave Stampe and Bernie Roehl. Because of its cost—free—it is the best choice for the garage-level virtual reality enthusiast. You can obtain the most recent copy of REND386 from either the Cyberforum libraries on Compuserve or the Internet site sunee.uwaterloo.ca. The files are typically listed as develx.zip and demox.zip, where x is the current version number. The most recent version as of this writing is 5. Figure 14.15 shows an example of a simple REND386 program that allows the renderer to display a world and the user to navigate through it. However, this program requires several files in order to display a world. The first of these is called a *world* file, which contains information about where to place objects in the virtual environment. Figure 14.16 is an example of a simple world file.

```
#include <stdio.h>
#include <stdlib.h>
#include <dos.h>
#include "rend386.h"
#include "userint.h"
#include "plg.h"
#include "splits.h"
#include "tasks.h"
#include "pointer.h"
#include "cursor.h"

/***************************************************************************
 This function is called when the user ends the graphics program.  It
 shuts done the graphics system and exits the renders and finally exits
 the progam.
 ***************************************************************************/
void closeall(){
 exit_graphics();
 reset_render();
 exit(0);
}


/***************************************************************************
```

FIGURE 14.15 *Skeleton program for REND386 rendering software*

```
 This function is from Rend386 DEMO2.C program and is used to get
 keyboard input from the user.
 *******************************************************************/
unsigned getkey(){
 unsigned c;
 union REGS regs;

 regs.h.ah = 2;
 int86(0x16, &regs,&regs );
 shifted = (regs.h.al & 3);
 if ((c=bioskey(0)) & 0xff) c &= 0xff;
 else if ( shifted ) c |= 1;
 return c;
}



/********************************************************************
 This function handles keys pressed by the user.Handle any user keys.
 *******************************************************************/
void handle_key ( unsigned int c ){
FILE *infile;

 switch ( c ) {
  case 'q':
  case 'Q':popmsg ( "Do you wish to quit? (y/n)" );
              if ( toupper(getkey())== 'Y' ) execution = 0;
              else redraw = 1;
              break;
  }
}



/********************************************************************
 This function performs the updating of the screen after any object or
 perspective movements.  The majority of the work is done in the
 function screen_refresh in the file render.c
 *******************************************************************/
void refresh_display(){

 fast_view_factors ( current_view );
 screen_refresh ( current_view );
}



/********************************************************************
 This function performs the functions of the program.  The loop terminates
 when execution = 1.
 *******************************************************************/
void main_loop(){
 while ( execution )
   {
   if (bioskey(1))    handle_key (getkey());
   if (redraw)          refresh_display();
   }
}



/********************************************************************
 This function is called to load video drivers.  The pointer
 v_driver_pointer is set to a handle representing the video driver.
 The variable v_driver_pointer is used by the files: main only.
```

FIGURE 14.15 *Continued*

```
*************************************************************************/
void load_video_driver ( char *dfile )
{
 v_driver_pointer = load_driver ( dfile );
 if ( v_driver_pointer == NULL )
 {
            fprintf ( stderr, "Bad video driver/n" );
            exit ( 1 );
 }
}


main(int argc, char *argv[]){
char *fname, *in_filename;
FILE *in;

 setup_render(40,800);
 atexit(closeall);
 set_global_split_root ( &split_tree );
 initial_world_split ( &split_tree );
 set_move_handler ( split_move_handler );
 objlist = new_objlist();


 fname = "rend386.cfg";
 if ((in = fopen ( fname, "r" )) == NULL )
   {
    fprintf ( stderr, "Configuration file not found!" );
    exit(1);
   }
 else
   {
    if ( read_world(in))
            {
                fprintf ( stderr, "Error reading configuration file!" );
                exit(1);
            }
    fclose ( in );
   }


 load_video_driver ( vdname );
 screeninfo = screen_data();
 highest_color = screeninfo->colors-1;
 preset_default_colors();

 frame_x = screeninfo->xmin;
 frame_y = screeninfo->ymin;
 frame_w = screeninfo->xmax - screeninfo->xmin+1;
 frame_h = screeninfo->ymax - screeninfo->ymin+1;

 default_view.left = screeninfo->xmin;
 default_view.top = screeninfo->ymin;
 default_view.right = screeninfo->xmax;
 default_view.bottom = screeninfo->ymax;
 default_view.aspect = screeninfo->aspect;


 if (enter_graphics()) {
   fprintf ( stderr, "could not enter graphics mode\n\n");
   exit(1);
   }
```

FIGURE 14.15 **Continued**

```
screen_clear_color = 0;

sky_color   = 1; ground_color = 2;


in_filename = fix_fname(argv[1] );
if ( strstr (in_filename, ".wld"))
   {
   if ((in = fopen ( in_filename, "r" )) == NULL )
            {
              fprintf ( stderr, "Error opening world file.\n" );
              exit(1);
            }
   if (read_world(in))
            {
              fprintf ( stderr, "Error reading world file.\n");
              exit(1);
            }
 }
initialize_screen_factors ( current_view );
fast_view_factors ( current_view );

main_loop();    /* start us off */

}
```

FIGURE 14.15 **Continued**

The two most widely used parts of the world file are those that load object and figure files. We have already seen what a PLG object file looks like from Figure 14.1. Let's look at creating an object using an object file.

Creating an Object

There are several different ways that we can create a 3-D object. The first is to draw the object on paper; depending on the object, this can either be an easy task or very hard, because paper allows for only 2-D representation. When the objects get so complex that designing them on paper becomes impossible, we

```
worldscale 1.0

hither       10
yon          20000000
skycolor     16
groundcolor 16

start 2000,1000,-400  0,0,0   1

ambient 76

object courtwall 32,48,4   0,0,0  800,0,4000     0 walls fixed
figure person 1,1,1 0,0,0 1000,0,1000
```

FIGURE 14.16 **Simple world file**

can turn to a CAD system, which will allow us to draw in three dimensions using the computer. The only problem is that the PLG format is not widely supported. In fact, the only CAD system that can produce PLG files is NorthCAD from Quest. For demonstration purposes, we will design a house on paper.

The first step is to draw a cube using the technique most of us were taught as children. Figures 14.17 through 14.22 show the steps necessary to draw a three-dimensional cube on paper. We then have to assign coordinates to each of the cube's vertices. The easiest way to do this is to assign the bottom left front corner to the coordinate 0,0,0. Figure 14.23 shows the bottom four vertices labeled with their coordinates. We can now move up to the top vertices by copying the bottom four coordinates except that we must substitute a value other than 0 for the *y* component. Figure 14.24 shows all of the vertices and their coordinates.

Next, we need to create a roof for our house. We can do this by placing a point centered above the cube and drawing lines from the top vertices to that point. We must also give this point a coordinate, as shown in Figure 14.25.

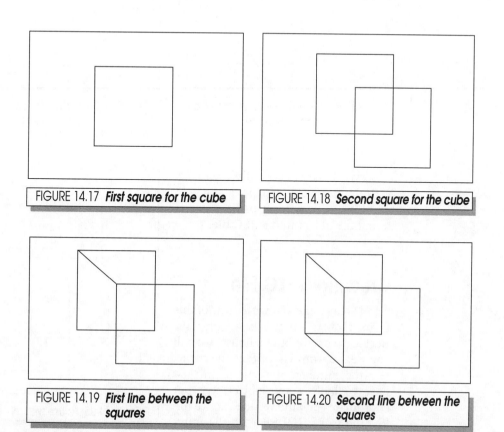

FIGURE 14.17 **First square for the cube**

FIGURE 14.18 **Second square for the cube**

FIGURE 14.19 **First line between the squares**

FIGURE 14.20 **Second line between the squares**

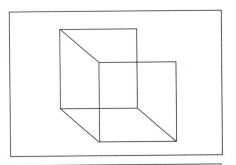

FIGURE 14.21 ***Third line between the squares***

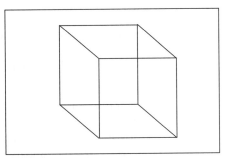

FIGURE 14.22 ***Final line between the squares***

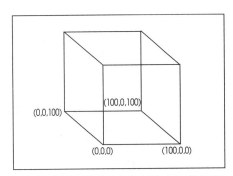

FIGURE 14.23 ***Cube with bottom vertices and coordinates***

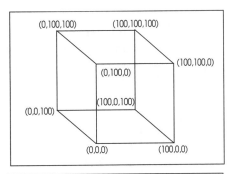

FIGURE 14.24 ***Cube with all vertices and coordinates***

We have successfully created a very simple object on paper along with all of its coordinates. Our next step is to put the object into a PLG file.

Creating a PLG File

All PLG files start out with a line of this form: NAME # Vertices # Polygons. Because we have built a house, we will choose the word HOUSE as the name. For the number of vertices, we just have to look at our object. We put coordinates on nine vertices, so we follow the word HOUSE with the num-

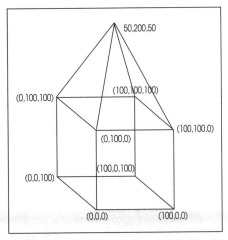

FIGURE 14.25 ***House with all coordinates***

ber 9. Next comes the number of polygons in the object. A polygon is a shape created from three or more points connected such that no lines intersect; a polygon with three vertices is obviously a triangle, and so on. If we look at our house again, we see that it has four sides, a floor, and a roof made from four polygons, so the total is nine polygons. We follow the second 9 with another 9 for our PLG heading: HOUSE 9 9.

After the heading line, we begin listing the vertices in our object. The order does not matter, but it is usually a good idea to follow some pattern. We would list the vertices for our house like so:

```
0 0 0
100 0 0
100 0 100
0 0 100
0 100 0
100 100 0
100 100 100
0 100 100
50 150 50
```

Once all of the vertices have been listed, we begin to create the polygons, each of which has a polygon description line with this format: color # vertices V1 V2 V3 .... The color of the polygons is based on the color scheme for REND386. I will not go into the scheme, but I will list the first 16 colors and their values:

Black = 0
Red = 1
Orange = 2
Pink = 3
Tan = 4
Light yellow = 5
Yellow = 6
Light green = 7
Green = 8
Cyan = 9
Light blue = 10
Blue = 11
Bright pink = 12
Magenta = 13
Grey = 14
White = 15

vertices is the number of vertices that make up the polygons, and V1 V2 V3 . . . are the index numbers of the vertices listed at the beginning of the PLG file. (The index to the vertex starts at 0, not 1.) The index numbers for the vertices must be listed in counterclockwise order as if you were looking directly at the polygons. So for the floor, we would imagine ourselves underground and

looking up at the bottom of the house. Our polygon description would be `color 4 1 0 3 2`. A polygon description line would be created for each of the polygons in our object. Once the object's PLG file is complete, we can add the object to the world file. All objects are added using an object descriptor and this format: `OBJECT plgname Sx, Sy, Sz Rx, Ry, Rz, Tx, Ty, Tz`

The word `OBJECT` is used to tell the parsing routines that this is an `OBJECT` descriptor line. Once the parser sees object, it expects the PLG filename for the object, which is used to open the object's file. The nine remaining values are used to determine specific characteristics of the object when it is placed in the world.

The first set, `Sx`, `Sy`, and `Sz`, are the scaling values of the object in each of the coordinates. These values are used to create differently sized versions of the object using the same PLG file. So if you want to have a great big house, just put a large value in each of the positions. The values 1,1,1 will call up the object exactly as you created it in the PLG file; values less than 1 will reduce its size. The `Rx`, `Ry`, and `Rz` values are used to rotate the object along each of the three coordinate axes. If you want an upside-down house, just use the values 180,0,0. The `Tx`, `Ty`, and `Tz` values are used to translate the object to a specific place in the world. This is how we create our virtual world.

Objects can be placed anywhere in the virtual world just by putting in the appropriate values for the translation. It is sometimes very useful to map out your virtual world on paper and then place the objects according to the map. Once you have placed the objects in the world file, you are ready to explore the world using the main program.

Navigation

The skeleton program in Figure 14.15 reads our world into many different internal structures. It renders the world based on where we are looking. In the REND386 system, this is called our *viewpoint*. Although the viewpoint has many different components, we can just look at four of them. The first is the position of the viewpoint, which is specified by three fields called ex, ey, and ez. We can place the viewpoint anywhere in the virtual world simply by placing the appropriate values into these fields. In addition, we can change the angle of the viewpoint with three other components: yaw, pitch, and roll.

As an example, our skeleton program has a viewpoint called `current_view`. If we wanted to place the viewpoint at the position 0,100,1000, looking straight ahead, we could do the following:

```
current_view → ex = 0;
current_view → ey = 100;
current_view → ez = 1000;
current_view → pan = 0;
```

```
current_view → tilt = 0;
current_view → roll = 0;
```

We would now have our viewpoint into the virtual world located at position 0,100,1000. We could instantaneously look behind us by changing our pan to `current_view → pan = 180;`. We would now be looking directly behind us. By changing the values of the viewpoint, we can simulate someone walking in the virtual world; by moving the viewpoint up in the air, we can fly. It's just a matter of assigning the correct values to the viewpoint data structure.

15

Playing
Racquetball

In the previous chapter, we discussed the concept of virtual reality rendering and explained the details of a shareware package called REND386. We are going to use this renderer to create an actual application—virtual racquetball. This is a good choice for several reasons:

- *We'll see VR theory put into action*
- *The polygon count necessary for virtual racquetball is low, so the speed of the game will be high, even on slower computers*
- *We will be able to use most of the hardware projects we have built*

Playing Racquetball

If you want to skip right to playing the game, refer to Appendix A, which talks about the disk and executing the program on it. You will need to have the Power Glove and its interface attached to the computer in order to play the game. The easiest way to play is to grab the racquet and then turn toward the side of the court. This gives you a chance to hit the ball when it comes from either the front or the back of the court.

Programming the Racquetball Game

Before we begin coding, we need to analyze the problem at hand. We want to simulate as closely as possible the real-world game of racquetball. This means several things:

1. *We need to have several pieces of equipment:*
   - *Racquet*
   - *Ball*
   - *A playing field or court*
2. *We need to be able to hold the racquet and hit the ball*
3. *The game should have a real sense of depth, not just two-dimensional graphics*

Let's look at each of these components separately. First of all, creating the equipment is a simple matter—we either design it on paper or use some type of software package to create it. Of particular concern is the racquetball, because we have only polygons to use as our "building blocks." We have to determine just how many polygons will be needed to create this spherical object.

Second, we must consider our virtual mobility. In the real world, we hold racquets in our hands, which are attached to our bodies. We have the ability to move a racquet in a swinging fashion while twisting our heads from side to side. If we wish to simulate this, we have to be able to differentiate between our heads, bodies, and hands.

Finally, we come to the question of three-dimensionality. During a racquetball game, a great deal of time is spent using depth perception to determine where the racquetball is in relation to ourselves. This will be just as important in our virtual game if it is to be convincing.

The racquetball court will be built using the REND386 system described in Chapter 14 and compiled using the Borland/Turbo C line of compilers. In order to recompile the code, you will need to obtain the REND386 development system from the sources given in Chapter 14.

Equipment Construction

The equipment for the racquetball game is simple enough that we can design it on paper with very little effort. We will begin with the racquetball court.

The Racquetball Court

One of the most important considerations when designing the racquetball court is realism. All of the dimensions should be scaled appropriately so that the user has a sense of actually being in a large playing area. This sounds nice in theory, but there are several problems to overcome in practice. The first is the size of the court. The program BIGCRT.EXE on the enclosed disk shows how a virtual court would appear if we created it using the approximate dimensions of a real court; the playing area is VERY large and not usable. The second program facing us relates to the first—we have no realistic way to navigate such a large area. No one has yet developed a tracking system that allows users to wander over large areas. The third problem is safety. If you are playing the virtual racquetball game while wearing a head-mounted display, you are not able to see obstacles and thus could hurt yourself.

The solution to these problems is to scale down the court to a size that allows users to stand or sit in one position and use the Power Glove to hit the ball. Although this limits the realism of the game, it makes it usable.

In REND386, each unit in the virtual world corresponds approximately to 1 millimeter in the real world. The dimensions of the racquetball court are going to be 3,200 units wide, 4,000 units in length, and 2,400 in height. This translates to 3.2 meters × 4.0 meters × 2.4 meters. The court appears as in Figure 15.1. Notice that there is no back to the court. It has been eliminated to maintain the user's sense of direction. If all of the walls were present, it would be very easy to get lost. The lack of walls will not affect the ball because we can control its movement through software manipulation.

We will begin our court construction with the floor, which is a simple polygon that can be created using the `polyobj` command in a world file. The complete floor command is

```
polyobj 4 sgray 800,0,0 800,0,4000 4000,0,4000 4000,0,0
```

In addition, there are several boundary lines on the floor that are used during a normal racquetball game. These lines are drawn with these commands:

```
polyobj 4 sred 800,0,3000 800,0,3100 4000,0,3100 4000,0,3000
polyobj 4 sred 800,0,2200 800,0,2300 4000,0,2300 4000,0,2200
polyobj 4 sred 1200,0,2300 1200,0,3000 1300,0,3000 1300,0,2300
polyobj 4 sred 3500,0,2300 3500,0,3000 3600,0,3000 3600,0,2300
```

Figure 15.2 shows the layout of the court with the floor completed.

Next we will add the side walls. Each of these is created from a single PLG file called courtwl2plg. This PLG file is the representation of a two-sided polygon 100 units in length and 50 units in height. We will use the scaling parame-

FIGURE 15.1 *Forward view of a virtual racquetball court*

FIGURE 15.2 *Floor of racquetball court*

ters in the object command of the world file. In addition, we have to rotate the walls into place. The commands that accomplish this are

```
split 800,1,0 1,0,0 0
object courtwal 40,84,4 0,270,0 800,0,0 0 walls fixed
split 4000,1,2000 1,0,0 0
object courtwal 40,48,4 0,270,0 4000,0,0 0 walls fixed
```

Figure 15.3 shows the court with the two new walls added.

Next, we add the front wall. This wall is made from a PLG file called courtwal.plg, which is exactly the same as the PLG file courtwl2.plg except that it uses a different `surfacedef` command in the world file for coloring the polygons.

You may have noticed that we have used several different colors for each of the walls of the court and not a uniform color throughout. The reason for this is that REND386 has a hard time with lighting. If you create two polygons, like our walls, and place them at angles to each other, like the corner of a house, you'll find that the system is unable to change the colors of the walls enough so that we actually see two different walls. Instead, we see one big glob of wall; the wall joint is invisible. Because of this, we have to color the walls manually to achieve the desired, realistic effect.

The front wall contains regulation marks just as the floor does, and these must be included when the wall is drawn. The commands for drawing the front wall are

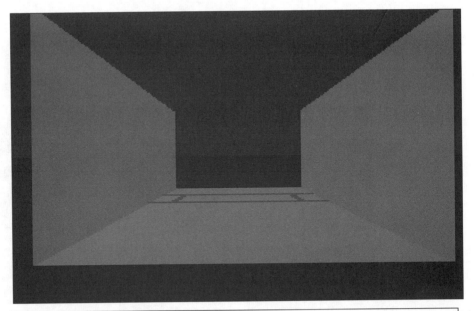

FIGURE 15.3 **Walls of racquetball court**

```
object courtwall 32,48,4 0,0,0 800,0,4800 0 walls fixed
object line 3200,100,10 0,0,0 800,300,3900 0 lines fixed
```

The last wall is the back wall. It is formed using the courtwl2.plg file, just like the side walls. The command for this wall is

```
split 4000,1,2000 1,0,0 0
object courtwl2 40,48,4 0,270,0 4000,0,0 0 walls fixed
```

Finally, we finish the court off with a ceiling. We use the `polyobj` command for the ceiling

```
split 0,2400,0 0,1,0 0
polyobj 4 sgray 4000,2400,0 4000,2400,2400 800,2400,4000 800,2400,0
```

Figure 15.4 shows the completed court.

The Ball

Now that we have a court, we need to create the ball. One of the hardest objects to create in a virtual environment (or in traditional graphics) is a circle or sphere. The reason for this is that to create the arc of the circle or sphere, we have to stairstep the pixels on the computer screen. Figure 15.5 shows a single section of a circle drawn on a typical computer screen.

FIGURE 15.4 *The completed racquetball court*

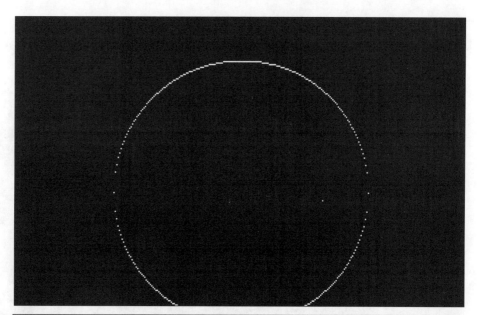

FIGURE 15.5 *A computer-generated circle*

Notice how the pixels change from horizontal to vertical in order to create the circle. Now imagine transforming this circle into a three-dimensional sphere. It would look pretty bad, right?

The situation is further complicated because we only have two-dimensional polygons with which to build our racquetball. One common solution to this dilemma is to use multiple angular bands of polygons. An easy way to visualize this is to think of a stop sign. If you laid a stop sign on the ground and magically pulled up all eight sides, you would have a band of eight polygons. Now, put a polygon on top of the stop sign and connect each of the sign vertices to the polygon vertices. You would create another band which is at an angle compared to the first band. If you did this to the bottom of the stop sign, you would have a crude sphere. Figures 15.6 through 15.8 show the sequence of operations just described.

To make the object look more like a sphere, all you have to do is create more bands of small polygons as well as add to the number of polygons per band. In the example above, we have a total of three bands each with eight polygons in it. This is the sphere we are going to use for our racquetball because we need to keep the polygon count down in our game. Figures 15.9 through 15.12 show several different spheres made using different band and polygon counts.

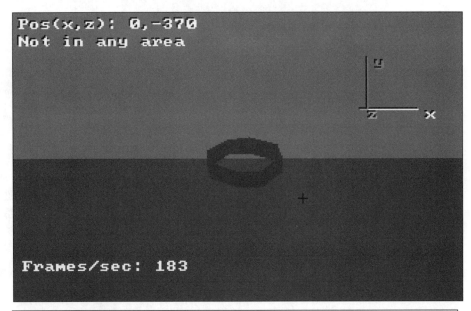

FIGURE 15.6 *Center band of a virtual sphere*

FIGURE 15.7 *Center and top bands of a virtual sphere*

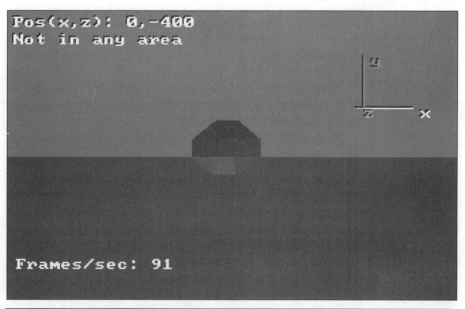

FIGURE 15.8 *Complete virtual sphere*

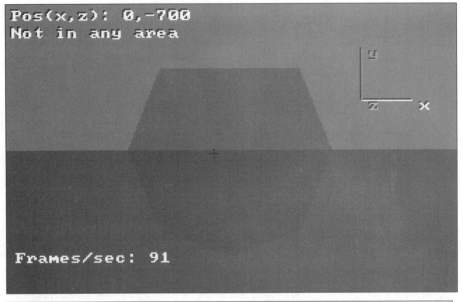

FIGURE 15.9 *A crude sphere*

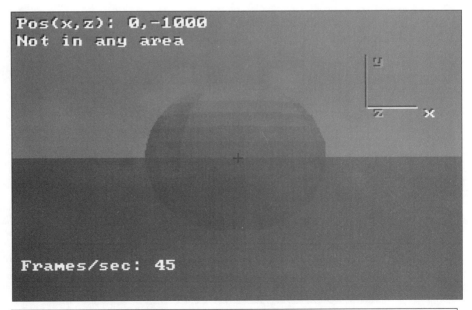

FIGURE 15.10 *A better sphere*

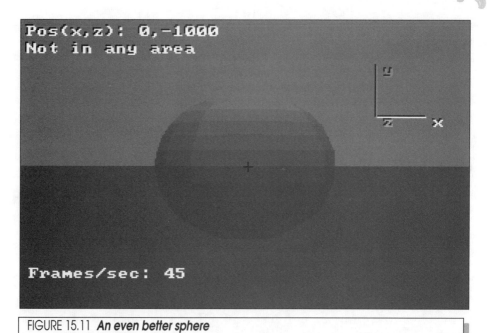

FIGURE 15.11 *An even better sphere*

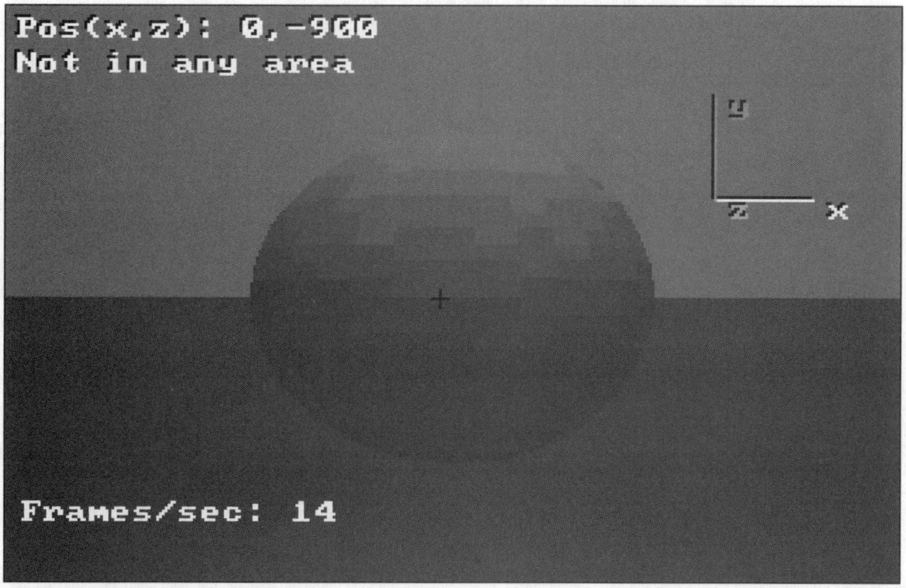

FIGURE 15.12 *Our final sphere*

The Racquet

The last piece of equipment that we need to build is the racquet. At first glance, you might think that a racquet would be quite complex to design for a virtual environment—the details could get overwhelming. A racquet is basically an ellipse with a straight handle attached to it. We can approximate this ellipse by using the stop sign again. If we were to take its two ends and pull them while allowing the mid-

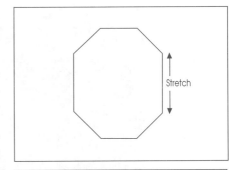

FIGURE 15.13 *A stretched stop sign*

dle section to stretch, the resulting shape would look pretty much like a racquet. Figure 15.13 shows the model.

The stretched stop sign will serve as the frame for our racquet. Because the racquet will be moved in all directions, we need to design it with objects that can be viewed from all sides. The basic object for this type of task is a cube. We will use eight cubes of different lengths to create the racquet shown in Figure 15.14.

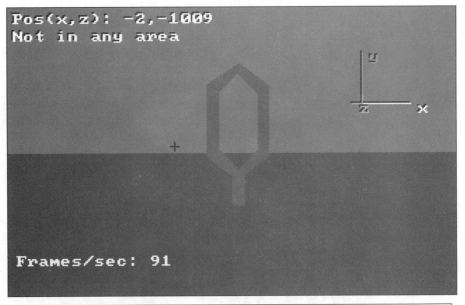

FIGURE 15.14 *Racquet frame*

With the frame completed, we just need to add the strings. In our virtual environment, we want everything to be as real as possible. Thus, when we have the racquet in hand, we should always be able to see its strings. If we were to create a single polygon for the strings—a very thin polygon—we would only be able to see them from one side. We would have to use a second polygon for the other side of the racquet. Along the same lines, if we were to look down on or up to the racquet, there would appear to be no strings because of the way the polygons were drawn. This means that we will need four polygons for each string! The total number of polygons needed just for the strings would add up to be more than what was needed for all the other objects.

Fortunately, there is a solution. REND386 has several features that are especially useful for drawing polygons. If you define a polygon with just one point, the system will not bother to perform any polygon code; it will simply plot the point in the appropriate location. If you define a polygon with two points—that is, a line—the system will draw the line where it's supposed to be. The line will be seen from all directions; therefore, we can use this type of polygon for our racquet strings. The finished racquet appears in Figure 15.15.

Now that we have all of the equipment necessary for playing racquetball, we need to put action into the system.

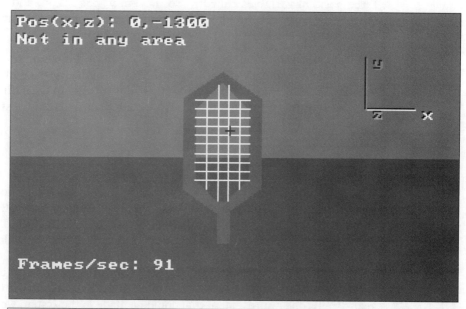

FIGURE 15.15 *Finished racquet*

Ball Movement

Because we are the only participants in our virtual environment, we need a way to move the ball around by ourselves. We only have one hand, and it's holding the racquet, so we will need to animate the ball itself. The system will automatically move the ball, and we will try to change its direction by hitting it. This is as close as we can get to a real racquetball game, which goes to show how complex simulating reality can be.

Animation

The ball will be animated through changes in its x,y,z coordinates. Obviously, if we change the x value, the ball will move from side to side. The y value will control the height of the ball above the floor, and the z value will control forward and backward motion. We will start the ball from a predefined position—in our case `1000,500,2000`.

The ball will move in a positive direction for all three components. Its actual movement is governed by three global variables, `inc_val_x`, `inc_val_y`, and `inc_val_z`. These variables are initialized to the values `50`, `40`, and `40`, respectively. When the program starts, the ball will be controlled by means of a function called `move_ball`, which adds the current increment variables to three position variables called `x_position`, `y_position`, and `z_position`. On the first call of the function, these variables will increase in value from their initialized values to `1050`, `540`, and `2040`, respectively.

This accumulation will continue until one of the boundary conditions is reached. The boundary conditions are defined by if. . .elseif statements. Let's look at the x direction conditions. If the ball is moving in the x direction, it has the possibility of hitting either the right or left wall. This can be stated as

```
if ( x_position > RIGHT_WALL )
{ }
else if ( x_position < LEFT_WALL )
{ }
```

The constants `RIGHT_WALL` and `LEFT_WALL` are defined to be 50 units inside of the actual location of the wall. The 50 units accommodates for the size of the wall and the ball so that the ball doesn't appear to go into the wall and bounce out of it. If either of the conditions is met, the increment value for the ball is reversed from positive to negative or from negative to positive. A test is done for each of the walls, the ceiling, and the floor of the court. In all cases, the ball will automatically change direction. Although the ball will appear to move quite realistically, one improvement that could be made in the system would be to add simulated gravity. Instead of simply changing directions and applying the increment value to the ball's position, a certain amount of gravity could be applied to it. You would then need some sort of way to pick up the ball from the floor.

At this stage in our project, we have a complete racquetball court and a ball that moves inside it. Next we need to be able to move ourselves around the court and control the racquet.

Body and Viewpoint Movement

We have to qualify the concept of movement in our virtual racquetball environment. In the real world, we have the ability to move our torsos, our limbs, and our heads independently. Thus we can walk, talk, and rotate our heads all at the same time. However, when we move our torsos using our legs, the rest of us comes along. Our heads do not keep talking and rotating on the corner while our torsos cross the street—although that would make for a very interesting virtual world. We need to be able to mimic our natural body movements in our virtual environment.

We start out by defining a body, which will have no objects attached to it except when we add the virtual hand, by using a segment. Recall from Chapter 14 that a segment is a data structure that we can use to manipulate objects or as a parent to other segments. It is the latter function that we are concerned with. Our body segment is defined as

```
SEGMENT*body_seg;
```

The variable `body_seg` is a pointer to a segment structure defined by **SEGMENT**. After the segment is defined, we need to create the actual data structure memory with the statement

```
body_seg = newseg (NULL);
```

Now that we have a body, we can begin to add the pieces necessary for complete movement in our virtual environment. The first thing we will add is our virtual hand. In the REND386 system, we have the ability to use the Power Glove as an input device, but one of the requirements for using it is that some fig file must be specified for its virtual representation. The system includes a virtual hand called HANDSM.FIG that is fairly realistic. We let the REND386 system know that we want to use HANDSM.FIG as our representation by setting the variable gpcursor to the string `handsm`. We also have to tell the system what system driver to use when controlling the Power Glove. The default is the Power Glove; the variable gpdname is set to `pglove`.

The initialization of the glove is performed using the function `gloveptr_init` statement, which requires a number of parameters and returns a `PDRIVER` pointer that we will use when accessing the glove. The system has defined the variable gd as a `PDRIVER` pointer as well as several others that are set for housekeeping purposes. The entire function call looks something like

```
gd = manip_device = menu_device = gloveptr_init ( gpdname, 2*65536L,
2*65536L, 2*65536L, 65536L,65536L,65536L);
```

We already know about the gpdname variable used in the function. The last six parameters are scaling values for the glove device. The first three values are the scaling for the *x,y,z* directional components. This means that for every unit the glove moves, the system will report that the virtual hand moves 2 units. This is advantageous because the glove's ultrasonic sensors have a small area of detection. After the glove has been initialized, we need to load the virtual representation of the hand using the statement

```
if(gd) load_glove_cursor(body_seg, manip_device, gpcursor);
```

Notice that we are giving the function our body segment, body_seg. The system will automatically create two more segments that become children to body_seg. Wrist_seg becomes a direct descendant of body_seg, and hand_seg becomes a descendant of wrist_seg. This means that if something is performed on the body_seg segment, the action will be passed to its children wrist_seg and hand_seg. The actual objects in the HANDSM.FIG files are attached to the hand_seg segment. What all this means is that we control the virtual hand using all three segments. If we move our bodies using body_seg, the virtual hands will naturally follow because body_seg is a parent. But we can also just move the virtual hand using the wrist_seg without moving our bodies. This is a very natural set-up for the hand.

The second task in setting up our body is to give it eyes. The REND386 system creates, or renders, the images based on where our eyes are looking—the *viewpoint*. We will use a variable called current_view to keep track of this. The viewpoint is not attached to the body as the glove is, so we will have to move it independently of the body but always at the same time. Now let's move everything into position.

We will begin by placing our body so that we'll have a good overall view of the court. This turns out to be at 2250,800,−300, which puts the center of our body in the middle of the court toward the back and about 3 feet up from the floor—just about the right height for the average person. Notice that the virtual hand will move to a position relative to the body_seg segment. The statements are

```
abs_move_segment ( body_seg, 2250,800,-300);
update_segment ( body_seg );
```

Next we move our viewpoint to the position 2000,1000,−400 with the statements

```
current_view → ex = 2000;
current_view → ey = 1000;
current_view → ez = -400;
```

We are ready to hit the ball, except that we don't have control over our racquet.

Movement Interface

Now that we have our body and viewpoint in the proper starting location, we need a way to move around. The most logical way to move is to use the joystick. The REND386 system allows us to do this by providing the functions necessary to locate and read from the joystick. We begin by locating it. The statement

```
if((joy_return = joystick_check()) = = 0)
```

will locate a joystick on the system if you have one attached. If `joy_return` is set to the value of 0, the system was unable to locate a joystick on the computer system. If this is the case, we will output a simple statement that says we were unable to find it, which means that the keyboard will have to be used for movement. If `joy_return` is not set to 0, then `joy_return` will be either a 1 or a 2. A value of 1 indicates that a joystick is plugged into joystick port 0, and a value of 2 indicates that a joystick is in port 1. Using this data, we can initialize the joystick with the statement

```
joystick_init (&joy_data,0) or joystick_init(&joy_data,1)
```

The Control Loop

Next we need to set up the system for movement. We will have four possible movements: forward, backward, left, and right. In addition, we will be able to move our viewpoint 90° to the left; this will allow us to look at the front of the court, keep our eyes on the ball, and move our body. The body's movement will be controlled by the joystick or the arrow keys on the keyboard.

To determine if the system needs to process a move, we will set up a control loop that watches the keyboard and the joystick. If a key is pressed or the joystick is moved, the system will react to it. The loop looks like

```
while ( running )
{
if(bioskey(1)) handle_key(getkey());
if(joystick_return) check_joystick();
refresh_display();
}
```

The Keyboard

The control loop will execute as long as the variable `running` is not 0. The loop begins by checking whether or not a key has been pressed; if not, then we do not need to do any further processing. If a key has been pressed, we need to process the key and any actions that the key is supposed to create. We perform the processing in a function called `handle_key`. The single parameter to this function

is the value of the key pressed. The `handle_key` function consists of a single `switch` statement that determines to which keys we are reacting.

```
switch(c)
{
        case 'q':
        case UP
        etc. . . .
}
```

One of the most important keys for us to respond to is the Q key. Pressing it is the only way for the user to quit the program. In this case, the system sets the `running` variable to 0 and returns control back to the main loop; as soon as this happens, the loop condition will become false, and the program will end. The other keys to which we want to respond are the movement arrows. These keys have the following numerical values:

```
UP      0 X 4800
DOWN    0 X 5000
LEFT    0 X 4B00
RIGHT   0 X 4D00
```

We have used the C define statement to define these as constant at the start of the program. When any of these keys are pressed, we need to move our body and viewpoint in the appropriate direction. Let's look at two of the keys.

UP and DOWN

When the user presses the UP arrow, our body and viewpoint should move forward in the virtual environment. Traditionally, we should be able to simply increase the z component in the body segment and the viewpoint. However, REND386 is based on a polar coordinate system, so a single movement in the z direction will not work on its own. We have to do some additional math. The code for moving forward is

```
x = 150 * sine(current_view →pan);
y = 150 * cosine(current_view →pan);
current_view →ex += x;
current_view →ez += z;
rel_move_segment ( body_seg, x, 0, z );
update_segment ( body_seg );
```

In programming for virtual reality, we always have to be aware of extra calculations in our programs. For example, our calculations for forward movement are based on the pan variable for viewpoint, and the values from that calculation are stored in temporary variables. In other words, we want to move forward based upon where we are currently looking. It would be very difficult to navigate (not to mention unrealistic) if we always walked forward regardless of where we were looking. In the real world, we almost always walk in the direction of our line of sight. Notice that we are putting a scaling value of 150 in the calculations. This is done so that our virtual stride increases from 1 millimeter to approximately 6 inches. If we were to increase this value, our movements in the virtual environment would be faster yet. However, as we increased the movement rate, the more choppy the scene would appear. Thus we want to pick a natural pace that makes the images appear to move smoothly. Moving backward is a simple matter of changing the sign of the scaling value from 150 to −150.

LEFT and RIGHT

We are again concerned about moving left and right relative to our current viewpoint. To see the importance of determining where you are looking, stand in one direction and move to the left. Note how you are moving. Now turn around 180° and move left. You are moving in the opposite direction than your first move. If you did not compensate for your direction, moving left would always take you in the same direction and would be very confusing. In terms of calculations, moving to the left or right is pretty much the same as moving forward or backward. To move to the left, the x and z calculated values would be

```
x = −150 * cosine(current_view → pan)
z = 150 * sine(current_view → pan);
```

Note that not only are the signs different but also the x value uses the cosine function, as opposed to the sine function, in the forward and backward movements. To move to the right, the signs on the scaling values would be switched.

Head Turn

One final key that we are going to look for is the Y key, which will turn your head in 90° increments. If you have ever wanted to see what was behind you without turning your body around, then this is your chance. We used the pan variable of our viewpoint in the movement code above. To change the location of our head in respect to the pan, we simply add or subtract a degree value such as

```
current_view → pan + = 90*65536L;
```

This statement will cause our viewpoint to change by a factor of 90°. The multiplication value `65536L` is a requirement of the number scheme employed by REND386 to speed up arithmetic. By putting this statement in our keyboard switch statement, we can turn our head toward the front of the court while our racquet is in position to hit the ball.

The Joystick

Now that the keyboard is all set up, we need to consider using the joystick. In our main execution loop, we make a call to the function `check_joystick` if a

joystick is present. Assuming that a joystick is available, the first thing we want to do is read its current status. The statement

```
joystick_read(&joy_data);
```

does just that and returns the data to the joystick variable we created earlier. The data appears in two fields of the `joystick_data` structure. `Joystick_data` is a data structure that contains the fields x and y. Fields x and y are the directional values for the location of the joystick. Because the joystick is an analog device, it can be noisy at times. For this reason, we want to filter out any readings that occur between 10 and −10 and then scale all of the other values back down into this range.

After we have the values for the joystick, we can move. First we will look at the left and right movements. To move left or right, the joystick is moved from side to side in the *x* direction. The system will respond with a positive *x* value if the joystick is moved to the right and a negative value if the joystick is moved to the left. The calculations for our movement are then

```
x = 3*x*cosine(current_view → pan);
z = −3*x*sine(current_view → pan);
```

If we move the joystick to the left, the *x* and 3*x* values will both be negative, and we will move to the left. If we move the joystick to the right, the *x* and 3*x* values will both be positive, and we will move to the right in our environment. We do the same type of calculations for the *y* value returned by the joystick.

Now everything is set for us to play racquetball except the movement of our virtual hand. How do we translate the glove's movement to the virtual hand? The REND386 system comes to the rescue again with a statement called `glove_update`. This statement is multifold. `Glove_update` reads the current status of the glove, determines its position, and updates our virtual hand. Once the function returns control back to the main program, we have to update the body segment manually using the `update_segment` statement. That's all there is to manipulating the glove. At this point, the system will allow you to move your body, your virtual hand, and your viewpoint anywhere in the virtual environment. The last step is to pick up the racquet and hit the ball.

Collision Detection

At the start, the racquet is floating in the air toward the front of the court, and the ball is moving around. Play begins when the user grabs the racquet with his or her virtual hand and begins hitting the ball. In order to grab the racquet with the virtual hand, the collision between these two objects must be detected. Once the user has the racquet in his or her hand, we have to continually test for a collision between the racquet and the ball. To do this, we use a simple method.

A function called `sphere_pretest` calculates the distance between any object and a point defined as some *x,y,z* coordinate position. If we want to determine if a collision has taken place between two objects, we supply the function with a pointer to one of the objects and the center point of the other object; the center point of any object can be obtained using the function `get_object_bounds`. In our case, we will find the current position of the ball and give the racquet as the object to the `sphere_pretest` function. The sequence is

```
get_object_bounds ( ball_object, &x, &y, &z );
dist = sphere_pretest ( racquet_object, x, y, z );
```

Once these two statements have finished executing, the variable `dist` will contain the distance between the two objects in units. To determine if they are colliding, we just look at the size of `dist` and the objects themselves. Because each object we are testing has a size in units, we need to specify a collision distance that takes these sizes into consideration.

In the racquetball game we have two different sorts of collision decisions. The first is between the virtual hand and the racquet, and the second is between the racquet and the ball. There is obviously no reason to test the racquet-and-ball collision until the racquet-and-hand collision has occurred. To control which decision is currently active, we introduce a variable called `NO_RACQUET`. If `NO_RACQUET` is not 0, then we do not have the racquet in our possession and must look for a collision between the racquet and the hand. Whether or not this has taken place will be determined on every iteration of the main loop. The decision statement we are using for the racquet-and-hand collision has two parts. The first is that the collision distance must be under 100 units, which means that the hand must be very close to the racquet. The second part of the decision statement is based on the glove's fingers. The REND386 Power Glove interface software has the ability to detect several crude gestures. The gesture that the glove makes in grabbing the racquet is a fist. When the hand is in a fist position and close enough to the racquet, a collision will occur, the racquet will become a child of the virtual hand, and thus the racquet will move whenever the hand moves. Because we have achieved a collision with the racquet, the variable `NO_RACQUET` will be set to 0.

When the `NO_RACQUET` variable is 0, the main loop looks for a collision between the racquet and the ball. The idea is basically the same as with the racquet and hand, except the collision distance is increased to 300 units for a better chance of hitting the ball. When a collision does occur between the racquet and the ball, the ball must react to the hit by moving in the opposite direction. To accomplish this, we determine the direction in which the ball was traveling when it was hit—whether its direction was positive or negative—and then reverse the direction by setting the `inc_val_z` variable, a variable used to track the ball's movement, equal to the opposite direction. In addition, we add some speed to the ball by setting `inc_val_z` equal to five times its normal speed of

10. Now each time the ball moves, this speed is decreased until the normal speed of 10 is achieved, thus making it seem as though the ball had actually been hit.

 ## Conclusion

That is the end of the racquetball game development cycle. There are numerous improvements that could be made if more memory was available in the computer. The complete racquetball game is available on the enclosed disk. Instructions and command-line options are discussed in Appendix A.

16

A Walk
in the
Park

For our second virtual world, we are going to introduce both a simple software environment (a park) and hardware capable of detecting and responding to human motion (a treadmill or bicycle and an inexpensive set of sensors that you'll learn how to build). Figure 16.1 shows a two-dimensional sketch of the park, which includes several attractions and a number of different-sized trees. The park also has a sidewalk, but one thing that it does not have is boundaries; we are free to walk anywhere we want. Let's continue by looking at different motion control devices.

Movement

As you know, to achieve the full sense of immersion, we must be able to manipulate things in the virtual world just as we would manipulate them in our real

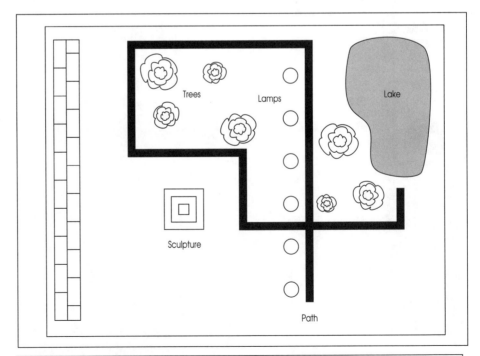

FIGURE 16.1 *Our virtual park*

world. Because manipulation requires movement, we therefore need to be able to move as naturally as possible in the virtual world. Most of the programs developed for the PC have dealt with motion through the keyboard; the racquetball game we developed in the previous chapter was set up so that pressing the F key caused the user to move forward. This is obviously *not* how we move in the real world.

The idea in the park world is to interface a treadmill, bicycle, Norditrak, or some other device with our virtual reality equipment so that we can simulate motion in the virtual world realistically. In order to translate our walking on the treadmill or pedaling on the bicycle into the virtual world, we must determine when a complete action has taken place on the motion device. On the treadmill, for example, the complete action is the cycle of a supporting roller, and on a bicycle, it is the cycle of one of the wheels. If we can measure the cycle of a wheel or roller, then we can determine when a person is standing still, walking, riding, or running.

Accurately measuring movement is important because we want the user to have as much control over his or her movements in the virtual world as possible. Unlike the keyboard-generated movement, which is only single speed, a person on a treadmill can walk slowly, quickly, steadily, or unsteadily.

Converting a Treadmill or Bicycle for VR !!!!

This section will discuss converting a treadmill and a bicycle (either an exercise bike or a normal bike with an exercise stand attached so that the back wheel can spin freely) for use with a virtual reality system.

Parts List for a Virtual Park	
❑ 2 perfboards	❑ 1 infrared LED and detector set (Radio Shack 271-142)
❑ 1 8255 interface circuit from Chapter 9	
❑ 1 bicycle, exercise bike, treadmill, or NordiTrak	❑ 1 9-V DC power supply
❑ 1 567 IC	❑ 1 555 IC
❑ 1 10-k potentiometer	❑ 1 741 op-amp IC
❑ 2 100-k resistors	❑ 1 1.2-k resistor
❑ 1 1-k resistor	❑ 1 10-k resistor
❑ 1 0.33-uf electrolytic capacitor	❑ 1 10-ohm resistor
❑ 1 1-uf electrolytic capacitor	❑ 1 2.2-uf electrolytic capacitor
❑ 1 6-V micro relay	❑ 2 0.1-uf ceramic capacitor

Movement-Sensing Circuit

We begin by building a movement-sensing system. Figure 16.2 is the schematic of an infrared transmitter. This circuit pulses the infrared LED at a rate of 4.8 kHz; each of the pulses lasts 45 milliseconds. One difficulty with this circuit is that it requires 9 V instead of 5 V, which prevents using the power supply from the computer. However, because the motion-sensing circuits will be attached to other machines, it is better that we not use the computer's power.

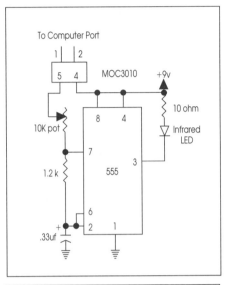

FIGURE 16.2 **Infrared transmitter**

Construction

Construction of this circuit is fairly straightforward. A small piece of perfboard is used to mount the components as shown in Figure 16.3. The circuit can be soldered or wirewrapped, depending on your preference. Refer to Appendix F for more information. Note that in Figure 16.3 the LED is bent 90° off one side of the board. This will allow us to mount the board in a small case. A hole for the LED should be cut in the side of the case (see Figure 16.4). This makes attachment to a treadmill or other motion device easier. The infrared LED package used in the author's prototype was Radio Shack 276-142, which also included a detector. The 9-V power source was taken from a wall-type transformer; a 9-V battery could also be used.

Receiver Circuit

The circuit that receives the pulses from the transmitter is a bit more complicated. Figure 16.5 is the schematic of the receiver circuit. It should be built as

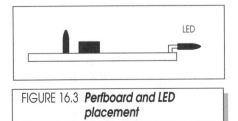

FIGURE 16.3 **Perfboard and LED placement**

FIGURE 16.4 **Case with LED**

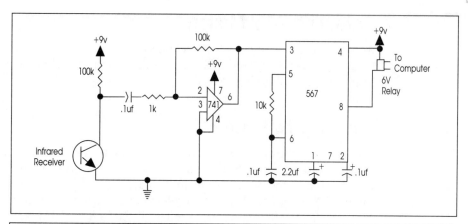

FIGURE 16.5 **Infrared receiver**

the transmitter was and inserted in a small 3" × 4" project box with a hole for the infrared receiver, similar to the hole for the LED, in Figure 16.4. The two circuits operate by aligning the infrared LED of the transmitter circuit with the infrared receiver. The application notes supplied with the infrared receiver indicate that the operational distance is 4 to 5 inches, but this can be increased with the use of focusing lenses.

In order for us to determine when the receiver has received a signal from the transmitter, we have to hook it up to our computer. A single input link from one of the 8255 chips we used earlier will work. You can use the 8255 from either the 3-D sound system or the head tracker we built previously. The easiest connection is through port C of our 3-D sound system 8255 interface chip. The input line from the 8255 is connected to one of the two input pins of the relay on the receiver. The other pin of the relay is connected to any ground (GND) line on the 8255. When the receiver receives a signal from the transmitter, it will trigger the relay; the 8255 will register the hit and send it to the computer. All we have to do is monitor the I/O byte for port C of the 8255. A simple monitoring program like the following should be used to calibrate the system:

```
void main()
{
  for(;;)
   printf ( "%d\n", inportb(0x223));
}
```

This program monitors the status of I/O port 0×223. Because there should not be voltage at any of the pins, the value recorded should be 0. Attach the receiver to input line 0 of port C. Now when the circuit is operating correctly, the value at port 0×223 should be a 1. To calibrate the system, turn the 10-K potentiometer on the transmitter until a 1 is displayed on the computer screen. If a 1 is never displayed, check your connection, make sure the LEDs are aligned properly, and try again.

Detecting Real Motion

Now that we have a circuit to detect motion, the next step is attaching the detector to our bicycle or treadmill. After we discuss the attachment, we will look at interpreting the data it gives us.

Attaching the Sensor

Treadmills come in either manual or automatic form. Automatic treadmills have a motor attached to them that forces the platform to move, thus making the user move, too. Manual treadmills have a platform of rubber that rests on top of a dozen or so rollers that diminish in size from the front of the treadmill to the back; we will use the larger rollers at the front of the treadmill. Obviously, all treadmills are different, and this may not work for the particular one you have. In that case, check the next section, "Treadmills with Solid Rollers," for a way to hook up the transmitter to the rubber of the treadmill that should work for all types. Figure 16.6 shows what a typical roller might look like.

We want to attach the transmitter somewhere in back of the roller and the receiver somewhere in front. As the roller turns, the infrared LED and detector will register a connection each time an open section of the roller appears. Because of the fast speed of the roller, you will want to cover all of the open spaces except one. Thus, each time a connection is registered, we will know that the roller has completed one single revolution. Otherwise, we would need to do some math to determine when a single revolution had occurred, and it is in our best interests to eliminate unnecessary tasks for the computer.

The attachment of the transmitter and receiver can be tricky because we must make sure that no pieces of the treadmill will catch on the boxes. In addition, you need to take into consideration the added weight of the user—how does the treadmill compensate for the weight? We do not want to smash the boxes against the floor each time someone uses the treadmill.

In the case of an exercise bicycle, the easiest thing to do is to attach the boxes to each side of the forks. Take a piece of cardboard about 3" × 3" and tape it to the spokes in the path of the LED and detector. Each time the cardboard passes through the path, a complete revolution will be registered. Figure 16.7 shows the layout.

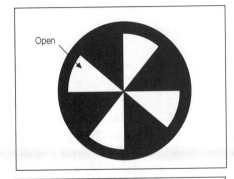

FIGURE 16.6 *Treadmill roller*

Treadmills with Solid Rollers

We know that all treadmills are not the same. Some treadmills have solid rollers, which will not work with our interface. In order to attach the interface to these treadmills, we need to take a look at the platform itself, which is usually a rubber-type belt that simply moves across the rollers.

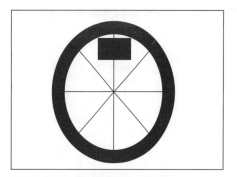

FIGURE 16.7 ***Cardboard insert***

To attach the interface to the rubber itself would be a feat because there would always be the possibility of stepping on the transmitter box. An alternative is to remove one of the rollers from either the top or bottom part of the treadmill and attach the transmitter in the roller's place. The receiver box would be attached opposite the transmitter either to the frame of the treadmill or to its side. This doesn't do much good because there would always be a connection between the LED and detector. What we need to do is attach a piece of cardboard or other material to the moving platform. We are doing the reverse of the roller attachment. In the case of the latter, the connection between the LED and detector is normally off and

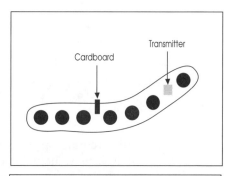

FIGURE 16.8 ***Complete revolution of treadmill runner***

comes on when the open part of the roller appears. In the case of the platform attachment, the connection is normally on and goes off when the cardboard passes between the LED and detector. Figure 16.8 illustrates this strategy.

Interpreting the Sensor's Readings

Now that we have the interface attached to our device, we need to interpret the results. The average person walks at a pace of 3 miles per hour. The following program can be used to translate the data from the interface into a miles per hour reading:

```
Program walktest;
uses crt;
convert  = --;      { feet per revolution }
sec_min  = 60;
min_hour = 60;
```

```
       mile_feeet = 5280;

var
  total, feet_per_sound, feet_per_hour, miles_per_hour,
  hour, min, sec, sec2, sec10 : integer;
begin
  while not key pressed do
    begin
      gettime (hour, min, sec, sec10);
      total :=0;
      while (abs(sec-sec2)<3) do
      {get revolution per second}
       begin
        if (port[610] = 1)inc (total);
        gettime(hour, min, sec2, sec10);
       end;
      {Get feet per second}
       feet_per_second :=(total DIV 3)*convert
      {Convert to feer per hour}
       feet_per_hour :=feet_per_second*sec_min*min_hour;
      {Convert to Miles per hour}
       miles_per_hour :=feet_per_hour*mile_feet;
       writeln ("Revs = ", total, " MPH = ", miles_per_hour);
    end;
end.
```

This program operates by recording how many revolutions occur each 3 seconds. This value, which must be measured on your treadmill for accuracy, is multiplied by the number of feet that the user moves each revolution of the roller. This multiplication gives us a feet per second reading, which is multiplied by the conversion values for seconds per minute and minutes per hour to give us feet per hour and then multiplied yet again by the conversion value for feet per miles to arrive at a final value of miles per hour.

If this is too much information, the first conversion of feet per second can be used. This will tell us exactly how much to move in the virtual world.

Using the PARK

The program PARK on the enclosed disk can be configured to use the sensors we have placed on our treadmills or bikes; based on the motion detected by them, the PARK program will generate your forward movement. Refer to Appendix A for instructions on executing the PARK program with the detection circuits as well as using a joystick with the program.

Programming a Joystick

You may be puzzled as to why we want to use a joystick for motion. Well, most people in motorized wheelchairs can move their chairs by using a small joystick at the end of one of the arm rests, and airplane pilots use joysticks, too. There may be a game there. . .

Initialization

Before a joystick can be used with a REND386 program, we have to determine if one is available. Now obviously we could look around the back of the computer and see if a joystick is attached, but the cleanest way is to ask the system itself. The routine `joystick_check` can be called to determine if a joystick is attached. The possible return values are 0 for no joystick, 1 for a joystick attached to port 0, 2 for a joystick attached to port 1, and 3 for both joysticks attached. After we determine where the joysticks are attached, we have to initialize a joystick data structure. The REND386 documentation includes one called `joystick_data`. In order to intialize the joystick properly, we must declare a variable of this type and pass it to the function `joystick_init`.

In our program, this is done with the following statements:

```
joystick_data joy_data;
if ((joy_return = joystick_check())   == 0 )
 {
 popmsg ( "Joystick was not found");
   delay ( 5000 );
   exit(1);
 }
 if ( joy_return & 1 )
   joystick_init ( &joy_data, 0 );
if ( joy_return & 2 )
   joystick_init ( &joy_data, 1 );
```

The variable `joy_data` is declared to be of type `joystick_data`. The code begins by determining the joystick port. (We are assuming that only one joystick is being used.) The return value of the function `joystick_check` is put into the variable `joy_return`. If the return value is 0, we indicate to the user that no joystick is available and exit the program. This is a drastic move because the program will still allow use of the keyboard.

We then initialize the appropriate joystick by ANDing the return value with a bit mask. If the joystick is at port 0, the least significant bit will be set. The AND will cause the if statement to be true, and the data structure will be initialized for the joystick at port 0. If the joystick is at port 1, the same thing will happen except at port 1, not port 0.

Joystick Read

Once the joystick data structure has been initialized, we are ready to begin receiving and interpreting data from it. The function `joystick_read` takes a joystick data structure and fills it with necessary information about the current state of the joystick. The three most commonly used fields of this data structure are *x*, *y*, and buttons. In order to use them, we must know what values they are returning to us. To this end, a simple test program was executed to read the joystick and report the values returned when the joystick was moved in all directions.

A joystick is a two-dimensional input device. The stick can move forward and backward, left and right. When the stick is moved to the farthest point left, the function `joystick_read` returns a value of −49. When the stick is moved to the farthest point right, the function returns 70. The value −49 is returned when the stick is moved forward as far as it can go, and a value of 32 is returned when the stick is moved to the back.

As you move the stick between the center position and any of the other positions, the `joystick_read` function will return a value between 0 and the values discussed above. This allows us to have some control over the amount of movement given to a particular joystick position.

For our demonstration program, we determine the amount to move in the scene by the value returned from the `joystick_read` function. One problem with the joystick is that it will not read a constant 0 for the *x* and *y* coordinates when you are not touching it; instead, it will skip around between −8 and 9 or so. For this reason, we have to set limits as to the usability of the information returned by the joystick. The REND386 demo program uses the following code:

```
x = joy_data.x;
y = joy_data.y;
if ( x>10 ) x -= 10;
 else
 {
  if ( x > -10) x = 0;
  else x += 10;
 }
 if ( y > 10 ) y -= 10;.
 else
 {
  if(y>-10) y = 0;
  else y+=10;
 }
```

The code begins by looking at the value in the *x* coordinate. If this value is greater than 10, 10 units are subtracted. The reason for this is that we are going to throw out anything in the range −10 to 10. By subtracting 10 units from any value greater than 10, we make up the values lost in the range. If the value is not greater than 10, it is checked against −10. If the value is in the range −10 to 10, *x* is set to 0, and nothing in the scene changes. If the value is less than −10, then 10 is added to the value to again replace values in the lost range. The code does the same for the *y* coordinate.

Once the coordinates have been "cleaned," we are ready to use them. In the RUNJOY.C demo program, the code to use is this:

```
switch ( joy_data.buttons )
{
 case 0:
    current_view->pan += ( x/10 * 65536L );
     current_view->ex -= ( y * thesin * 50L );
     current_view->ez -= ( y * thecos * 50L );
  redraw = 1;
 break;
 case 1:
    current_view->ex += (x * 50L * thecos);
     current_view->ez -= (x * 50L * thesin);
  redraw = 1;
 break;
}
```

Because the joystick has only a two-dimensional base from which to work, we have to use the buttons to change the function of the stick movement. If none of the buttons are down, the buttons field of the joystick data structure will be data. In our case, if no buttons are down, the *x* coordinate controls the yaw of the eye, and the *y* coordinate controls its forward and backward movement. If the button on top of the joystick is down, the buttons field will return a value of 1. In this case, the *x* coordinate controls the left or right movement of the eye, and the *y* coordinate has no function.

Once it has been determined what function the coordinates have, the actual eye must be moved. In all cases, the value of the coordinate, either x or y, is used as a scaling function for the movement. For all movements other than yaw, the value is multiplied by 50. Thus, a little pressure on the joystick causes a little movement, whereas a lot of pressure causes a large movement.

A Fast-Paced Robot Combat Game

Our final project will be to set up Shooter, a virtual reality game. It also allows you to use much of the hardware you built in previous chapters. The objective of this application is not only to entertain but also to demonstrate the techniques used to build virtual environments with objects that move on their own.

Programming the Game

Shooter involves a lot of activity—movement through the virtual world, firing projectiles, and sensing when objects collide. We'll look at all these issues in detail as we discuss how to write this type of software.

The Playing Field

Figure 17.1 is a diagram of our playing field. As you can see from the figure, the field is 100,000 units long by 100,000 units wide. This provides an area large enough to give some freedom yet restricts the users so that they do not get entirely lost out in cyberspace. The surface of the playing field is like a checkerboard, only expanded dramatically. The reason for this has to do with how we perceive depth. In our virtual playing field, there will be times when you move your viewpoint to a position where all obstacles (and your opponent) are out of view. When this happens, you will find yourself in a scene like Figure 17.2. The sky is one color, in this case blue, and the floor looks like a checkerboard. If you continued to move forward in this scene, you would still have a sense of depth because the checkerboard would provide a frame of reference. The floor beneath you would be first one color and then another. And all the while you moved on, the other sections of the

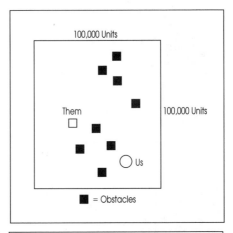

FIGURE 17.1 *The playing field for Shooter*

FIGURE 17.2 ***Empty playing field with checkerboard floor***

checkerboard would be moving relative to you. Contrast this landscape to the one in Figure 17.3.

If you were faced with this scene and continued to move forward, you would have no idea as to where in the virtual world you were. The sky would appear as a solid blob of color, and so would the floor, which means that you would have no idea if you were moving forward, backward, left, or right. It is for this reason that we need to apply some type of pattern or texture to the floor. If the pattern is moving in one direction, then we know we are moving in the other direction.

The floor is composed of 64 polygons, each of which is one of two colors. No two polygons of the same color can be adjacent to each other. Each polygon measures 80 units $\times$ 80 units, so the entire checkerboard measures 640 units $\times$ 640 units. Because the playing field is 100,000 units $\times$ 100,000 units, we have to scale the checkerboard up by a factor of 156.25. As we have seen previously, if we want to load an object into our world, we just put a line in the world file and it will be automatically loaded in. However, for this application we are going to load some of the objects and figures under the main program's control in order to separate them from the objects in the world file. The code necessary to read a PLG file automatically is

FIGURE 17.3 *Empty playing field with single color floor*

```
void get_floor()
{

 FILE *in;
 OBJECT *floor;

 set_loadplg_offset ( 0,0,0 );
 set_loadplg_scale ( 8,8,8 );
 if ((in = fopen ( "shootflr.plg", "r" )) == NULL )
   {
    fprintf ( stderr, "Unable to open floor file.\n" );
    exit(1);
   }
 floor = load_plg ( in );
 if ( load_err != 0 )
   {
    fprintf ( stderr, "Error loading floor.plg file.\n" );
    exit(1);
   }
 fclose ( in );


 add_obj_to_split ( &split_tree, floor );
}
```

The code begins by setting the desired offset of the object we are loading. The numbers that we put in the offset command are added to the vertices in the object file in order to place the object in a different position. We want to have the object placed in its original position so we keep the offset values at 0,0,0. Next we set the scaling values. We figured out that the necessary scaling for the floor was 156.25, so this value is entered for the x and z coordinates only. If we were to enter the value in the y position, we would get a playing field that was 100,000 units tall.

Once the initial read values are set, we open the object file using the C file command `fopen`. If the routine returns a NULL, then there is a problem with the filename and the program exits. If the `fopen` returns a valid file handle, it is passed to the PLG reading routine `load_plg( );`. Once this routine returns from reading the PLG file, we can check the variable `load_err` to determine if the object was read successfully. After the object file is closed, it is added to the renderer's list of objects to render by the function `add_obj_to_split();`.

That's all it takes to manually read in a PLG file. We now have a floor for our playing field. The next task is to place obstacles on it.

The Obstacles

We're going to use simple, cubelike columns that are tall and wide enough for the players to hide behind them. Normally, we would want to have a very complex and exciting environment in which to play, but because we have to redraw our environment each time we move, we want to keep the polygon count low. This is the main reason why we chose to use cubes for obstacles. Figure 17.4 shows the obstacle description lines as they appear in our world file for this application. All of the blocks are created from a single PLG object file and only differ in their dimensions. Figure 17.5 shows how the obstacles look on the playing field.

The last object that we need to create is the representation for our opponent.

The Robot

As we are playing the game, we will want to be able to shoot our opponent; therefore, we need to have some type of visual representation for our opponent that will move whenever he or she moves. It will be more enjoyable if that representation actually looks something like our opponent. We could keep the polygon count very low and simply have him or her be a tall, thin block, as shown in Figure 17.6.

```
object cube 5, 100, 5 0, 0, 0 2500, 0, 2540 768
object cube 15, 50, 15 0, 0, 0 3000, 0, 9000 768
object cube 15, 50, 15 0, 0, 0 4000, 0, 32894 768
object cube 15, 50, 15 0, 0, 0 4000, 0, 42000 768
object cube 15, 50, 15 0, 0, 0 -6000, 0, 29500 768
object cube 15, 50, 15 0, 0, 0 -2000, 0, 4800 768
object cube 15, 50, 15 0, 0, 0 75000, 0, 48990 768

object cube 15, 50, 15 0, 0, 0 -4000, 0, -3000
object cube 15, 50, 15 0, 0, 0 2400, 0, -17000
object cube 15, 50, 15 0, 0, 0 5430, 0, -42000
object cube 15, 50, 15 0, 0, 0 32000, 0, 8000
object cube 15, 50, 15 0, 0, 0 32000, 0, -8000
object cube 15, 50, 15 0, 0, 0 18000, 0, 2700
```

FIGURE 17.4 **Obstacle description lines**

FIGURE 17.5 **Obstacles in view**

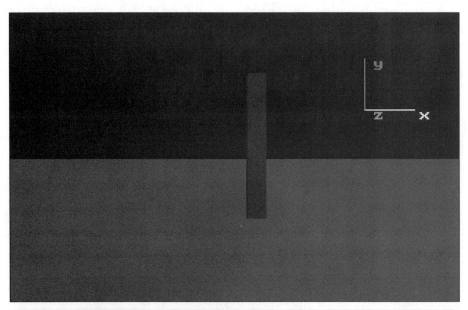

FIGURE 17.6 **Human representation—tall, thin block**

This design would make for a high-speed game, but it really isn't very interesting visually. Another option could be to use a robotlike character. Figure 17.7 shows a robot used in the demonstration program for Version 4.01 of REND386. This is a much better representation than the tall, thin block, but we can do even better. Figure 17.8 shows a humanoid object that is more realistic than the two previous ones and does not have a large polygon count. By far the most complex part of the object is the head. Recall from the discussion of the racquetball in Chapter 15 that spheres are reproduced by combining many polygons; a realistic human head would require hundreds or thousands of them. This object is the one we are going to use in our game. We will load it manually from within the program because we need to perform some special operations on it. This is the code that reads in the opponent's representation:

```
SEGMENT *read_other_guy(int person)
{
 FILE *in;
 SEGMENT *other_guy_seg;
 OBJECT *chest;

 if ((in = fopen ( "otherguy.fig", "r" )) == NULL )
   {
     fprintf ( stderr, "Unable to open otherguy file.\n" );
     exit(1);
   }

 set_readseg_objlist ( objlist );
```

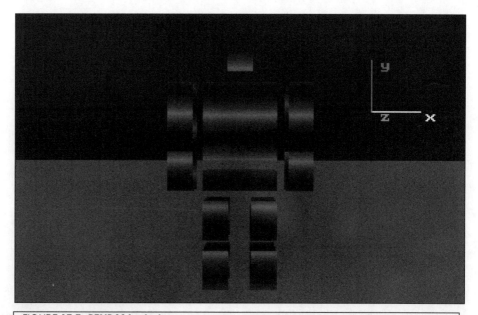

FIGURE 17.7 *REND386 robot*

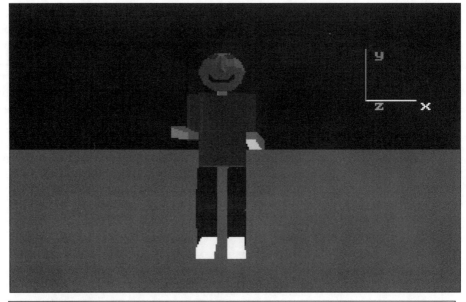

FIGURE 17.8 ***The opponent—our final choice***

```
set_readseg_scale ( 2, 2, 2 );
other_guy_seg = readseg (in, NULL);
if ( readseg_err != 0 )
  {
    fprintf ( stderr, "Error loading otherguy.plg file.\n" );
    exit(1);
  }

chest = seg_get_object ( find_segment_by_name ( other_guy_seg, "chest"
));
chest->oflags = 1;

left_leg = find_segment_by_name ( other_guy_seg, "left thigh");
right_leg = find_segment_by_name ( other_guy_seg, "right thigh" );

/* rel_rot_segment ( left_leg, -20*65536L,0,0, RXYZ );
rel_rot_segment ( right_leg, 20*65536L,0,0, RXYZ );
update_segment ( left_leg );
update_segment ( right_leg ); */

update_segment ( other_guy_seg );


return other_guy_seg;
}
```

The first half of the code does the actual reading of the figure field and puts it
into the list of objects for the renderer to render. The second half of the code is

what we need to concentrate on. In order to make the opponent's representation more realistic, we will animate it so that its legs move whenever the figure moves. Let's look at how we do this.

Figure 17.9 shows how the representation is constructed. When we did the actual read of the figure file, the routine returned to us a segment pointer that is attached to the root of the figure; if we manipulate this pointer, we manipulate the entire figure. To find the legs, we use the routine `find_segment_by_name()` which takes as parameters the root segment and the name of the segment we are trying to find. The right leg is found with this command:

```
right_leg = find_segment_by_name ( other_guy_seg, "right thigh" );
```

The variable `right_leg` is a segment pointer that is attached to the right leg. We can use it to manipulate the right leg only. Once both legs are found, we are ready to begin playing.

Movement

The whole idea of the game is movement. We want to be able either to move toward and find our opponent or to flee and hide from him or her. At the same time, however, our opponent is doing the same in relation to us. This means that we will have to manipulate their representation in our environment as well as our own which is what we'll focus on next.

Our Movements

We can move in the virtual environment by using two different controls: the keyboard or the joystick. We have already looked at the calculations that determine how the joystick and keyboard move us in the virtual world, so we will skip that part. Because so much will be happening in our playing field, we need to have a way of moving that doesn't take much time. In other words, if you move the joystick forward, you should move forward; but if at the same time your opponent is also moving forward, his or her representation on your computer screen must also move. We cannot move ourselves and then, when we are finished, move the opponent. All movements must be in real time.

```
{
    name = chest;
    {
     name = neck;
      { name = head; }
     name = rightupr;
      { name = rightlow; }
     name = leftupr;
      { name = leftlow;  }
     name = right thigh;
      { name = rightleglow;
        { name = rightshoe; }}
     name = left thigh;
      { name = leftleglow;
        { name = leftshoe; }}
    }
}
```

FIGURE 17.9 **Opponent figure segments**

To accomplish this, we will use this very simple tasking system in a main loop of the program:

```
if (still_to_move_u !=0) handle_us_move();
if (still_to_move_t !=0) handle_them_move();
if (still_to_move_b !=0) shoot_it();
if (still_to_move_tb !=0 ) other_guy_shoot_it();
```

To see how the tasking system works, let's look at what happens when we press the F key, which is used to move our viewpoint forward. When it is pressed, the following statements are executed:

```
hit =0;
still_to_move_u += 300;
```

The statement that is important is the second one. We add 300 units to the variable `still_to_move_u`. When the system returns from the keyboard routines to the `main_loop`, the tasking system will look at the variable `still_to_move_b` and, because it is not 0, will execute the routine `handle_us();`, which looks like this:

```
void handle_us_move()
{
 long x, z;
 OBJECT *obj;


  x = MOVE_STEP * sine(current_view->pan);
  z = MOVE_STEP * cosine(current_view->pan);
  current_view->ex += x;
  current_view->ez += z;
  walk_split_tree ( split_tree, check_list );
  if ( hit )
    {
        current_view->ex -= x;
        current_view->ez -= z;
        still_to_move_u = 0;
    }
  else
    {
        com_tx(1);
        abs_move_segment ( body_seg, current_view->ex, 0, current_view-
>ez );
        update_segment ( body_seg );
        still_to_move_u -= MOVE_STEP;
        if ( still_to_move_u < 0 ) still_to_move_u = 0;
        redraw = 1;
    }
}
```

The first part of the routine checks to see if we have collided with any of the obstacles. We will discuss this in more detail later. Once the routine has determined that we have not run into anything, it moves our viewpoint 300 units forward. At the same time, it transmits the character l to the other machine. This l tells the other machine that it should move our representation 300 units on the other person's computer display.

To keep the game simple, we have only allowed two other movements. By pressing the left and right arrows, you can yaw your viewpoint left and right. Because you will probably not sit in one position and spin your viewpoint, all yawing movements are done when the key is pressed and not queued, as is the case for forward movements.

The Opponent's Movements

Our opponent's movements are handled by the following routine:

```c
void move_other_guy()
{
  long tan_val;
  switch (random(10))
  {
    case 0:
    case 1: still_to_move_t += MOVE_STEP;
            break;
    case 2: other_guys_view.pan += PAN_ANGLE;
            rel_rot_segment ( other_guy, 0, PAN_ANGLE, 0, RYXZ );
            update_segment ( other_guy );
            redraw = 1;
            break;
    case 3: other_guys_view.pan -= PAN_ANGLE;
            rel_rot_segment ( other_guy, 0, -PAN_ANGLE, 0, RYXZ );
            update_segment ( other_guy);
            redraw = 1;
            break;
    case 4:
    case 5:
    case 6:
    case 7: if (current_view → ex > other_guys_view.ex)
        {
            other_guys_view.ex += 50;
            rel_move_segment ( other_guy, 50, 0, 0 );
            update_segment ( other_guy );
        }
        else
        {
            other_guys_view.ex -=  50;
            rel_move_segment ( other_guy, -50, 0, 0 );
            update_segment ( other_guy );
        }
        if (current_view → ez > other_guys_view.ez)
        {
            other_guys_view.ez += 50;
            rel_move_segment ( other_guy, 0, 0, 50 );
            update_segment ( other_guy );
        }
```

```
    else
    {
        other_guys_view.ez -= 50;
        rel_move_segment ( other_guy, 0, 0, -50 );
        update_segment ( other_guy );
    }
        update_segment ( other_guy );
        redraw = 1;
        break;
    case 9: still_to_move_tb = 4000;
    break;
    }
}
```

Collision Detection

When we talked about our movements earlier, we left out discussing collision detection. We need to cover that here. When we are moving our viewpoint, we don't want to move through the obstacles. Remember that we put our obstacles in the world file, which is read by the program. These obstacles are put into the rendering loop, just like all other objects. Because they are going to be used as something other than just stationary objects, we need a way to designate them. All PLG objects have a set of 16 flags that are use for various purposes. Thankfully, some of these are available for our use. When our main program starts up, we will read the contents of the world file and set a flag in all of the objects in the file, indicating that they are indeed obstacles. The code that does this is

```
walk_split_tree ( split_tree, check_obj );
```

This statement tells the system to take a walk through the current list of objects to be rendered and pass each one of them to the function check_obj:

```
void check_obj ( OBJECT *obj )
{
obj →oflags = obj →oflags | 0X0008;
}
```

The function sets the fourth bit to a 1, indicating that the object is an obstacle.

When we move forward, the function handle_us has to check whether or not we are against an obstacle. It does this by executing another walk statement:

```
walk_split_tree ( split_tree, check_list );
```

This time, all of the objects in the list to be rendered are sent to the function check_list. We need to remember that unlike the first walk through the objects, we now have ALL of the objects in the render list, including the representations of our opponent and the floor. When these were read into the render list, their fourth bit was not set to a 1.

The function `check_list` is

```
int hit = 0;
void check_list ( OBJECT*obj )
{
 if((obj →oflags & 0×0008 ) && (!hit))
 {
 dist = sphere_pretest ( obj, 1200*sine(current_view →
pan)+current_view →ex, current_view →ey, 1200*cosine(current_view →
pan)+current_view →ez );
 if (( dist > 50 ) && ( dist < 2050 )) hit = 1;
 }
}
```

This function has elements that we discussed in designing the racquetball application—namely, the `sphere_pretest` routine. Notice that in order for the distance to be calculated between our current position and some object, it's fourth bit must be set to a 1. Therefore, the routine will not even test an object for a collision unless it has been previously designated as an obstacle.

Conclusion

The game has many components other than just the movements of our viewpoint and the opponent's representation. We also have to consider bullets being fired as well as when they collide with the opponent. However, this collision detection is exactly the same as for the obstacles. Developing a virtual reality game that is fun to play yet does not execute at a snail's pace can be quite a challenge. Shooter makes an attempt to be somewhere in the middle.

Appendices

Appendix A

Installing Software from the Disk

Installing software from the enclosed disk is a simple process. All you have to do is indicate which drive is to be used; the installation program will then automatically create all the subdirectories and install the software on that drive. The disk is not copy protected, and you may freely make backup copies for your use only. However, the software on the disk is compressed into one large archive file, so you must always use the installation program on the disk to copy software to your hard drive.

You can customize the installation so that only the software you choose ends up in the subdirectories you specify. Later you can go back and install other software. In the installation program, use the arrow keys to move around, and press ENTER to select an option. You can also press ALT-X at any time to quit.

To install software from the disk:

1. *Insert the disk in your floppy drive. At the DOS prompt, switch to that drive by typing* A: *or* B:.
2. *Type* Install. *The installation program will start, and you will see the welcome screen. Press ENTER to continue.*
3. *An Options screen will appear. If you want to install all the software automatically, simply highlight the Start Installation option and press ENTER. To customize the installation process, follow the remaining steps.*
4. *To change the hard drive to which the software is installed, select the Select Destination Drive option. Your drives will be shown along with the amount of free space on each. Highlight the drive you want and press ENTER.*
5. *To change the default subdirectories where each piece of software is installed, select Edit Destination Path. Highlight the path you want to change and press ENTER; edit the path, and then press ENTER again. When you're finished, select Continue Installation.*

6. *If you are reinstalling software from the disk, you can use the Toggle Overwrite Mode to determine whether or not files from the diskette should automatically overwrite existing ones on your hard drive. If you have altered any of the programs, choose either the Prompt to Overwrite or Never Overwrite options to protect your work.*
7. *If you only want to install some of the software on the disk, choose Select Groups to Install and then highlight the software you want. Press Continue to go back to the Options screen.*
8. *When you have made all the selections you want and are ready to install the software, highlight Start Installation and press ENTER.*

Chapter 2

The programs on the enclosed disk for Chapter 2 deal with the operation of the Power Glove and the parallel port interface that we constructed. There are three executable and two information files.

TEST.EXE

The TEST.EXE program is the simplest one for testing the Power Glove's connection with the host computer. To execute the program, plug the Power Glove interface into the parallel port of the computer and into the small interface box on the triangle sensors of the Power Glove. Plug the power supply into the glove and wait for a beep. Execute the program by typing `test` followed by pressing the RETURN key.

The program will clear the screen and begin displaying numbers relating to the *x,y,z*, roll, finger, and button values from the glove. Press the CENTER button on the glove to reset the system. To quit the program, press any key on the computer's keyboard.

LOWRES.EXE

The LOWRES.EXE program is an example of the joystick mode of the Power Glove. Attach the Power Glove to the computer as described in the TEST.EXE section, type `lowres`, and press the RETURN key.

The program will clear the screen and begin scrolling numbers down the left side of the screen. As you move the Power Glove, the numbers will change from 0s to 1s, depending on your movements. To quit the program, press any key on the computer's keyboard.

GLOVREND.EXE

The GLOVREND.EXE program is an example of using the Power Glove with the rendering package REND386. Again, we want to make sure that the Power Glove is attached to your computer and the power supply has been hooked up. To execute the program, type `glovrend` and press the RETURN key.

The program will clear the screen, and you will see this message: `looking for glove`. Point the glove at the triangle sensors. The glove will beep, and the screen will clear. Within a second or two, a brown virtual hand will appear on the screen. It will move anywhere that you move the Power Glove; make a fist, and the virtual hand will make a fist. To recenter the glove and the virtual hand, press the CENTER button on the Power Glove's control pad. To quit the program, press the Q key on the computer's keyboard, followed by the Y key.

The source code for the GLOVREND.EXE program is called GLOVREND.C.

Menelli

The menelli directory contains files with instructions for building a serial port interface for the Power Glove. To uncompress the files, type `lharc x menelli` and press the RETURN key. A number of files will be created on your drive.

Glove

The glove directory contains the source code and header files for the TEST.EXE program described above. The files glove.c, glove.obj, and glove.h can be used to add Power Glove support to any program compiled with the Borland C line of compilers. The TEST.EXE program is an example of using the Power Glove in a normal DOS program. To recompile the TEST.EXE program using the glove.c, obj, h files, type `bcc -o test.c glove.obj` and press RETURN. This command will invoke the Borland C command-line compiler to compile the program TEST.C, which uses the file glove.obj.

JET.EXE

Although somewhat crude, this program will allow you to pilot a virtual jet fighter. Using the Mattel Power Glove, you can control its movements as well as fire on targets.

The Power Glove should be connected to the parallel port using the interface cable we discussed in Chapter 2. Before you begin the program, make sure that the glove is connected and that power has been supplied to it.

The program is executed by typing `jet jet.wld <return>` in the jet directory.

Piloting the jet is very simple. Once the program starts, you will see a control stick in the lower middle part of the screen. To fly, place your virtual hand on the top of the control stick and grip. Once you have done this, you can move your hand in the direction that you want to go. To stop flying, simple release your grip. To change the speed of the jet, use the index finger of the virtual hand to touch the top red button to the right of the control stick. A floating menu will appear that allows you to change the jet's speed. Touch the top button to accelerate, touch the middle button to decelerate and touch the bottom button when you are finished.

In addition to flying, you can fire missiles. Press B on the keyboard, and an explosion will appear in the distance. To change the missile's range, press the middle button on the main control panel. Another floating menu will appear that allows you to adjust for your target.

The last button allows you to leave the menu.

It is possible to hit and remove the different mound formations that appear in the landscape, but it's not easy. (These mounds are formed using the program MAKECLD.EXE included in the distribution.)

The bottom button on the control panel allows you to leave the simulation; you can also do so by pressing Q on the keyboard.

Chapter 3

In Chapter 3, we discussed how the mouse works, how to use it for virtual reality applications, and how to build a 3-D mouse using pieces from a Power Glove. There are five programs mentioned in the chapter.

MOUSE1.EXE

The MOUSE1.EXE program gives the basic raw output from a mouse connected to the computer. The program is executed by typing `mouse1` and pressing RETURN. The program will display the current x,y, and button values from the mouse. The x and y numbers represent how much the mouse has been moved. If you move the mouse to the left very gently, the numbers will be very low. If you move the mouse very quickly and over a larger area, the numbers will get bigger. Mouse movements to the left and right register as x values, whereas up and down movements will register as y values. To exit the program, press any key.

To execute the program correctly, you must have a mouse and mouse driver software installed on your computer. Refer to the documentation that came with your mouse to determine how to install the mouse driver software.

MOUSEZ.EXE

The MOUSEZ.EXE program is like the MOUSE1.EXE program except that we have given the right mouse button a second job. Execute the program by typing `mousez` and pressing RETURN. The program will begin displaying the same numbers as above, plus a value for z. If you move the mouse left and right, you will get the same x values as described earlier. If you move the mouse up and down, you will get y values. To get z values, hold down the right mouse button and then move the mouse up and down. You are using the right button to simulate the movement of the mouse into and out of the z axis, which would extend into and out of the surface on which you currently have your mouse. To exit the program, press any key.

3DMOUSE.EXE

The 3DMOUSE.EXE program is used with the 3-D mouse built in Chapter 3. To execute the program, type `3dmouse` and press RETURN. You must have the Power Glove interface connected to the computer as well as a power supply applied to the glove. This program will display the $x,y,z,$ and button values for the 3-D mouse. Remember that we have taken the tracking mechanism from a Power Glove and attached it to the mouse. To exit the program, press any key.

RENDMS1.BAT

The RENDMS1.BAT program is used to manipulate a virtual hand using an ordinary mouse. To execute the program, type `rendms1.bat` and press RETURN. The program expects to find a mouse driver installed in your computer. The program will clear the screen, look for your mouse, and load in the files it needs to run. After a short time, a virtual hand will appear on the screen that will respond to the movements of the mouse.

If you move the mouse to the left and right, the virtual hand will respond by moving left and right along the x-axis. Up and down movement of the mouse will cause the virtual hand to move forward and backward along the z-axis. To get the virtual hand to move up and down along the y-axis, press the right button on the mouse and then move it up and down. The right button causes the up and down movement to change from the z-axis to the y-axis.

You can also make the virtual hand grip and ungrip by pressing the left mouse button. If you press the left button down, the virtual hand will grip. The hand will remain gripped until the left button is released.

To exit the program, press the Q key on the computer's keyboard, followed by the Y key.

RENDMS2.BAT

The RENDMS2.BAT program is used to manipulate a virtual hand using the 3-D mouse built in Chapter 3. To execute the program, type `rendms2` and press RETURN. The program looks for the Power Glove to be attached to the parallel port and for a mouse attached to a serial port. The virtual hand will track the movements of the 3-D mouse based on the ultrasonic tracking mechanism.

As with RENDMS1.BAT, the virtual hand can be gripped and ungripped by pressing the left mouse button. If you press the left button down, the virtual hand will grip. The hand will remain gripped until the left button is released.

To exit the program, press the Q key on the computer's keyboard, followed by the Y key.

Chapter 4

G3DMATE.EXE

The program G3DMATE.EXE is a demonstration virtual chess game that allows you to pick up and move chesspieces using the Global 3-D Controller. The program has several command-line switches that must be used to tell the program where your Global 3-D Controller is attached. The command-line switches are always put after the name of the program to be executed.

1. *In order for the program to operate correctly, you must have a Global 3-D Controller attached to one of the four COM ports on the PC. We will use a command-line switch to tell the computer to which of the ports the controller is attached. The switches available are*
   – 1 = controller is on COM1
   – 2 = controller is on COM2
   – 3 = controller is on COM3
   – 4 = controller is on COM4
   If your controller is attached to COM1, you would execute the program by typing `gdcmate – 1` *followed by pressing the RETURN key. Substitute the appropriate switches for the different COM ports.*

2. *You will see the opening screen.*
3. *You will be asked to select the black or white player by typing b or w, respectively.*
   NOTE: You and your opponent must select opposite sides.
4. *You are asked to type 1, 2 3, or 4 for the modem's COM port. Select a COM port number by typing the correct number between 1 and 4.*
   NOTE: MATE uses both a mouse and the modem. They must be on opposite COM ports. If your mouse is on COM1, then your modem must be on either COM2 or COM4. If there is a conflict, MATE will stop.
5. *You will see a message explaining the coloring scheme used in MATE.*
   NOTE: The gray chesspieces correspond to the white player; the red chesspieces correspond to the black player.
   Press any key to continue.
6a. *You will see the message* LOADING.
   Please wait until the program starts up. It will take a few seconds.
   NOTE: During the startup process, the program will check the COM port you selected. If a problem is detected, the program will exit, and you will see a chart listing the COM ports and instructions. Try starting the program again and make sure you type the correct COM number. If the program still does not run, please check carefully for any COM conflicts, then try again. Remember, your mouse COM port and your modem COM port must be different; otherwise, they will conflict and the program won't run.
6b. *You will see the message* Null modem/Modem.
   If you are not going to play over the modem, press N.
   If you are going to practice, but without using the modem, press N.
   Pressing N will save time by skipping the modem-checking routine.
   To play over the modem, press M.
   This starts a modem check by the computer.
7. *If the program sees no COM port conflicts, you will see a chessboard with red and gray pieces on it. In the middle of the screen, you will see a chart listing representations—faces—that you may select, for example, a mouse's face, a cat's face, and so on.*
8. *Select the face you wish. Your opponent will see it, and you will see the face your opponent has chosen.*
   They can be the same or different.
   Type the corresponding number to choose your representative face.
9. *Now you are ready to practice. After practicing, you will be ready to dial your opponent and interact in this virtual reality environment. (See the "Practice" section of this appendix.)*
10. *When you are ready, you can either call your opponent by voice and then let the program take over the phone line (O key) or let the program dial your opponent (D key).*
11. *In the shareware version, when the remaining time has reached one minute a counter will appear in the top right corner of the screen. When the counter reaches zero, the program will exit.*

HELP H
Press the H key at any time after MATE has begun to see the HELP screen.
The following is a list of keys and a short description.
A—answer opponent's computer
B—back to original positions
C—color change (switch sides)
D—dial opponent's computer
E—return viewpoint and hand to original position
G—disconnect modem
H—help screen
L—load previously saved game (disabled in shareware version)
M—send message
O—originate after voice connection
P—change modem speed
Q—quit and exit
R—restart timer
S—save game (disabled in shareware version)
T—timer: set number of minutes per move
U—display timer
X—activate null modem cable connection
Z—answer null modem activation

Practice—Mouse Movements

Before you actually dial an opponent, you should practice moving and picking up pieces. Above the chessboard in front of you is a virtual representation of your hand, with four fingers and a thumb. This hand is controlled by using the Global 3D Controller. Remember, you will not see your opponent until you have dialed and connected with your opponent.

Global 3D Controller and Hand Motions

If you move the Global 3D Controller to the left, your virtual hand moves to the left. If you move the Global 3D Controller to the right, your virtual hand moves to the right. Try both motions with the Global 3D Controller.

If you move the Global 3D Controller forward or backward, your virtual hand moves forward and backward. Try this and watch your virtual hand move.

If you move the Global 3D Controller up or down, your virtual hand moves up and down. The Global 3D Controller will not move your virtual hand below the chessboard.

Grabbing and Moving Pieces

Now, practice picking up a chesspiece. If you press the ; key on the keyboard, your virtual hand will make a gripping motion. Press the ; key and watch your virtual hand grip. To pick up a chesspiece, move the Global 3D Controller and maneuver your virtual hand close to a chesspiece. When it is close enough to the chesspiece, the back of your virtual hand will turn blue, and the Global 3D Controller will transmit a tiny vibration to your (real) hand. When you see the virtual hand turn blue, press the ; key to grab the piece. Then move the Global 3D Controller to move the piece. When you have moved the chesspiece to the desired square, just press the ; key again. The piece will stay where you have put it.

To capture one of your opponent's pieces, grab and move the opponent's piece off the board and then grab and move your piece to the corresponding square.

Joystick/Keyboard—Viewpoint Movements

In addition to being able to move your virtual hand, you have the ability to move your viewpoint. Both the joystick and the keyboard can be used to control your viewpoint position.

The Joystick

Regardless of direction, the farther you push on the joystick, the faster you move. For slow movement, push just a little. To move forward or backward in the virtual environment, move the joystick forward or backward. Try pushing and pulling the joystick and watch your viewpoint move forward and backward. To move your viewpoint to the left or right, move the joystick to the left or right.

The next movements depend on button 0 of the joystick, which is usually located on top of the joystick itself. If you move the joystick forward or backward while holding button 0 down, you rotate your viewpoint down or up. This is just like rotating your head forward or backward, except that in the virtual environment we have the ability to rotate a full 360°.

NOTE: Your hand does *not* follow while rotating because you are just rotating your head, not your entire body. Try holding down button 0 on top of the joystick and watch your viewpoint rotate as you push or pull the joystick.

If you move the joystick left or right while holding button 0 down, you yaw your viewpoint left or right. This is like looking left or right.

The last movements to be discussed depend on button 1 of the joystick, which is usually located on the base of the joystick. If you move the joystick forward or backward while holding down button 1, your viewpoint will move up or down.

There is no action for the left/right movements of the joystick while holding button 1 down.

The Keyboard

All of the joystick movements can be duplicated using the keyboard. If your keyboard does not have separate cursor keys, turn the number lock off and use the number pad cursor keys.

The keys are

LEFT arrow—move left
RIGHT arrow—move right
UP arrow—move forward
DOWN arrow—move back
SHIFT LEFT arrow—yaw, or look, to the left
SHIFT RIGHT arrow—yaw, or look, to the right
SHIFT UP arrow—rotate down
SHIFT DOWN arrow—rotate up
PAGEUP key—move up
PAGEDOWN key—move down

Setting Modem Speed—P

The P key allows you to change the speed setting of the modem. You are allowed to change the modem speed up to 14,400 baud. The game is set up for 2,400 baud initially (default protocol: 8 data bits, no parity, and 1 stop bit).

Dialing Your Opponent—D

The D key allows you to dial an opponent's phone number. You are asked for the number, and you can then enter one up to 25 characters in length. Once the number is entered, press ENTER. The modem will pick up and dial. If you have already connected by voice, then use the O key instead of D. (See the "Alternative Connection" section.)

Once your opponent's modem picks up the line, you will see the message `waiting to connect..` After a little information is passed between the computers, your opponent's representation will appear onscreen. Press any key to continue.

Answering an Opponent's Call—A

If you are designated to answer the computer link from your opponent, press the A key when your phone starts to ring. You will see the same messages as the dialer.

Alternative Connection—O

If you and your opponent have already established a voice connection, you do not have to hang up to play MATE. One player presses the O key to originate a modem call. The other player presses A to answer the call. After the modems have picked up, place your phone handset on its cradle. Do *not* pick up the phone handset after the connection is established. Use the M key instead to send messages.

Once connected, you and your opponent can start playing chess. (Remember that the white player always goes first.) You'll see your opponent's representation, or "face", and s/he will see yours. You will see both your opponent's virtual hand and your own. And you'll see what s/he is doing—moving, turning, gripping, and so on.

During MATE, you have several things you can do besides play chess.

NOTE: The following options are listed under the HELP menu. To see the help menu, press the H key.

Quit—Q

The Q key will exit you from the MATE game. You will see the message `Are you sure?` If you do not want to quit, press N; otherwise, press Y. The system will automatically hang up the modem for you, and you will be returned to the operating system. Make sure to save your game before quitting MATE.

Reset Game—B

The B key will reset the MATE game. You *and* your opponent will be returned to the original positions. All of the chesspieces will be returned to their home positions. Make sure to save your game before pushing this key.

Switch Side—C

The C key will reset the game as above *and* change each of you to the opposite color. Make sure to save your game before pushing this key.

Original Position—E

The E key will return your viewpoint and virtual hand to their original positions. However, this will *not* change the position of your opponent or the position of any of the chesspieces. Make sure to save your game before pushing this key.

Hang-up—G

The G key will hang up the modem but you will stay in the MATE game.

Each of you can save the game either before or after pressing G.

Load Previous Game—L

The L key allows you to load a previously saved game. You will be asked for the complete filename. Type the 8-character name, the period, and the 3-character extension. For safety reasons, each player must separately load a previous game. You can load a previous game either when you first execute MATE or when you are on line.

This feature is disabled in the shareware version.

Send Message—M

The M key allows you to send a message to your opponent. You will see a text box. Enter a message up to 33 characters in length. Press ENTER to send the message to your opponent. He or she must press a key to erase the message from both screens.

Save Game—S

The S key allows you to save a current game. You will be asked for the complete filename. Type the 8-character name, the period, and the 3-character extension. For safety reasons, each player must separately save a current game. Make sure you save a game before exiting from the game, or the information will be lost, erased, and gone forever.

This feature is disabled in the shareware version.

Timer—T, U, and R

❑ *Set Timer Length—T*
   The T key allows you to set the number of minutes for the timer, which is used to limit the time for competition moves. Before starting the timer, agree with your opponent about the number of minutes to be allowed per move. You will be asked to enter the number of minutes per move; the maximum is 255.
   Only one player has to set the time. The system will transfer the correct setting to the other computer automatically.
❑ *Start timer—U*
   The U key starts the timer, which will appear on both screens and will automatically start with the white player.
❑ *Reset timer—R*
   The R key restarts the timer. When you have finished your move, restart the timer. Because of lag time that can be experienced with the system, the timer may not change to the other player immediately. Just be patient—it will change.
   If the timer expires, the opposite player must press a key to make the message display. The timer will automatically start for the other player.

NULL MODEM—X and Z

You may have occasion to play MATE with two computers in the same room. Connect the two computers with a NULL MODEM cable. The cable must have pins 2 and 3 interchanged and at least one of the ground pins connected straight through.

To activate the cable connection instead of the modem, one player presses the X key and the other presses the Z key. (Do not use the D and A sequence—those are for dialing and answering with the modem.) The connection will proceed the same way as a modem connection.

RENDG3D.EXE

The RENDG3D.EXE program is an example of using the Global 3D Controller in a REND386 program. RENDG3D.EXE uses the same command line switches as GDCMATE.EXE. To execute the program using the Global 3D controller in COM1, type rendg3d −1 and press RETURN. Substitute the appropriate command-line switch for the other COM ports.

CYBERMAN.C

This source code tells you how to communicate with the Logitech CyberMan through the mouse driver.

G3DCNT.C, G3DCNT.H

This source code tells you how to communicate with the Global 3D Controller.

SERIAL.C, SERIAL.H

This source code is public-domain serial port code that is used in the Global 3D Controller examples.

Chapter 5

G3DMATE.EXE

A complete description of this program is given under Chapter 4 programs.

FORCEFD1.BAT

The FORCEFD1.BAT program executes a force feedback program that simulates feedback from a virtual environment. The program requires a mouse be connected to the computer. To execute the program, type `forcefd1` and press RETURN. The program will clear the screen and present you a virtual floor with a red cube and a blue cube on it.

The object of this virtual world is to demonstrate the idea of visual feedback using a virtual hand. When the virtual hand gets within a certain distance of the cubes, the back of the virtual hand will turn blue. This is a tactile feedback indicator.

The movements of the mouse control the virtual hand in the following manner:

❑ *Mouse movement left and right = virtual hand movement left and right*
❑ *Mouse movement up and down = virtual hand movement forward and backward*
❑ *Mouse movement up and down with right button pressed = virtual hand movement up and down*

The left mouse button controls the gripping of the virtual hand.

FORCEFD3.BAT

The program FORCEFD3.BAT is a second program for demonstrating the concept of feedback. The program expects to find a mouse attached to your computer. To execute the program, type `forcefd3` and press RETURN.

You will be presented with the same virtual floor and cubes as above. The mouse and virtual hand work just the same. However, the weight of the cubes is different.

Move the virtual hand to the red cube, press and hold the left button when the back of the hand turns blue, and move the mouse up and down. Notice that the cube and virtual hand move freely. Now drop the red cube by releasing the left mouse button, move the virtual hand to the blue cube, press and hold the left button when the back of the hand turns blue, and move the mouse again. Notice how heavy the blue cube is.

This is an example of force feedback in a virtual environment using software.

Chapter 15

RB.EXE

The RB.EXE program is a virtual reality racquetball game that uses various pieces of equipment we have interfaced to the computer or built. The program requires one of three command-line switches that determine which interface device will be used to control the virtual hand in the program. The options are

–P = use Power Glove connected to parallel port
–M = use Mouse
–G = use Global 3D Controller

For example, if you are going to use your mouse to control the virtual hand, type `rb –M` and press RETURN. The system will look for your mouse.

Before we describe the game, recall the following:

❑ **When using the Power Glove, simply gripping and releasing your hand will cause the virtual hand to grip and release.**
❑ **When using the mouse, the left button controls the gripping and releasing.**
❑ **When using the Global 3D Controller, the ; key on the keyboard controls the gripping and releasing.**

The system will search for the glove and then present the game to you. Your first step is to grab the racquet. Using the keys detailed below, you move to the left and forward until the hand is even with the racquet's handle. Once this is achieved, grip the glove, and the racquet will be attached to your hand. As a helpful indicator, the distance number at the top of the screen will be between 0 and 350 when you are close to the handle.

Once you have the racquet, the number at the top will be the distance indicator between the middle of the racquet's net and the ball. The first thing you should do is press the Y key to turn your body to the right and then use the arrows to turn your head to the right until you see your hand. Position your view so you can see your hand and as much of the court as possible. There are two ways to hit the ball. The first is to hit the ball with the front of your racquet, which will cause the ball to speed toward the front of the court. The second way is to hit the ball with the back of your racquet, which will cause the ball to speed to the back of the court. The ball will gradually slow down in each case.

The easiest way to use the game is to set up the glove to the right of your computer and then face the monitor. This way, you can move your body with the keys and the glove at the same time. It takes some getting used to, but after a while you can run around the court pretty easily.

The action keys are

L,l—move body to the left
R,r—move body to the right
F,f—move body forward
B,b—move body backward
Y,y—turn 90° to the right
RIGHT arrow—turn head to the right
LEFT arrow—turn head to the left
UP arrow—tilt head up
DOWN arrow—tilt head down

Chapter 16

PARK.EXE

The PARK.EXE program is a simple virtual reality world that allows you to experiment with 3-D viewing. The program allows the following command-line switches:

−S = use shutter glasses
−1 = shutter glasses interface is attached to COM1
−2 = shutter glasses interface is attached to COM2
−G = use Global 3D controller on COM1
−I = use Global 3D controller on COM2
−H = use VictorMaxx StuntMaster HMD

To use the program with the shutter glasses on COM1, type `park −S −1` and press RETURN.

Keyboard Controls

The keyboard in the PARK program controls the viewpoint of the user. You can change your viewpoint by simply pressing a key. The keys defined in the program are

f—your viewpoint moves forward
b—your viewpoint moves backward
l—your viewpoint moves to the left
r—your viewpoint moves to the right
UP arrow—your viewpoint pitches (looks) up
DOWN arrow—your viewpoint pitches (looks) down
LEFT arrow—your viewpoint yaws (looks) left
RIGHT arrow—your viewpoint yaws (looks) right
q—you exit the program

Joystick Controls

The joystick is used to move your viewpoint just like the keyboard, except that it is more natural—moving the joystick to the left, right, up, or down will move your viewpoint in that direction. To perform the pitching and yawing, press the button on top of the joystick and move forward and backward to pitch your viewpoint and move the joystick left and right to yaw left and right.

Global 3D Controller Controls

The Global 3D Controller is by far the most natural way to move in the park. You can move your viewpoint forward, backward, left, and right just as you would use a normal joystick. You yaw your viewpoint by twisting the Controller's control ball left and right. You pitch your viewpoint by twisting the Controller's control ball forward and backward. You can also move your viewpoint up and down by pushing or pulling on the control ball.

Chapter 17

SHOOT.EXE

The SHOOT.EXE program is a single-user shoot-em'-up game that pits you against a computer-controlled robot. The program allows for a number of command-line switches, such as

> *−H = use VictorMaxx StuntMaster HMD*

To use the program with the shutter glasses on COM1, type `shoot −S −1` and press RETURN.

Keyboard Controls

The keyboard in the SHOOT program controls the viewpoint of the user. You can change your viewpoint of the virtual world by simply pressing a key. The keys defined in the program are

> *f—your viewpoint moves forward*
> *l—your viewpoint moves to the left*
> *r—your viewpoint moves to the right*
> *SPACE bar—a bullet is fired straight ahead of you*
> *q—you exit the program*

Joystick Controls

The joystick is used to move your viewpoint just like the keyboard, except that it is more natural. Moving the joystick to the left, right, and up moves your viewpoint in that direction. To fire your gun, press the button on top of the joystick.

This game contains a number of obstacles that you can hide behind. Occasionally, you will find that you cannot get around an obstacle once you have gotten to it. The trick to getting around the object is to move your viewpoint left or right until the object is out of your view and then move forward. Because you cannot move backward, this is the only way to get away from an obstacle.

ATTACK.EXE

As a special bonus, we have included a complete modem-to-modem shared virtual reality game called Virtual Attack that you can play against a friend. The game can be found in the /attack directory once the enclosed disk is installed on your hard drive. The world file, its associated PLG object file, and the collision detection code for this game were developed by Todd Porter. Many thanks to him for allowing me to use it.

Virtual Attack is a two-level shoot-'em-up game. The first level has a large playing field and four automatic slides that take you to each of the four second-level platforms. The object of the game is to shoot your opponent.

To play the game, you will need an IBM 80386 (or higher) computer, a modem, a telephone line, and an opponent with the same set-up. To begin, follow these steps:

1. *Execute the game by typing* ATTACK *and pressing RETURN. The game will load in some necessary files and present you with a dialing message box. The program normally relies on use of the keyboard and the joystick. If you want to use the Global 3D controller, start the game with the command* ATTACK −G *followed by RETURN. If you want to use the CyberMan, start the game with the command* ATTACK−C *followed by RETURN.*
2. *Enter the comm port that your modem is connected to.*
3. *Press M if you are using a modem, or N if you are using a null modem.*
4. *When you begin, you will be in practice mode.*
5. *To connect with your opponent over a null modem, one of you should press X, and the other should press Y. Go to step 8.*
6. *To connect with your opponent over a modem, press D to dial, and then enter your opponent's phone number.*

7. *Once your opponent's phone starts ringing, he or she should press the letter A on their keyboard to answer the call.*
8. *After the modem has established a connection, the computer systems will transfer a little information and then its time to start playing.*

Play

Playing Virtual Attack is very simple. You have the ability to move your body in all directions and to fire a gun. The movements are controlled differently for each of the input devices used. If you are using the keyboard, follow this guide:

LEFT arrow—yaw Left
RIGHT arrow—yaw Right
UP arrow—move forward
LEFT SHIFT LEFT arrow—move left
LEFT SHIFT RIGHT arrow—move right
LEFT SHIFT UP arrow—pitch up
LEFT SHIFT DOWN arrow—pitch down
SPACEBAR—fire gun
M—send message to your opponent
H—help

You gun will fire in the direction that you are looking. If you pitch up or down, the gun will fire its bullet according to the degree of pitch.

If you are using the joystick, your forward, backward, left yaw, and right yaw movements are all controlled by its position. The gun is fired by pressing the button on top of the joystick. Movements to the left or right are controlled by pressing one of the buttons on the base of the joystick and then moving it left or right. You can pitch your view up or down by pressing one of the buttons on the base of the joystick and moving it up or down.

If you are using the Global 3D Controller, your movements are directly controlled by the movement of the controller itself. Because the controller does not have a button for firing the gun, we will use the SPACEBAR as the fire button.

If you are using the Logitech CyberMan, your movements are also directly controlled by the movement of the controller itself. However, the CyberMan has three buttons on top of it, the left button is used to fire your gun.

Slides

When play begins, one person will be on the bottom level and the other person will be on one of the top-level platforms. In order to move between platforms, simply move forward toward one of them. When your movement puts you at the edge of any of the slides, the computer system will automatically raise or lower you to the appropriate level.

You don't need to worry about falling off any of the levels either, because the computer will automatically keep you within the playing field.

Quit

To quit the game, press Q on the keyboard, followed by Y. The system will automatically hang up your modem.

Appendix B

VR Companies

Adams Consulting Group
Consultants in virtual reality
3952 Western Ave.
Western Springs, IL 60558
(708) 246–0766

Advanced Gravis
*Developer of PC input devices and 3-D
    sound cards*
101–3750 North Fraser Way
Burnaby, B.C.
CANADA V5J 5E9
(604) 431–5020
(604) 431–5155 (fax)

Alternate Worlds Technology
Arcade developers
6900 Greenmere Boulevard
Prospect, KY 40059
(502) 495–7186
(502) 423–8318 (fax)

Ascension Technology Corp.
Magnetic trackers
PO Box 527
Burlington, VT 05402
(802) 655–7879

Autodesk, Inc.
Developers of 3-D graphics tools
2320 Marinship Way
Sausalito, CA 94965
(415) 332–2344

Avatar Partners
Developers of virtual reality applications
16050 Kings Creek Road
Boulder Creek, CA 95006
(408) 338–6294

Bio Control Systems, Inc.
Developers of biofeedback-type devices
430 Cowper Street
Palo Alto, CA 94301
(415) 355–9195
(415) 329–8494 (fax)

Boffin Limited
Source for NTSC converters
2500 West County Road 42 * #5
Burnsville, MN 55337
(612) 894–0595
(612) 894–6175 (fax)

Cerebel Information Arts
Publisher of a catalog for VR products
675 Massachusetts Ave.
Cambridge, MA 02139
(617) 576–6700

Clarity
Auditory interfaces
Nelson Lane
Garrison, NY 10524
(914) 424–4071

Covox, Inc.
Developers of sound products
675 Conger St.
Eugene, OR 97402
(503) 342–1271
(503) 342–1283 (fax)

Crystal River Engineering
*Developers of advanced 3-D sound
  products*
12350 Wards Ferry Rd.
Groveland, CA 95321
(209) 962–6382
(209) 962–4873 (fax)

CyberEvent Group, Inc.
Hosts VR events
355 Degraw St.
Brooklyn, NY 11231
(718) 802–9415
(718) 802–9415 (fax)

CyberNet
Force feedback devices
1919 Green Rd.
Ann Arbor, MI 48105
(313) 668–2567
(313) 668–8780 (fax)

Dean Friedman Productions, Inc.
Video virtual reality
33 Dirubbo Drive
Peekskill, NY 10566
(914) 736–3600
(914) 739–2986 (fax)

Digital Image Design, Inc.
Developers of input devices
170 Claremont Avenue
New York, NY 10027
(212) 222–5236
(212) 864–1189 (fax)

Digital Media Group
111 Fourth Ave.
New York, NY 10003
(212) 388–0122

Dimension International
*Developers of superscape rendering
  software*
Zephyr One, Calleva Park
Aldermaston, Berkshire, ENGLAND
RG7 4Q2
+44(0) 734–810077
+44(0) 734–816940 (fax)

Division, Ltd.
Developers of VR hardware and software
Quarry Rd.
Chipping, Sodbury
Bristol, ENGLAND BS17 6AX
(44) 454–324527
(44) 454–323059 (fax)

Domark Software, Inc.
Developers of virtual reality studio software
1900 S. Norfolk St, #202
San Mateo, CA 94403
(415) 513–8929
(415) 571–0437 (fax)

Evans & Sutherland
*Developers of high-performance graphics
  machines*
600 Komas Dr.
PO Box 59700
Salt Lake City, UT 84108
(801) 582–5847
(801) 582–5848 (fax)

Fake Space Labs
*Developers of head-mounted displays and
  the Boom head tracker*
935 Hamilton Ave.
Menlo Park, CA 94025
(415) 688–1940
(415) 688–1949 (fax)

Flogiston Corp.
Developers of VR equipment
462 Cape Hill
Webster, TX 77598
(713) 280–8554

Focal Point
Developers of 3-D sound products
1402 Pine Avenue, Suite 127
Niagara Falls, NY 14301
(716) 285–3930

Global Devices
Developers of input devices
6630 Arabian Circle
Granite Bay, CA 95746
(916) 791–3533

Horizon Entertainment, Inc.
Supplier of VR arcade systems
501 North Broadway
St. Louis, MO 63102
(314) 331–6049

ISCAN, Inc.
Developers of head-mounted displays
125 Cambridgepark Drive
Cambridge, MA 02140
(617) 868–5353
(617) 868–9231 (fax)

Leep Systems, Inc.
Developers of head-mounted displays
241 Crescent Street
Waltham, MA 02154
(617) 647–1395
(617) 899–9602 (fax)

Lefton Graphics Systems
Developers of PC-based rendering software
2118 Central SE, Suite 45
Albuquerque, NM 87106
(505) 843–6719
(505) 843–9394 (fax)

Lightscape Graphics Software, Ltd.
Developers of visualization software
2 Berkeley Street, Suite 600
Toronto, Ontario
CANADA M5A 2W3
(416) 862–2628
(416) 862–5508 (fax)

Liquid Image Corporation
Developers of head-mounted displays
582 King Edward Street
Winnipeg, Manitoba
CANADA R3H 0P1
(204) 772–0137
(204) 772–0239 (fax)

Logitech
Developers of PC hardware, 3-D mice, and CyberMan
6505 Kaiser Drive
Fremont, CA 94555
(510) 795–8500
(510) 792–8901 (fax)

Meckler
Publishers of various VR information and conferences
11 Ferry Lane West
Westport, CT 06880
(203) 226–6967
(203) 454–5840 (fax)

MicronGreen, Inc.
Developers of 3-D modeling software
1240 N.W. 21st Ave.
Gainesville, FL 32609
(904) 376–1529
(904) 376–0466 (fax)

Networked Virtual Art Museum
Studio for Creative Inquiry
Carnegie-Mellon University
Pittsburgh, PA 15213
(412) 268–3452

n-Vision, Inc.
Developers of head-mounted displays
800 Follin Lane, Suite 270
Vienna, VA 22180
(703) 242–0030
(703) 242–5220 (fax)

Pixsys
Developers of an optical tracking system
5680 B Central Ave.
Boulder, CO 80301
(303) 447–0248

Polhemus Laboratories, Inc.
Developers of head tracking systems
PO Box 5
Cambridge, VT 05444
(802) 644–5569
(802) 644–2943 (fax)

Reflection Technology
Developers of Private Eye
240 Bear Hill Road
Waltham, MA 02154
(617) 890–5905
(617) 890–5918 (fax)

RPI Advanced Technology Group
Developers of VR hardware and software
PO Box 14607
San Francisco, CA 94114
(415) 777–3226

SAI
27107 Richmond Hill Rd.
Conifer, CO 80433
(303) 838–6346

Sarcos
Developers of feedback devices
261 East 300 South, Suite 150
Salt Lake City, UT 84111
(801) 531–0559
(801) 531–0315 (fax)

Sense8 Corporation
Developers of VR rendering software
4000 Bridgeway, #101
Sausalito, CA 94965
(415) 331–6318
(415) 331–9148 (fax)

Shooting Star Technology
Developers of arm-based head trackers
1921 Holdom Ave.
Burnaby, B.C.
CANADA V5B 3W4
(604) 298–8574
(604) 298–8580 (fax)

Silicon Graphics, Inc.
*Developers of high-performance graphics
    machines*
2011 North Shoreline Blvd.
Mountain View, CA 94039
(415) 960–1980

SimGraphics Engineering Corporation
*Custom designers of graphics-based
    applications*
1137 Huntington Drive
South Pasadena, CA 91030
(213) 255–0900
(213) 255–0987 (fax)

Simsalabim Systems
Developers of 3-D viewer
PO Box 4446
Berkeley, CA 94704–0446

Software Systems
Developers of modeling tools
1884 The Alameda
San Jose, CA 95126
(408) 243–4326

SophisTech Research
Developer of sourcebooks
6936 Seaborn Street
Lakewood, CA 90713–2832
(310) 421–7295
(310) 425–0890 (fax)

Spaceball Technologies, Inc.
Developers of input devices
600 Suffolk St.
Lowell, MA 01854
(508) 970–0330

Spectrum Dynamics
Supplier of VR hardware and software
2016 Main Street, Suite 1207
Houston, TX 77002–8843
(713) 752–0761
(713) 658–3889 (fax)

Stereographics Corporation
Developers of 3-D systems
2171–H East Francisco Blvd.
San Rafael, CA 94901
(415) 459–4500
(415) 459–3020 (fax)

Straylight
Developers of VR rendering software
150 Mount Bethel Road
Warren, NJ 07059
(908) 580–0086
(908) 580–0092 (fax)

3DTV Corporation
Supplier and developer of 3-D systems
PO Box Q
San Rafael, CA 94913–4316
(415) 479–3516
(415) 479–3316 (fax)

Viewpoint
Developers of 3-D datasets
870 West Center
Orem, Utah 84057
(800) 328–2738
(801) 224–2272 (fax)

Virtual Images, Inc.
Developers of VR arcade systems
4356 Langport Rd.
Columbus, OH 43220
(614) 459–1232
(614) 459–1232 (fax)

Virtual Reality, Inc.
Developers of head-mounted displays
486 Washington Ave.
Pleasantville, NY 10570
(914) 769–0900
(914) 769–7106 (fax)

Virtual Reality Laboratories, Inc.
Developers of visualization software
2341 Ganador Court
San Luis Obispo, CA 93401
(805) 545–8515
(805) 781–2259 (fax)

**Virtual Reality Special Interest Group
  (VR SIG)**
Los Angeles Chapter
Virtual Ventures
1300 The Strand, Suite A
Manhattan Beach, CA 90266
(310) 545–0369

**Virtual Reality Special Interest Group
  (VR SIG)**
Louisville Chapter
PO Box 43003
Louisville, KY 40253
(502) 495–7186

Virtual Reality Special Interest Group (VR SIG)
Chicago Chapter
3952 Western Ave.
Western Springs, IL 60558
(708) 246–0766

Virtual Research
Developers of head-mounted displays
1313 Socorro Ave.
Sunnyvale, CA 94089
(408) 739–7114

Virtual Scene Systems
Developers of image-processing tools
18 Waterhouse Road
Bourne, MA 02532
(508) 759–2459
(508) 759–2257 (fax)

Virtual Southwest Realities, Inc.
Suppliers of VR hardware and software
2920 E. Northern, Suite 104
Phoenix, AZ 85028
(602) 971–9299
(602) 971–8232 (fax)

Virtual Technologies
Developers of glove input devices
PO Box 5984
Stanford, CA 94309
(415) 321–4900
(415) 321–4912 (fax)

Virtus Corp
Developers of walkthrough software for Macintosh
117 Edinburgh St., Suite 204
Cary, NC 27511
(919) 467–9700
(919) 460–4530 (fax)

The Vivid Group
Developers of video gesture systems
317 Adelaide Street West, Studio 302
Toronto, Ontario
CANADA M5V 1P9
(416) 340–9290
(416) 348–9809 (fax)

VREAM Inc.
Developers of VR rendering software
2568 N. Clark St, #250
Chicago, IL 60614
(312) 477–0425

VRex, Inc.
Developers of 3-D overhead projectors
8 Skyline Drive
Hawthorne, NY 10532
914–345–8877
914–345–9558 (fax)

VRontier Worlds of Stoughton, Inc.
Developers of VR hardware and software
809 E. South St.
Stoughton, WI 53589
(608) 873–8523
(608) 877–0575 (fax)

W Industries Limited
Developers of VR arcade systems
Virtuality House
3 Oswin Rd
Brailsford Industrial Park
Leicester
ENGLAND LE3 1HR
(0533) 542–127
(0533) 548–222 (fax)

Worldesign
Consultants in VR
128 NW 56th Street
Seattle, WA 98107–2023
(206) 782–8630

Xtensory, Inc
Developers of feedback systems
140 Sunridge Dr.
Scotts Valley, CA 95066
(408) 439–0600
(408) 439–9709 (fax)

XYTRON Ltd.
Developers of CRT displays
13010 San Fernando Rd.
Sylmar, CA 91342
(818) 362–8341
(818) 367–2970 (fax)

Appendix C

Other Sources of Information

Publications

Publication: *CyberEdge Journal*
Address: #1 Gate Six Road, Suite G
Sausalito, CA 94965
(415) 331–3343
(415) 331–3643 (fax)

Publication: *PCVR Magazine*
Address: See Appendix E

Publication: *PixElation*
Address: VRASP
c/o Karin August
PO Box 4139
Highland Park, NJ
08904–4139

Publication: *Presence*
Address: MIT Press Journals
55 Hayward St.
Cambridge, MA 02142
(800) 356–0343
(617) 258–6779

Publication: *Modern Media*
Address: Magellan Marketing, Inc.
32969 Hamilton Courts,
Suite 215
Farmington Hills, MI 48334
(313) 488–0330

Publication: *Virtual Reality Report*
Address: Meckler Publishing
11 Ferry Lane
Westport, CT 06880
(203) 226–6967

Publication: *VR Monitor*
Address: Matrix Information Services
18560 Bungalow Drive
Lathrup Village, MI 48076
(313) 559–1526

Publication: *VR News—Virtual Reality Newsletter*
Address: PO Box 2515
London, N4 4JW
ENGLAND

Publication: *Virtual World Builder* (biannual catalog)
Address: Spectrum Dynamics
2 Greenway Plaza Ste. 640
Dallas, TX 77046–0203
(713) 520–5020

Publication: *Virtuoso* (bimonthly magazine)
Address: Spectrum Dynamics
2 Greenway Plaza, Suite 640
Dallas, TX 77046–0203
(713) 520–5020

On-Line Services

Service: AOL—America On-Line
Forum: VIRTUS
Contact: (800) 827–6364 (voice)

Service: BIX
Forum: join virtual.world
Contact: (800) 695–4882 (2400 data)

Service: Compuserve
Forum: GO CYBERFORUM

Service: Diaspar Virtual Reality
    Network
Forum: various
    (714) 831–1776 (voice)
    (714) 376–1200 (2400 data)
    (714) 376–1234 (14.4k data)
    telnet: diaspar.com
    (192.215.11.1)
    Sign on as DIASPAR

Service: The WELL
Forum: GO VR
Contact: (415) 332–4335 (voice)
    (415) 332–6106 (data)
    telnet: well.sf.ca.us
    Sign on as NEWUSER

BBS

BBS: Amulet BBS
Data: (310) 453–7705

BBS: SENSE/NET
Data: (801) 364–6227

BBS: Toronto VR SIG
Data: (416) 631–6625

BBS: *PCVR Magazine Support
BBS*
Data: (608) 877–1017

Internet FTP Sites

Site: avalon.chinalake. navy.mil
Address: 129.131.31.11
Directories: /pub

Site: cogsci.uwo.ca
Address: 129.100.6.10
Directories: /pub/vr

Site: cs.unc.edu
Address: 152.2.128.159
Directories: /pub/virtus
    /pub/hmd

Site: ftp.apple.com
Address: (130.43.2.3)
Directories: /pub/vr

Site: ftp.ipa.fhg.de
Address: 129.233.17.68
Directories: /pub/VIRTUAL-REALITY

Site: ftp.ncsa.uiuc.edu
Address: 141.142.20.50
Directories: /vr

Site: ftp.u.washington.edu
Address: 140.142.56.1
Directories: /public/virtual-worlds

Site: karazm.math.uh.edu
Address: 129.7.128.1
Directories: /pub

Site: sunee.uwaterloo.ca
Address: 129.97.50.50
Directories: /pub/vr
    /pub/rend386
    /pub/.. - various directories

Site: sunsite.unc.edu

Address: 152.2.22.81
Directories: /pub/academic/computer-
                science/virtual-reality

Site: taurus.cs.nps.navy.mil
Address: 131.120.1.13
Directories: /pub/ascension_bird

Site: wuarchive.wustl.edu
Address: 128.252.135.4
Directories: /graphics

Internet USENET Groups

Newsgroup: sci.virtual-worlds
Newsgroup: sci.virtual-world.apps
Newsgroup: alt.cyberpunk
Newsgroup: alt.cyberspace
Newsgroup: alt.3d

Electronic Mailing Lists

List: Glove-list
Contact: send email to
                listserv@boxer.nas.nasa.gob
Message: subscribe glove-list <your
                full email address>
Post: send message to glove-
                list@boxer.nas.nasa.gov

List: Head Tracking
Contact: send email to trackers-
                request@gucis.queensu.ca
Message: Informal request for activa-
                tion
Post: send message to
                trackers@gucis.queensu.ca

List: REND386
Contact: send email to rend386-
                request@sunee.uwaterloo.ca

List: sci.virtual-worlds
Contact: send email to
                listserv@uiucvmd.bitnet
Message: subscribe virtu-l <Your full
                email address>
Post: send message to
                scivw@stein.u.washington.
                edu

List: sci.virtual-worlds.apps
Contact: send mail to
                listserv@uiucvmd.bitnet
Message: subscribe vrapp-l <Your full
                email address>

Electronics Sources

All Electronics Corp.
Electronic parts
PO Box 567
Van Nuys, CA 91408
(800) 826–5432
(818) 781–2653 (fax)

Allied Electronics
Electronic parts
7410 Pebble Drive
Fort Worth, TX 76118
(800) 433–4700

American Design Components
Parts and computer systems
400 County Avenue
Secaucus, NJ 07094
(800) 776–3700
(201) 601–8990 (fax)

AMP Incorporated
Pziedo film distributor
PO Box 799
Valley Forge, PA 19482–0799

Circuit Cellar Ink
Best magazine for experimenters
4 Park St.
Vernon, CT 06066
(203) 875–2199
(203) 872–2204 (fax)

COMB
Liquidator
720 Anderson Ave
St. Cloud, MN 56395
(800) 328–0609

Damark
Liquidator
7101 Winnetka Ave. N.
PO Box 29900
Minneapolis, MN 55429–0900
(800) 729–9000

Digi-Key Corp.
Electronic parts
701 Brooks Ave. South
PO Box 677
Thief River Falls, MN 56701–0677
(800) 344–4539
(218) 681–3380 (fax)

Easy Tech, Inc.
Electronic parts
2917 Bayview Drive
Fremont, CA 94538
(800) 582–4044
(800) 582–1255 (fax)

Edmund Scientific
Optics and other technical supplies
101 East Gloucester Pike
Barrington, NJ 08007–1380
(609) 573–6260
(609) 573–6293 (fax)

Electronic Goldmine
Electronic parts
PO Box 5408
Scottsdale, AZ 85261
(602) 451–7454
(602) 451–9495 (fax)

Grayhill, Inc.
Switches, relays
561 Hillgrove Ave.
PO Box 10373
La Grange, IL 60525–0373
(708) 354-1040
(708) 354-2820 (fax)

Jameco
Electronic parts and computers
1355 Shoreway Road
Belmont, CA 94002
(800) 831–4242
(800) 237–6948 (fax)

JDR Microdevices
Electronic parts and computers
2233 Samaritan Drive
San Jose, CA 95124
(800) 535–5000

Marlin P. Jones & Associates
Electronic parts
PO Box 12685
Lake Park, FL 33403–0685
(407) 848–8236
(407) 844–8764 (fax)

Mouser Electronics
Electronic parts
PO Box 699
Mansfield, TX 76063–0699
(800) 346–6873

Newark
Electronic parts
4801 N. Ravenswood Ave.
Chicago, Il 60640–4496
(312) 784–5100
(312) 784–5100, ext. 3107 (fax)

Parts Express, Inc.
Electronic parts
340 E. First St.
Dayton, OH 45402–1257
(513) 222–0173
(513) 222–4644 (fax)

R&D Electronics
Electronic parts
1224 Prospect Ave.
Cleveland, OH 44115
(216) 621–1211
(216) 621–8628 (fax)

Unicorn Electronics
Electronic parts
10010 Canoga Ave., Unit B-8
Chatsword, CA 91311
(800) 824–3432
(800) 998–7975 (fax)

Appendix E

PCVR Magazine

For those wanting to keep on the cutting edge of this state-of-the-art technology, there is no better resource than *PCVR Magazine*, a new virtual reality publication that introduces high-tech virtual reality equipment, theories, and software to the layperson by simplifying procedures, languages, and materials. Up until now, the equipment for virtual reality systems usually costs over $25,000 which pretty much limited exploration of this field to universities and businesses. *PCVR Magazine* changes this situation by bringing the technology into your home. By following step-by-step instructions, a complete virtual reality system can be built for under $3,000—including the personal computer required to execute the system.

For $26 a year, subscribers receive six issues that contain editorials, thought-provoking columns, hardware/software topics, tutorials, and do-it-yourself projects.

The hardware projects have covered connecting the Sega 3-D glasses and Mattel Power Glove to an IBM personal computer, building a head-mounted display, and constructing a head-tracker device. These hands-on projects use off-the-shelf components, which enables nontechnical people to have access to virtual reality equipment in their own homes.

The tutorials explain the major technical areas of virtual reality without the jargon usually associated with industry journals.

PCVR Magazine intends to bring virtual reality out of science laboratories and into the general computer community.

Subscription information (six issues):
$26.00 U.S./Canada
$38.00 overseas

Back Issues—all are available:
$4.50 U.S./Canada
$6.50 overseas

Payment: Check or money order drawn on U.S. bank in U.S. dollars. Visa, Mastercard, and American Express also accepted.

PCVR Magazine can be contacted at
PO Box 475
Stoughton, WI 53589
Phone/Fax: (608)877-0909
EMAIL: PCVR@FULLFEED.COM

Issue 1—Power Glove Interface. Interfacing the Power Glove to the IBM PC—Creating a Virtual Hand using Borland C 2.0—Graphics Source Code and Packages

Issue 2—Power Glove Software. Creating a Better Virtual Hand—A Virtual Handshake—A PCVR Board—Graphics—Basics

Issue 3—Head-Mounted Display and 3-D Glasses. Interfacing the Sega Glasses to the PC—Building a Head-Mounted Display—Basics—REND386 and the Sega Glasses—A 3-D Pointing Package for REND386 and the

Power Glove—A PLG/FIG Virtual Hand—Graphics—Basics—Games

Issue 4—REND386 Version 3.0 Renderering Software. The Power of REND386—REND386 Program Skeleton—Compiling with REND386—Creating Objects in REND386—REND386 and Figures—REND386 Sega/Power Glove Interfaces—Building a Head-Mounted Display, Part 2—Graphics

Issue 5—Head Tracking. Survey of Available Head-Tracking Technology—Building a Boom Head Tracker for $10.00—Virtual Imagination—Building a Head-Mounted Display, Part 3—Graphics—Working with REND386

Issue 6—3-D Sound. Theory of 3-D Sound—Current 3-D Sound Products—3-D Sound System—The Power Glove Serial Interface: Touching the Future—REND386 Skeleton Program—Graphics—Working with REND386—Software Library—My Virtual Playground

Issue 7—VR Motion. Interfacing a Motion Device—A Demo World for Motion—Using a Treadmill for Motion—Using a Joystick for Motion—Visual Perception of Spatial Information—A C++ Power Glove Driver—Graphics—Working with REND386—My Virtual Playground

Issue 8—PCVR Renderer. The PCVR Renderer—Building the PCVR Renderer—PCVR Renderer Objects—Visual Perception of Spatial Information, Part 2—VR Insider—Graphics—Working with REND386—My Virtual Playground

Issue 9—Build an HMD for $450.00. Build a Virtual Reality Headset Yourself—Personal Virtual Reality Video Controller—Lenses and Mirrors and HOEs, Oh My—VR Insider—Working with the PCVR

Renderer—Graphics—Working with REND386—My Virtual Playground

Issue 10—Voice Recognition. Adding Voice Recognition to REND386—Covox Voice Recognition Software—Visual Perception of Spatial Information, Part 3—Debugging Virtual Worlds with REND386—Lepton Virtual Reality Toolkit—Book Review—VR Insider—Working with REND386—My Virtual Playground

Issue 11—Connectivity. Adding Serial Access to REND386—Building Cyberspace—Cyberterm: A Terminal into Cyberspace—Terrain Mapping with REND386—What's New—Book Review—Software Review—VR Insider—Graphics—Working With REND386—Conference Report—In the Industry—My Virtual Playground

Issue 12—Input Devices. Rebuilding the Power Glove—Interfacing the Global 3D Controller—Interfacing the Logitech CyberMan—What Are Strain Gages?—Survey of Input Devices—Cyberterm, Part 2—Terrain Mapping—Book Review—Product Review—VR Insider—Virtual Tele-News—Making REND Work—In the Industry—My Virtual Playground

Future Issues:

Issue 13—Head Tracking

Issue 14—Feedback

Issue 15—Arcade Systems

Issue 16—Glove Technology

Issue 17—Applications

Issue 18—3-D Sound

Issue 19—Head-Mounted Displays

Issue 20—VR Operating Systems

Appendix F

Building Circuits

For those new to building their own electronic circuits, I would like to touch on a couple of points in general and then look at each of the projects outlined in the book specifically.

Solder or Wirewrap?

Determining whether to solder the circuits or to use wirewrap is a personal decision. In some cases, as we will see later, you will want to use both. I find that I can wirewrap a project much more quickly and cleanly because I don't have much practice soldering. Also, by wire-wrapping you don't have to worry about heating an electronic part to the point that it becomes damaged. For the beginner, I would recommend wirewrapping for the simple reason that you can undo the connection in the event that something doesn't work correctly the first time around. Once the circuit is built and functions as it should, you can always go back and solder the connections in place.

Tools

All of the tools that you will need for the projects in this book can be purchased at your local Radio Shack. The following list includes the tools' Radio Shack part numbers.

Soldering
15-watt pencil soldering iron—64-2051—
$7.49
.062" size solder—0.5 oz—64-001—$0.99

Wirewrapping:
Wirewrapping tool—276-1570—$6.95
Wirewrapping wire—276-501—$2.39 (This wire comes in three different colors. Any color will do.)

Parts

A good number of the parts used in the projects can be found at Radio Shack as well. However, some of the parts, such as the intergrated circuits, are not off-the-shelf items. I would recommend that you purchase them from one of the electronics companies listed in Appendix D. Digi-Key is especially good, and their prices are better than Radio Shack's.

The projects should be built on a breadboard, which is a board with holes in it that allow the components to be placed. You can purchase them at either Radio Shack or another source.

Tips for Soldering

As I mentioned before, I am not an expert solderer, but I have learned several things that I will pass on to newcomers:

Always use a socket for integrated circuits. You do not want to solder directly to the chip if you have not soldered before. In addition, using a socket makes it easy to replace the chip if something goes wrong.

Always solder your power and ground points. This helps to prevent short circuits.

If your circuits work correctly, come back and solder the wirewrapped connections to ensure that they do not loosen.

Tips for Wirewrapping

Wirewrapping can be a simple process if you use patience.

Try to let the wirewrapping tool do the job of wrapping the wire on the component. Don't force the wrapping, or the wire may break.

For faster wrapping, cut several lengths of wire before beginning a project.

Avoid wirewrapping a connection that will be under tension, such as a cord that will be pulled.

Chapter 2

In Chapter 2, we build the PC cable for the Power Glove as well as a power source. I would recommend soldering the connections between the DB-25 and the Nintendo cable. The entire connection can be placed into the hood of the DB-25, thus eliminating the need for an interface box.

Be sure to solder all of the connections so that they form a strong bond, because the connections will be under some tension.

Chapter 6

In Chapter 6, we build the shutter glasses interface. This project should be wirewrapped on a breadboard. The entire interface can be put into a 2" × 3" prototype box, available from Radio Shack. Avoid the boxes made from metal because you run the risk of your circuit touching the box and causing a possible short.

Be careful when locating the connection points on the stereo jack. Use a multimeter to determine which connecting point goes with the appropriate tip, middle, and ground points.

Chapter 7

In Chapter 7, we build the interface for the VictorMaxx StuntMaster. This interface consists of a cable with several different plugs and jacks attached to it. Use a multiwire cable available from Digi-Key to keep the costs down.

Chapter 8

In Chapter 8, we build the head-mounted display. This project requires more woodworking than electronic work.

Chapter 10

In Chapter 10, we build the 3-D sound system. As mentioned in the chapter, this project should be built on a PC XT prototyping board, available from Radio Shack. The board is not inexpensive, costing $27.95, but it makes for easy interfacing to the PC.

Chapter 12

In Chapter 12, we build the arm-based head tracker. This project uses the same interface as the 3-D sound system. You should have enough room on the prototype card to add this project as well. On the other end of the tracker, make sure that the connection points on the potentiometer don't hit each other when the tracker is operational.

Chapter 16

In Chapter 16, we build the motion detectors. The most important thing here is to build the interfaces so that they will fit inside two small boxes. Use wirewrapping and the 2" × 3" boxes.

Glossary

Accommodation—Change in the focal length of the eye.

Ambient light—A nondirectional light applied to a world so that it appears to be equally bright everywhere.

Artificial reality—Term introduced by arts and computer visualization scholar Myron Krueger in the mid-1970s to describe his computer-generated responsive environments based on a nonintrusive system that tracks people with pattern-recognition techniques and video cameras.

Augmented reality—A technique whereby a computer-generated image is projected onto glasses worn by the user; allows for computer data to be displayed on top of or over the real world.

Binaural—Sound that incorporates information about the human ears and head; stereophonic.

Boom—A type of tracking device that attaches to the user via mechanical arm.

Convergence—The point at which the left and right images are fused into a single image.

Convolvotron—A hardware system that uses the concept of convolving to create 3-D sound.

Cyberspace—A virtual environment shared by human users that is constructed from a group of computer networks.

Cyber sickness—Headaches or nausea caused by using a simulator or being immersed in a virtual environment.

DataGlove—A glove wired with sensors and connected to a computer system for gesture recognition.

DataSuit—A system like the DataGlove except that it is fitted for the entire body, not just the hand.

Depth cuing—The use of shading, texture, color, interposition, and many other visual characteristics to provide a cue for the z-coordinates, or distance, of an object.

Exoskeletal devices—Mechanical systems that attach to the outside of the body to perform some task such as force feedback.

Eyephone—A head-mounted display (HMD) designed by VPL.

Eye tracking—Determining where a user is looking.

Field of view—An angular measurement in degrees of the visual field.

Force feedback—The resistance created by an object being manipulated and transferred to the user via mechanical means.

Frustum of vision—The field of view where all objects in the environment are visible.

Gesture—A sign or signal or symbol usually made using the hand or gloved hand.

Goggles—Anther common term for head-mounted displays.

Haptic interfaces—Interfaces that provide a sense of both tactile and force feedback.

Head-mounted display (HMD)—A display system for presenting images to a user while blocking all other sources.

Head-related transfer function (HRTF)—A mathematical function that represents the characteristics of a sound that has reached the user's ears.

Head tracking—Determining where in three-dimensional space a user's head is located.

Heads up display (HUD)—A device that projects an image onto a space in our real world.

Immersion—A feeling of being within and able to manipulate an environment.

Interaural amplitude—The difference between the intensity of sound in your ears.

Interaural time—Differences between the arrival time of sound in your ears.

Internet—A worldwide digital network.

Lag—A delay created between an action and its detection.

Liquid Crystal Display (LCD)—Display devices that use bipolar films sandwiched between thin panes of glass.

Motion parallax—The apparent difference in degree of movement of objects at various points in space when the user's viewpoint is moved in the x-axis.

Motion platform—A controlled system that simulates movement in the real world.

Navigation—In virtual reality, this term refers to moving through virtual space without losing one's way.

Occlusion—The concealing or hiding from view of one object by another.

Perspective—The rules that determine the relative size of 2-D objects to give the impression of 3-D distance.

Pitch—Rotation about the x-axis (also referred to as *tilt*).

Portals—Locations in a virtual environment that serve as doorways to a different world.

Projected reality—A VR system that uses projection screens rather than head-mounted displays.

Real time—A system that does not have lag. Typically on the order to 30 frames per second.

Render—To convert a numeric representation of an object to a visual representation.

Roll—The rotation about the z-axis.

Shutter glasses—LCD screens or rotating shutters used to see stereoscopically.

6 DOF—Six degrees of freedom: Yaw, pitch, roll, up–down, left–right, forward–backward.

Stereopsis—Binocular vision of images with horizontal disparities.

Tactile feedback—Transmitting the texture of a virtual object to a user.

Texture mapping—Adding a bitmap to an object to give it added realism.

3-D sound—Sound that is filtered or convolved so that it appears to be originating from a specific location in space.

Tracker—A device that determines the position of objects in the real world and conveys this information to a computer for processing.

Viewpoint—The point of view of the user in the virtual world.

Virtual reality—An immersive, interactive simulation of realistic or imaginary environments (as defined by Jaron Lanier).

Virtual environments—Realistic simulations of interactive scenes.

Visualization—In VR, the use of computer graphics to make visible numeric or other quantifiable relationships.

Voxel—A cubic volume pixel for quantizing 3-D space.

Wireframe—The lines that make up the outline of an object.

Yaw—Rotation about the y-axis (also referred to as *pan*).

Bibliography

HMD

Chung, J.C. 1989. Exploring virtual worlds with head-mounted displays. *Three-Dimensional Visualization and Display Technologies:SPIE* 1083:42–52.

Howlett, Eric M. 1990. Wide angle orthostereo. *Stereoscopic Displays and Applications:SPIE* 1256:210–23.

Lipscomb, James S. 1989. Experience with stereoscopic display devices and output algorithms. *Three-Dimensional Visualization and Display Technologies:SPIE* 1083:28–33.

Martin , Stephen W., and Richard C. Hutchinson. 1989. Low-cost design alternatives for head-mounted stereoscopic displays. *Three-Dimensional Visualization and Display Technologies:SPIE* 1083:53–58.

Noble, Lowell. 1987. Use of lenses to enhance depth perception. *True 3D Imaging Techniques and Display Technologies:SPIE* 761:126–28.

Pausch, Randy, et al. 1991. A practical, low-cost stereo head-mounted display. *Stereoscopic Displays and Applications II:SPIE* 1457:198–207.

Rebo, Robert K. 1989. A helmet-mounted virtual environment display system. *Helmet-Mounted Displays:SPIE* 1116:80–84.

Robinett, Warren, and Jannick P. Rolland. 1991. A computational model for the stereoscopic optics of a head-mounted display. *Stereoscopic Displays and Applications II:SPIE* 1457:140–60.

Teitel, Michael A. 1990. The Eyephone, a head-mounted stereo display. *Stereoscopic Displays and Applications.:SPIE* 1256:168–71.

Head Trackers

Ferrin, Frank J. 1991. Survey of helmet tracking technologies. *Large-screen projection, avionic, and helmet-mounted displays:SPIE* 1456:86–94.

Mase, Kenji, et al. 1990. A realtime head motion detection system. *Sensing and Reconstruction of Three-Dimensional Objects and Scenes:SPIE* 1260:262–69.

Raab, Frederick H., et al. 1979. Magnetic position and orientation tracking system. *IEEE Transactions on Aerospace and Electronic Systems* AES-15, No 5:709–18.

Wang, Jih-fang, et al. 1990. Tracking a head-mounted display in a room-sized environment with head-mounted cameras. *Helmet-Mounted Displays II:SPIE* 1290:47–57.

Shutter Glasses and Stereo Programming

Baker, John. 1987. Generating images for a time-multiplexed stereoscopic computer graphics system. *True 3D Imaging Techniques and Display Technologies: SPIE* 761:44–52.

Clapp, Robert E. 1987. Stereoscopic perception. *True 3D Imaging Techniques and Display Technologies:SPIE* 761:79–82.

Hodges, Larry F. 1991. Basic principles of stereoscopic software development. *Stereoscopic Displays and Applications II: SPIE* 1457:9–17.

———. 1992. Tutorial: Time-multiplexed stereoscopic computer graphics. *IEEE Computer Graphics and Applications*. 3:20–30.

Hodges, Larry F., and David F. McAllister. 1985. Stereo and alternating-pair techniques for display of computer-generated images. *IEEE Computer Graphics and Applications* 9:38–45.

Lipton, Lenny. *Programmer's guide: the creation of software for stereoscopic computer graphics*. Stereographics Corporation.

McAllister, David F. 1992. On minimizing absolute parallax in a stereo image. *Stereoscopic Displays and Applications III:SPIE* 1669:20–29.

Basic VR

Benedikt, Michael, ed. 1992. *Cyberspace: First steps*. Cambridge: MIT Press.

Bishop, Gary, et al. 1992. Research directions in virtual environments: Report of an NSF invitational workshop. *Computer Graphics* 26:153–77.

Ditlea, Steve. 1993. Virtual reality: How Jaron Lanier created an industry but lost his company. *UPSIDE*. 6:8–21.

Earnshaw, Roe A., Michael Gigante, and Huw Jones, eds. 1993. *Virtual reality systems*. New York: Academic Press.

Grimes, Jack. 1992. Virtual reality goes commericial with a blast. *IEEE Computer Graphics & Applications* 3:16–17.

Haggerty, Michael. 1992. Serious lunacy: Art in virtual worlds. *IEEE Computer Graphics & Applications* 3:5–7.

Hamit, Francis. 1993. *Virtual reality and the exploration of cyberspace*. Indianapolis, IN: Sams Publishing.

Haywood, Thomas P. 1993. *Adventures in virtual reality*. Indiana: Que.

Heim, Michael. 1993. *The metaphysics of virtual reality*. New York: Oxford University Press.

Jacobson, Linda. 1994. *Garage virtual reality*. Indianapolis, IN: Sams Publishing.

Kalawsky, Roy S. 1993. *The science of virtual reality and virtual environments*. New York: Addison-Wesley.

Pimentel, Ken, and Kevin Teixeira. 1993. *Virtual reality: Through the new looking glass*. New York: McGraw-Hill.

Rheingold, Howard. 1991. *Virtual reality*. New York: Summit Books.

Stampe, Dave, Bernie Roehl, and John Eagan. 1993. *Virtual reality creations*. California: Waite Group Press.

Starks, Michael. 1991. Stereoscopic video and the quest for virtual reality: An annotated bibliography of selected topics. *SPIE Stereoscopic Displays and Applications II* 1457:327–37.

Wexelblat, Alan, ed. 1993. *Virtual reality: Applications and explorations*. New York: Academic Press.

Wodaski, Ron. 1993. *Virtual reality madness*. Indianapolis, IN: Sams Publishing.

Feedback

Brooks, Frederick P., et al. Project GROPE—Haptic displays for scientific visualization. *Proceedings of SIGGRAPH '90*, 177–85.

Iwata, Hiroo. Artificial reality with force-feedback: Development of desktop virtual space with compact master manipular. *Proceedings of SIGGRAPH '90*, 165–70.

3-D Audio

Begault, Durand R. 1991. Challenges to the successful implementation of 3-D sound. *Journal of the Audio Engineering Society* 39: 864–70.

Blauert, J. 1993. *Spatial hearing*. Cambridge: MIT Press.

———. 1970. Sound localization in the median plane. *Acustica* 22:205–13.

Bosi, Marina. 1990. An interactive real-time system for the control of sound localization. *Computer Music Journal* 14:59–64.

Cooper, Duane H. 1982. Calculator program for head-related transfer function. *Journal of the Audio Engineering Society* 30:34–38.

———. 1983. Letters to the editor. *Journal of the Audio Engineering Society* 31:760.

Gatehouse, R. Wayne, ed. 1982. *Localization of sound: Theory and application*. Amphore Press.

Kendall, Gary S., and C.A. Puddie Rodgers. 1981. The simulation of three-dimensional localization cues for headphone listening. *Proceedings of the 1981 International Computer Music Conference*, 225–43.

Kuhn, George F. 1977. Model for the inter-aural time differences in the azimuthal plane. *Journal of the Acoustical Society of America* 62:157–67.

Moore, F. Richard. 1983. A general model for spatial processing of sounds. *Computer Music Journal* 7:6–15.

———. 1978. An introduction to the mathematics of digital signal processing. Part I. *Computer Music Journal* 2:1, 38–47.

———. 1978. An introduction to the mathematics of digital signal processing. Part II. *Computer Music Journal* 2:38–60.

Sakamoto, Naraji, Toshiyuki Gotoh, Takuyo Kogure, Masatoshi Shimbo, and Almon H. Clegg. 1981. Controlling sound-image localization in stereophonic reproduction. *Journal of the Audio Engineering Society* 29:794–98.

———. 1982. Controlling sound-image localization in stereophonic reproduction:Part II. *Journal of the Audio Engineering Society* 30: 719–21.

Shaw, E. A. G. 1974. Transformation of sound pressure level from the free field to the eardrum in the horizontal plane. *Journal of the Acoustical Society of America* 56:1848–61.

Stockham, Thomas G. 1966. High-speed convolution and correlation. *Proceedings of the Spring Joint Computer Conference*, 229–32.

Ward, Wayne Hinson. 1984. A signal processing model of auditory lateralization. *Master's thesis, University of Colorado, Boulder.*

Wenzel, Elizabeth M., Frederic L. Wightman, and Scott H. Foster. 1988. A virtual display system for conveying three-dimensional acoustic information. *Proceedings of the Human Factors Society*, 86–90.

Wightman, Frederic L., and Doris J. Kistler. 1989. Headphone simulation of free-field listening I:Stimulus synthesis. *Journal of the Acoustical Society of America* 85:858–67.

———. 1989. Headphone simulation of free-field listening II:Psychophysical validation. *Journal of the Acoustical Society of America* 85:868–78.

Yost, William A., and George Gourevitch. 1987. *Directional hearing.* Springer-Verlag.

Index

Now that you've built the hardware, here's the book on how to design your own <u>virtual reality software!</u>

The Virtual Reality Programmer's Kit

by Joe Gradecki

Author of *The Virtual Reality Construction Kit* and publisher of *PCVR Magazine*

The Virtual Reality Programmer's Kit is a complete book/disk set for creating your own virtual worlds on the PC. This book shows you how to build everything from simple three-dimensional worlds that support a mouse or Power Glove, to sophisticated multi-user environments that can be played over modems.

The book also discusses how to:

▶ Manage the trade-off between graphical detail and rendering speed

▶ Benchmark your VR world for other people's computers

▶ Design interactive worlds that keep people intrigued

▶ Write device drivers for a variety of VR gear, including a mouse, head tracker, Power Glove, and 3-D sound system

Everything you need to create your own virtual worlds is included on the disk!
The virtual reality development software on the disk is perfect for people with no programming experience and makes creating virtual worlds easier for experienced C programmers. There is a wealth of C code on the disk that can be placed into your own software projects.

The disk includes:

▶ 3 virtual worlds (ready-to-run and in C code)

▶ Utilities that make it easier to build objects for your worlds

▶ Device drivers for a variety of VR gear (C code)

▶ Benchmarking software

| Available August 1994 | ISBN 0 471-05253-1 | 29.95 with 3.5 disk |

Price is subject to change

The Virtual Reality Construction Kit
by Joe Gradecki

Here are scenes from two of the virtual worlds included on disk. In Virtual Attack, you can link up with a friend over modem or serial connection in a head-to-head combat game. Search the multi-platform playing field to find your opponent before he finds you.

VIRTUAL ATTACK

To relax after a tough day on the combat grounds, walk among the trees or down the railroad tracks of this virtual park.

A RELAXING PARK